Europe as the
Western Peninsula
of Greater Eurasia

Europe as the Western Peninsula of Greater Eurasia

Geoeconomic Regions in a Multipolar World

Glenn Diesen

ROWMAN & LITTLEFIELD
Lanham • Boulder • New York • London

Published by Rowman & Littlefield
An imprint of The Rowman & Littlefield Publishing Group, Inc.
4501 Forbes Boulevard, Suite 200, Lanham, Maryland 20706
www.rowman.com

6 Tinworth Street, London, SE11 5AL, United Kingdom

British Library Cataloguing in Publication Information Available

Library of Congress Cataloging-in-Publication Data

Names: Diesen, Glenn, author.
Title: Europe as the western peninsula of greater Eurasia :
  geoeconomic regions in a multipolar world / Glenn Diesen.
Description: Lanham : Rowman & Littlefield, [2021] |
  Includes bibliographical references and index. | Summary: "This book
  examines how the EU as a geoeconomic region will be impacted by the
  Russian-Chinese cooperation to construct a Greater Eurasia"—Provided by
  publisher.
Identifiers: LCCN 2021020047 (print) | LCCN 2021020048 (ebook) |
  ISBN 9781538161760 (cloth) | ISBN 9781538161777 (epub)
  ISBN 9781538161784 (pbk)
Subjects: LCSH: Geopolitics—Eurasia. | European Union countries—
  Foreign economic relations—Asia. | Asia—Foreign economic relations—
  European Union countries. | Eurasia—Boundaries. | Eurasia—Economic
  conditions. | Eurasia—Politics and government.
Classification: LCC HF1531.Z4 A7876 2021 (print) | LCC HF1531.
  Z4 (ebook) | DDC 320.1/2095—dc23
LC record available at https://lccn.loc.gov/2021020047
LC ebook record available at https://lccn.loc.gov/2021020048

Contents

Foreword   vii

Introduction   xi

1: Theorising the Geoeconomics of Regions   1

2: Eurasia as a Geoeconomic Region   19

3: The Dominance of the West as a Maritime Region   39

4: Restoring Political Subjectivity in Greater Eurasia   65

5: The Chinese-Russian Partnership for Greater Eurasia   91

6: China as a European Power   115

7: Eurasian Russia Skewing the Balance of Dependence in Europe   131

8: The Three Levels of Trans-Atlantic Fragmentation   153

9: Developing Strategic Autonomy for European Sovereignty   173

Conclusion: Adapting to Greater Eurasia   191

Bibliography   195

Index   219

Foreword

I have been watching Professor Glenn Diesen's academic work for almost a decade with growing interest, and it is a great pleasure for me to write a foreword to his new book. Glenn Diesen is one of the most prominent representatives of the modern school of geoeconomics founded by outstanding American thinker and strategist Edward Luttwak.

The balance of dependence concept proposed and elaborated by Professor Diesen in his previous works is one of the most productive—and closest to reality—theories that explain the modern world.

Diesen's concept helped me and my Russian colleagues to better understand the essence of the current stage in Russia's turn to the East and advance it further. The turn was conceived in the mid-2000s and began in earnest in the 2010s mainly as a way to enter rapidly growing Asian markets, including through accelerated growth of Russia's Siberia and Far Eastern regions which had been hit the hardest by the economic collapse of the 1990s. The ups and downs of crises in the EU, Russia's prevailing economic partner at that time, were the last to be taken into account. There were also concerns, also largely sidelined, over excessive dependence on the West amid growing mutual alienation and Western partners' dissatisfaction with Russia's refusal to obediently follow their policies, as most former socialist countries in Central and Eastern Europe were doing. It was not until 2012-2013, when the Western press and foreign policy leaders of most Western countries started pounding away at Moscow massively, that the turn to the East began to take on geopolitical dimensions. It finally assumed both the economic and geopolitical dimensions after the reincorporation of Crimea into Russia, thus putting an end, at least for the time being, to the expansion of Western alliances, primarily NATO, into territories that Russia considered vital for its national security. Further expansion, as many in Moscow believed, was fraught with a big war.

So, one can even say that Russia has once again safeguarded peace in Europe as it did before by defeating Napoleon and Hitler.

Western sanctions and downright hostile policies have accelerated Russia's turn to the East. In fact, by the beginning of 2020, Russia's trade with Asia had exceeded that with Europe, although the latter had amounted to almost two-thirds of Russia's foreign trade turnover in the late 2000s, and the former was around one-fifth. The network of gas and oil pipelines in Asia and LNG plants make it possible to redirect export flows between the two parts of Eurasia.

It was only then, including after reading Diesen's fascinating books, that Russian strategists started hitherto almost intuitive attempts to avoid unilateral dependence on European markets and move into the rising Asian ones. Having strengthened its position in the world and entered alternative export and import markets with high-quality, but relatively cheaper goods, Russia radically changed the existing balance of dependence and the overall balance of power in relations with the West, especially Europe.

Russia's turn to the East and China's westward turn towards Eurasia through the Belt and Road Initiative was accompanied by even more significant changes in the entire system of international relations—the end of the West's five-hundred-year dominance, including the liberal order of the last seventy years. For Russia, which was not its part, it did not seem liberal, that is, free, because it provided for unitarianism in politics, economy, ideology, and culture. Nor was it an order, given dozens of wars unleashed by the United States and its allies, which claimed many millions of human lives. In recent decades alone the West committed acts of aggression against the remnants of Yugoslavia, Iraq, and Libya. There were also dozens of coups, recently called colour revolutions, which most often plunged entire countries, regions, and their peoples into suffering and poverty. The West also supported the coup in Ukraine in 2014, which has turned this country, previously mid-developed by European standards, into almost the poorest one on the subcontinent in terms of per capita income, and steadily going down towards a failed state.

The West's—and before that Europe's—five-century political, economic, cultural, and civilizational dominance was deeply rooted in military superiority over the rest of the world, which Europe had acquired in the 16th-17th centuries. Not only the Portuguese, British, Spanish, and French Empires but also the Russian Empire came into existence due to superiority in armament and military organization. This allowed them to syphon off world GNP and strengthen their own states. At first, they plundered their colonies, but in the second half of the 20th century, the system of dominance became more sophisticated and worked through Western economic institutions—the Bretton Woods system. And yet, military superiority remained the foundation of dominance. Striving to survive, the Soviet Union, and then China created nuclear weapons, and this foundation began to crumble. The West started to lose wars, power escalation became much more difficult. The non-West had grown bolder. Suffice it to recall anti-colonial revolutions, the non-aligned movement, or the Arab oil embargo of the 1970s. Then for a historical second, it seemed that superiority had been regained. The Soviet Union collapsed, and Russia, plunged into a deep crisis, temporarily lost its ability to pursue an effective deterrence policy. But after the bombing of Yugoslavia, the US secession from the ABM Treaty, and the invasion of Iraq, Russia covertly launched a new rearmament cycle to create hypersonic missiles, gliding warheads, etc. These weapons, now being deployed, have apparently deprived the West of its military superiority completely. At the same time, either due to oversight or ideological narrow-mindedness, the West let China make a leap forward. Before that, it had rejected Russia's attempt to become part, albeit independent, of the West, thus pushing it towards the non-West. Now China and Russia, having created a de facto alliance, have fundamentally changed the balance of power in the world.

Whether a Greater Eurasia partnership will take place (this concept was born in Russia and supported by China, and from the very beginning geographically included Europe or its part), or the centre of the world economy and politics, and eventually culture, will be in Eurasia, and not Europe, as it was for the last five centuries, or the Atlantic over the last 65-70 years, depends on many things. First and foremost, it will depend on whether China will be able to move away from its old tradition of the Middle Kingdom, that is, a great power that surrounds itself with vassals. It will not be able to do that. To the west of its borders, it will meet the resistance of large powers-civilizations with a thousand-year-long history and significant resources. This is already happening with India, but there will also be Iran, Turkey and, of course, Russia with its genetic striving for sovereignty and proven ability to protect it.

If China chooses the "first among equals" principle, which is more likely, a partnership will be created, with Russia taking the convenient position of a North Eurasian balancer and a cultural, transport, and military-strategic unifier and guarantor.

Europe and European countries will have to decide whether they want to take an active part in building a new partnership or whether it will be built without them and then partially against them, without taking their interests into account.

Europe's movement towards Greater Eurasia can be artificially delayed by provoking some kind of crisis like the Missile Crisis in the 1970s that halted Greater Europe's march towards detente and deprived Western Europe of a chance to acquire the power of agency.

If Europeans keep hoping to revive the bygone comfortable times and stay in limbo as they did for the last ten years, then EU countries will enter Greater Eurasia one by one or in groups. The future tentative border of Greater Eurasia can already be seen. It will pass along the French-German border or include Germany if it finally makes up its mind.

The best option for the European Union's Europe would be to take an active part in building a new partnership. In this case, the EU will get a new goal and legitimacy. At the same time, this scenario does not imply disengagement from the United States, of course. That would be highly irrational. But in order to choose this scenario, Europe will have to stop falling further into the civilizational crisis and give up attempts to unite against make-believe enemies—Russia or China. It is not at all obvious whether Europeans can do this.

But for Russia, the best scenario would be a friendly Europe with its markets and cultural influence balancing out China's growing power in Greater Eurasia.

I think this scenario would be a saver for Europe as well. But I am not going to advise anything to our European neighbours, who were our friends not so long ago and hopefully will be our good neighbours and partners in a future Greater Eurasia. Europeans themselves must make their own decisions and bear responsibility for their consequences or lack thereof.

Sergey Karaganov
Honorary Chairman of the Presidium of the Council on Foreign and Defense Policy
Dean of the Faculty of World Economy and International Affairs of the National Research University Higher School of Economics (NRU HSE)

Introduction

The transformation of Eurasia demonstrates why geography continues to be a central aspect of great power politics. The Russian-Chinese strategic partnership forms the core of a larger Greater Eurasian region, which relies on geoeconomic power to integrate Europe and Asia into a Eurasian supercontinent. Europe subsequently finds itself torn between two geoeconomic regions – as a sub-region of the trans-Atlantic region and the Greater Eurasian region. To survive as a geoeconomic region in a multipolar world, Europe must assert strategic autonomy and diversify its partners for economic connectivity to avoid excessive reliance on a single state or region.

Until recently, the EU appeared destined to be a leading power that would shape the world. However, the European continent now risks becoming a political object, a chessboard for the great powers, as the US and rising powers in the east become more brazen in their effort to assert their geoeconomic influence over Europe. A report to the European Council in 2010 cautioned that the EU must become "an assertive global actor" or be relegated to "an increasingly irrelevant western peninsula of the Asian continent" (European Council 2010). In February 2017, leaked German documents referred to as *Strategic Perspective 2040*, detailed contingency plans in case the West would disintegrate and the EU would collapse. The documents also consider the scenario of European states gravitating towards Russia and joining an eastern bloc of countries.

EUROPE AS A GEOECONOMIC REGION

Regions are conceptualised here as geoeconomic constructs. Economic nationalists acknowledged in the 19th century that industrialisation was a central component of nation-building. British regional geoeconomic primacy in Europe and beyond relied on its domineering manufacturing industry, rule over the seas as a commercial and military advantage, and the prominence of its banks and currency. The "American System" and the German, French and Russian equivalents recognised to various degrees that autonomy and influence relied on the three pillars of geoeconomic power: strategic industries, transportation corridors and financial instruments. The geoeconomics of nation-building was soon thereafter also used to construct geoeconomic regions. These ideas also influenced Japan's economic nationalism to assert strategic autonomy in the 19th century, and then to construct an East Asian geoeconomic region.

The contemporary West as a united region is largely an accident of history. After the First World War, there were five major geoeconomic regions in the world centred on three continents – the British Empire, the French Empire, Germany with Eastern Europe, the US with Latin America, and Japan with East Asia. All five regions had an imperial structure where the dominant power relied on coercion to preserve control over the vassals and keep out rivals. The Second World War devastated Western Europe and East Asia, which enabled the US to cement primacy over these two regions through security dependencies and geoeconomic control over strategic industries, transportation corridors and financial instruments. The main three geoeconomic regions in the world – North American, Western Europe, and East Asia, were organised into US-centric inter-regional frameworks. The main adversaries of the US were communist states, which relegated geostrategic rivalry primarily to the realm of militarised geopolitics. Furthermore, the military confrontation with communist rivals mitigated geoeconomic rivalry between the US hegemon and its dependent allies.

The former centuries of world politics were defined by Euro-centrism as European powers acquired military and maritime supremacy from the early 16th century and subsequently used the entire globe as the chessboard for great power politics. Europe was inhabited by the sole political subjects, the actors that organise the world, and the non-European world were demoted to political object, those who were organised into regional structures by foreign powers. The destructiveness of the Second World War largely made Europe an object of great power politics, as the decision-making and regional structures were imposed by the US and the Soviet Union.

Incrementally, Europe has regained its status as a political subject through regional integration within the wider trans-Atlantic region. The EU has been instrumental to improve symmetry in relations with the US to create an internal balance of power within the trans-Atlantic region. The establishment of the European Union (EU) as an autonomous geoeconomic region has been a central achievement to operate as an integral sub-region of the West under the patronage of the US.

The US supported an EU-led Europe and Japan-led East Asia to the extent they demonstrated commitment to inter-regional formats under US leadership. During the bipolar era the US sought to strengthen European junior allies as a bulwark against the Soviet Union, and after the Cold War to assert collective hegemony over the pan-European space. The subsequent concentration of geoeconomic power in the US gave birth to a liberal international economic system that also benefitted the Europeans.

The current transition towards a global multipolar distribution of power takes Europe into uncharted waters, and European unity demands adjusting to new realities. In a multipolar world, excessive dependence on the US is no longer sustainable. The US will demand greater geoeconomic loyalty in its rivalry with China and Russia that diminishes the EU's strategic autonomy and its ability to diversify its partnerships to the extent Europe becomes a province of the US. Weakened by excessive geoeconomic reliance on the US, the EU will not be able to harness political loyalty from its member states. By positioning itself as an instrument of US hegemony, the EU will embrace zero-sum policies towards China and Russia that will subsequently incentivise the Eurasian duo to engage in wedge tactics.

In a multipolar world, Europe must establish itself as an independent pole of power with sufficient strategic autonomy and diversified economic connectivity with the other poles of power. As an independent pole of power, the EU can provide material benefits to its member states and adopt a swing power strategy to incentivise benign relations with external powers such as the US, Russia, and China. A swing power strategy entails increasing or decreasing economic connectivity with any region in response to actions towards the EU. Once Europe weds itself permanently to solely one region, both the partner region and adversaries lose their incentives to accommodate European strategic interests.

CHINESE AND RUSSIAN REJECTION OF THE UNIPOLAR ERA

An underexplored phenomenon in international relations is the absence of a shared narrative regarding the inclusion of China and Russia in the US-led international economic system. Every American administration considered themselves to have reached out to China since the 1970s and to Russia since the 1990s. Although, both Beijing and Moscow consider themselves to have been presented with a dilemma of either accepting the role of political objects or be contained. The failure to adequately incorporate Russia as the largest state in Europe and China as the largest state in Asia made the unipolar system temporary and unstable.

China and Russia remained the sole great powers, independent of the US, in the post-Cold War era under US global primacy. By definition, great powers can exercise influence at a global level and act independently even in defiance of the hegemon. Neither Russia nor China could therefore be adequately be accommodated in an international system centred around the US. China was initially cultivated as a potential partner in the unipolar system at the lower end of supply chains in the international division of labour to supply cheap commodities. Albeit, after climbing up global value chains and growing out of its junior role, China is asserting itself as a political subject capable of dismantling the geoeconomic foundations of US global primacy. Russia was marginalised in the new Europe immediately after the Cold War as the dividing lines on the continent were merely moved towards Russian borders. The West envisioned a socialising role for itself as relations with Russia were organised as a subject-object / teacher-student relationship. Russia would not have a seat at the table, rather its participation in international security was largely limited to improving its governance per Western precepts. The unipolar format in Europe necessitated a perpetually weak Russia that would abide by institutions that did not grant Moscow representation.

Neither China nor Russia as great powers could permanently accept the role as political objects in the unipolar era and have aimed to break out of containment. Although, their approach has differed greatly. Enjoying a stable status quo in East Asia, China was content to bide its time hide and hide its strength until it was in a favourable position to reorganise regions. In contrast, Russia has been punching above its weight to balance a revisionist and expansionist NATO and EU that unilaterally fill the vacuum left behind after the collapse of the Soviet Union.

China's initial development strategy did not entail challenging the US-led international economic order. The US dominated the world's strategic industries and China competed at the lower end of value chains with cheap production, China relied on transportation corridors under the administration of the US and accepted the primacy of US-led financial institutions. Yet, the format for interdependence was not durable. China accrued the productive power of the world, accumulated a vast amount of foreign reserves, and rapidly climbed up global value chains. In contrast, the costs of global primacy began to weigh down on the US as its deficits grew exponentially and socioeconomic tensions within society began to challenge political stability. The global financial crisis of 2008 and the enduring failure of the US to restore fiscal discipline made the US-Chinese interdependent partnership untenable. Much like Germany outgrew the "peaceful rise" model of Bismarck by 1890 that had aimed to avoid conflict with other powers, so did China's "peaceful rise" come to an end by challenging the geoeconomic primacy of the US after 2008.

The Chinese government invests vast amounts of money to restructure geoeconomic regions. Strategic industries are falling under Chinese control as the China 2025 initiative directs funds to assert technological dominance in artificial intelligence, robotics, and the other leading technologies associated with the Fourth Industrial Revolution. Chinese-centric transportation corridors are constructed under the multi-trillion-dollar Belt and Road Initiative that reorganises transportation corridors by both sea and land. In very explicit terms, the new Silk Road seeks to revive the transportation corridors of the ancient Silk Road, which collapsed and thus handed over geoeconomic dominance to western maritime powers. New financial instruments are also developing rapidly as China constructs international development banks, payment system, and internationalises its currency.

After decades of failing to reach a post-Cold War settlement with the West to include Russia in Europe, Moscow has grown increasingly disillusioned. Russia strived towards a Greater Europe as a continuation of Gorbachev's Common European Home. However, a NATO-centric and EU-centric Europe depends on preventing new centres of power from emerging to ensure the regional gravitational pull towards the West. The EU, therefore, envisioned post-Cold War Russia as a political object of European politics, rather than a political subject with a seat at the table. Russia marginal role in the new Europe required establishing asymmetrical interdependence between the EU and Russia to maximise the autonomy and influence of Brussels and minimise the autonomy and influence of Russia. Hence, the EU has sought to reduce its dependence on Russia, while increasing Russia's reliance on the EU. Moscow's final hope for gradual integration with the West collapsed in 2014 when Western states supported regime change in Ukraine to push Kiev to make the "civilizational choice" between the West and Russia.

THE RUSSIAN-CHINESE STRATEGIC PARTNERSHIP FOR GREATER EURASIA

The recent Chinese-Russian partnership sets the foundation for a new Greater Eurasia region, which aims to elevate Beijing and Moscow as political subjects in the international system. The Russian Foreign Minister, Sergey Lavrov (2012), argued that adjustments are necessary to adapt to unexpected new realities:

the globalization process has taken a turn quite different from that anticipated by its adepts twenty years ago. It was believed then that after the breakup of the Soviet Union and the socialist system the developed Western countries and large corporations would freely spread their influence around the world and that the liberal-democratic system would be the only beacon for all peoples "lagging behind." In reality, however, many developing countries have largely benefited from the globalization, as they have created modern industries and significantly improved the well-being of their populations, whereas developed countries have gone through the processes of de-industrialization, reduction of the middle class and growing social stratification.

A continental shift is underway as Russia has suspended its 300-year-long Western-centric foreign policy, and its post-Cold War Greater Europe Initiative, and replaced it with the Greater Eurasia Initiative. China is recognised as an indispensable partner as it has both the intention and capacity to develop an entirely new multipolar geoeconomic architecture where Moscow can have a seat at the table. While the unipolar system relied on containing Russia, the multipolar system in partnership with China restores Russia as a political subject.

A Greater Eurasian region, that integrates Asia and Europe, is currently being negotiated and organised with a Chinese-Russian partnership at the centre. Eurasian geoeconomic instruments of power are gradually forming the foundation of a super-region with new strategic industries, transportation corridors and financial instruments. Across the Eurasian continent, states as different as South Korea, India, Kazakhstan, and Iran are all advancing various formats for Eurasian integration.

After centuries of attempting to re-establish itself as a European maritime power to escape economic isolation, Russia sees an unprecedented historical opportunity by looking towards a more accommodating and benign East for economic connectivity. By integrating Europe and Asia into a Eurasian region, Russia can reposition itself from the dual periphery of Europe and Asia towards the centre of a super-region. President Putin announced Russia's objective to establish a Greater Eurasian partnership at the St. Petersburg Economic Forum in June 2016. Putin argued that the Russian-led Eurasian Economic Union (EAEU) would be an important component that would establish a close partnership with countries such as China, India, Iran and Pakistan to form a Greater Eurasia (Kremlin 2016). While Beijing and Moscow share the ambition to construct a larger Eurasian region, their formats differ. The common denominator of both formats is the necessity of a Sino-Russo partnership to integrate Eurasia. China and Russia have subsequently been working towards avoiding zero-sum approaches to Central Asia and the wider Eurasian space.

The ambition to integrate Europe and Asia into one Eurasian supercontinent is hardly a new concept. In the early 19th century, Napoleon and the

Russian Tsar conspired to send an army through Central Asia to reach British India, and thus challenge the strategic significance of Britain's control over the seas. In the mid-19th century, Friedrich List proposed an Anglo-Germanic Eurasian land corridor from Belgium to Bombay to counter the rapid rise and expansionism of the US. The Russian-British "Great Game" of the 19th century was largely about constructing rival regions. Russia aimed to reach and control the southern and eastern edge of Eurasia through land corridors, while Britain sought to control the supercontinent from the sea. Leading German strategists such as General Haushofer advocated, well into the Second World War, in favour of a Eurasian bloc in partnership with Russia, China, India, and Japan, to counter the dominance of maritime powers. The Chinese-Russian partnership for Greater Eurasia is significantly different as it is not a European imperial project, rather an endeavour to restore the political subjectivity of Eurasia.

The rise of China represents the end of 500years of Western dominance and Asia as a region is rapidly falling under Chinese stewardship and thus breaking away from US hegemony. The next step in Greater Eurasia is to integrate Europe into Greater Eurasia with a sophisticated geoeconomic infrastructure of strategic industries, transportation corridors and financial power.

EUROPE BETWEEN THE TRANS-ATLANTIC REGION AND GREATER EURASIA

Greater Eurasia challenges the geoeconomic architecture of the trans-Atlantic region, which makes Europe a contested sub-region pulled towards the two larger regional constructs. The theoretical assumption of geoeconomic regions is that economic dependence is followed by political loyalties.

European states are currently installing Chinese 5G technology; Greece, Italy, Poland, Austria, Luxembourg, and Switzerland have joined the Chinese Belt and Road Initiative; in 2015 all of the major US allies in Europe joined the Chinese-led Asian Infrastructure Investment Bank (AIIB), and in December 2020 the EU and China agreed on the Comprehensive Agreement on Investment (CAI). Turkey will have the Russian S-400 missile defence system delivered, and Germany is completing the North Stream 2 pipeline with Russia. The Europeans have pursued the aforementioned Eurasian economic connectivity irrespective of US disapproval and threats of sanctions.

The EU leading concept is "strategic autonomy" from the US to establish "European sovereignty." Technological sovereignty is deemed to be imperative towards this end. Eurasian transportation corridors, including the harmonisation of Russia's Northern Sea Route with China's Polar Silk Road to develop an Arctic transportation corridor, will create new arteries of trade for

Europe outside US control. The EU aims to shed the extraterritorial legislation of the US by setting up an alternative payment system to SWIFT and also
decoupling from key US digital platforms to protect data.

The US endeavours to prolong its dominant position by creating new
regions. A key initiative is to reimagine and reinvent the Asia-Pacific region
as the Indo-Pacific region as an anti-Chinese bloc while hardening Europe's
position against both China and Russia. However, in both Asia and Europe,
the US is demanding more from its allies at a time it has less to offer in terms
of security guarantees and generous trade agreements. The EU's decision to
continue economic integration with China, which is deemed to be less of a
threat due to mere geography, will continue to fuel discord between the US
and the EU.

The US demand for greater geoeconomic loyalty from its European partners, and preparedness to use economic coercion towards this end, threatens
to weaken the EU as an autonomous region within the trans-Atlantic region.
As the Europeans' geoeconomic loyalty towards Washington wanes, the
US relies increasingly on economic coercion against its European allies
that undermines the US posture as a benign hegemon. Furthermore, the US
military threats and economic coercion against several Eurasian powers
such as Russia, China, and Iran function as an incentive for further Eurasian
integration.

Can the cohesion and strategic autonomy of Europe be preserved in a multipolar world? Or will a fragmented Europe become the arena for a geoeconomic rivalry between the trans-Atlantic region and Greater Eurasia?

THE GEOECONOMIC OF REGIONS

The book is structured into three sections: The first three chapters outline the
theory and history of Eurasia and Europe as geoeconomic regions; the following two chapters explore the Russia-China strategic partnership for Greater
Eurasia; the last four chapters assess the process of transforming Europe into
the western peninsula of Greater Eurasia.

Chapter 1 theorises the geoeconomics of regionalism. The strategic
autonomy and influence of geoeconomic regions depend on a balance of
dependence at both the internal and external level. The balance of dependence
refers to a geoeconomic understanding of the realist balance of power. In an
asymmetrical interdependent partnership, the more powerful and less reliant
side in a dyad can extract political power. The more dependent side therefore
has systemic incentives to restore a balance of dependence by enhancing
strategic autonomy and diversifying economic partnerships to reduce reliance on the more powerful actor. The external balance of dependence refers

to the development of geoeconomic regions as instruments for skewing the symmetry in relations with external powers. The internal balance of dependence refers to the relations between members of a region. Members of a geoeconomic region will reduce their loyalty towards a region under a skewed balance of dependence unless the loss of sovereignty is offset by material benefits from membership in the region.

Chapter 2 analyses Eurasia as a geoeconomic region. The concept of a Eurasian region that unifies Europe and Asia has through history been an alternative to the dominance of maritime powers in the oceanic-centric world economy. The invention of railways enables modern powers to recreate the mobility of ancient nomadic powers that endowed them with commercial and military competitiveness. After centuries of efforts by Western European countries to exclude the Russians from the maritime corridors of Europe, Russia began looking towards reviving Eurasian land corridors throughout the 19th century to challenge the primacy of oceanic states. From the 1840s to the 1940s, the Germans also began devising various schemes over the following century to construct a Eurasian continental bloc. Britsh and American strategies have been deeply influenced by the prospect of an emerging Eurasian region, as a direct threat to their advantageous position in the oceanic world order.

Chapter 3 explores the evolution of Europe as a geoeconomic region. Europe has historically had a proclivity to be organised by maritime powers due to the commercial and military advantages. Yet, administrating the continent from the maritime periphery has demanded the preservation of dividing lines among land-powers to prevent alternative regions from emerging. Napoleon's Continental System was the initial of constructing a European region with geoeconomic means that could rival an oceanic British-led Europe. The German Zollverein, which commenced in 1834, attempted to recreate the geoeconomic conditions of the Continental System. The failure to accommodate Germany's spectacular industrial rise within a European region contributed to two world wars. Under US patronage, a continental European geoeconomic region, the EU, emerged with unifying strategic industries, transportation corridors, and financial instruments. Yet, the EU's "peaceful rise" within the West implied not challenging the authority of the US.

Chapter 4 explores Russian and Chinese efforts to restore their political subjectivity. The unipolar system after the Cold War could not adequately accommodate Russia and China as political subjects. Both Moscow and Beijing were presented with an ultimatum of accepting their status as political objects or be contained and confronted. Russia enjoyed less economic power and was under greater pressure to contest the unipolar system as NATO expands towards Russian borders and peels off its neighbours in zero-sum formats. In contrast, China could bide its time and pursue a "peaceful rise" in terms of accruing internal geoeconomic power before outgrowing and challenging the unipolar structures. Systemic pressures have pushed both Russia and China towards Eurasianism as a geographical solution to an increasingly untenable US-centric order.

Chapter 5 analyses the Chinese-Russian partnership for Greater Eurasia. A strategic partnership between China and Russia lays the foundation for a multipolar Greater Eurasian region that integrates Asia and Europe into a larger geoeconomic region. China endeavours to displace the US as the leading geoeconomic power in the world, while Russia also develops a favourable position at the centre of an integrated Eurasian continent. These concepts for Greater Eurasia have similarities and differences, which makes Eurasian integration largely contingent upon harmonising their interests. The Sino-Russian strategic partnership at the centre of Greater Eurasia is currently laying the foundation for a partnership in the tech-sector, reorganisation of supply chains, cooperation on transportation corridors, and establishment of new financial instruments such as joint investment banks, money transfer systems, and diversification of currencies that also includes gold accumulation and digital currencies. The Chinese-Russian core lays the foundation for a gravitational pull to integrate the wider Eurasian continent.

Chapter 6 explores China as a European power. The economic interdependence between the EU and China becomes increasingly asymmetrical in China's favour. The reorganisation of the fundamental regional geoeconomic structures in Europe strengthens Beijing's authority in Europe vis-à-vis Brussels. First, Chinese strategic industries and leading technologies that underpin them are penetrating the European market. Second, the Belt and Road Initiative introduces new and rival land- and maritime-transportation corridors to Europe. Last, China's new financial instruments in Europe following the global financial crisis have been instrumental to finance regional Chinese infrastructure projects and create dependence on Chinese capital. Efforts by Brussels to scale back on China's growing clout on the continent can be countered and circumvented by Beijing through bilateral agreements and the 17+1 format with Central and Eastern European countries.

Chapter 7 examines why Russia's Eurasian orientation restructures relations with Europe. Russia's Eurasian economy shifts the symmetry of dependence primarily by reducing Russian reliance on Europe, while Russia's increased influence in Europe has less impact on the balance of dependence. Russia's pivot to the east does not entail "leaving Europe," rather the end of a Western-centric foreign policy is intended to make Europe matter less to Russia. Russia's strategic industries are largely limited to weaponry and energy, although with potential in the digital sector. Energy will remain a key influence in Europe, which will have more political significance by establishing Russia as a swing-supplier of both oil and gas. The east-west

Eurasian transportation corridor is supplemented with a north-south corridor in cooperation with Iran and India. Furthermore, the coordination of Russia's Northern Sea Route and China's Polar Silk Road can become the "roof" on top of Greater Eurasia, which under Russian control can produce both economic and political power. The principal political influence derives from Russia's ability to end its commitments to the Helsinki order and establish itself as an international conservative power.

Chapter 8 analyses the three-level fragmentation of the trans-Atlantic region. The influence of Greater Eurasia depends on the cohesion of the trans-Atlantic region, which is deteriorating. First, there is a decoupling of Europe from the US as the rise of China creates different interests. The US has less to offer by shifting focus to Asia, yet demands greater geoeconomic loyalty from Europe. Concurrently, Europe has a greater need to develop strategic autonomy and frustrations grow on both sides of the Atlantic. Second, Europe itself is fragmenting as excessive widening and deepening of European integration has fuelled internal divisions. The effort to create a homogenous supranational union does not function as the economies of member states are too different and the internal balance of dependence has skewed excessively in Germany's favour. Relative economic interdependence within the geoeconomic region has declined, the failure of developing sufficient technologies sovereignty within the EU, and the ability to deliver material goods for its member state diminish political loyalties towards Brussels. Last, growing polarisation within Western states results from the excesses of neoliberal economic policies.

Chapter 9 explores Europe adapting to a multipolar system by developing strategic autonomy for European sovereignty. The failure to assert strategic autonomy sovereignty will condemn Europe to become a political object where the great powers compete for influence. In response to this challenge, the EU has seemingly made a complete ideological reversal by transitioning from post-sovereign ideas to the objective of asserting European sovereignty. These changes will impact the internal cohesion of the EU and its relations with external partners. Strategic autonomy is achieved by engaging independently with all major poles of power, yet without being permanently tied to any of them. Will the EU be able to remain an autonomous geoeconomic region within Greater Eurasia, will the EU retreat under US patronage to balance Eurasian powers?

It is concluded that the unipolar era appears to unravel as fast as the bipolar era - with equally profound consequences. Europe must adapt to the multipolarity of Greater Eurasia by acting in accordance with the balance of dependence logic.

1

Theorising the Geoeconomics of Regions

Geoeconomics means that political power derives from controlling markets rather than using military power to control territory. The international system gravitates towards geoeconomics when military weapons become increasingly destructive and there is a high degree of economic interdependence between states.

Geoeconomics explores political economy through the prism of realist theory. Liberal economic theory depicts economic interdependence through the lens of absolute gain from increased market efficiency. Geoeconomics stipulates that focus must be devoted to relative gain above absolute gain as the international system consists of states that compete against each other for power and survival. In an interdependent economic relationship, each side gains some influence over the other and thus also loses some autonomy. Under asymmetrical interdependence, where one side is more dependent than the other, the less dependent states can increase both autonomy and influence. States can be said to act geoeconomically when they intervene in the economy to skew the symmetry of economic interdependent relationships to maximise their autonomy and influence. Asymmetrical interdependence thus enables economic power to be converted into political power.

Regionalism is a crucial instrument of geoeconomic power. Regionalisation refers to a natural process of integration in which economic and social activities are not restrained by national borders due to mere geographical proximity. In contrast, regionalism entails a deliberate and policy-guided approach by governments to enhance socioeconomic and political connectivity within a region. Geoeconomic regionalism entails government policies to increase economic connectivity within a specific region to enhance their collective autonomy and influence in the wider world.

The economic nationalism of the 19th century recognised that industrialisation was linked to nation-building as sovereign states required a certain degree of economic autonomy. The economic infrastructure of states rests on three pillars—strategic industries, transportation corridors, and financial instruments. The theory on geoeconomic regions, outlined in this chapter, argues that these three geoeconomic levers of power also lays the foundation for region-building.

An analysis of geoeconomic regions demands a dual-level analysis of the external and internal balance of dependence. Geoeconomic regions are developed to use the collective strength of members to improve the external balance of dependence with the wider world. Yet, states also seek a favourable internal balance of dependence among other members of the geoeconomic region. The internal and external balance of dependence is intrinsically inked as geoeconomic regions must successfully mobilise the resources of their member states to skew the symmetry of interdependence with external powers.

This chapter first conceptualises geoeconomics and the balance of dependence as a political economy consistent with the assumptions of political realism. Second, geoeconomic regions are argued to be an important tool for geoeconomic power by emulating the logic of collective strength through military alliances. Third, geoeconomic regions are assessed by their external and internal balance of dependence. Last, geoeconomics is operationalised and measured by strategic industries, transportation corridors, and financial instruments. These three pillars of geoeconomic power are used by the dominant power to pursue hegemony, by the economic nationalists to enhance sovereignty, and for geoeconomic regions to advance collective power. It is concluded that the balance of dependence explains why geoeconomic regions rise and fall.

GEOECONOMICS AND THE "BALANCE OF DEPENDENCE"

Geoeconomics directs focus to relative gain as political power derives from creating asymmetrical interdependence. From early mercantilism to more modern neo-mercantilism and geoeconomics, the realist understanding of political economy mimics political realism. The Cold War offered a brief break from geoeconomics as the main rivals of the capitalist states were communist.

After the Cold War, Luttwak (1990: 19) announced the return of geoeconomics as "states will tend to act 'geoeconomically' simply because of what they are: territorially defined entities designed precisely to outdo each other on the world scene." Liberal theory on economics neglects the anarchic structure of the international system, and as Huntington (1993: 72) aptly argues:

"the idea that economics is primarily a non-zero-sum game is a favourite conceit of tenured academics."

States must embrace trade and economic connectivity with other states as market efficiency is required for prosperity and influence, yet economic dependence creates vulnerabilities and reduces political autonomy (Gilpin 2011: 80). By skewing the symmetry in an interdependent relationship, a state can maximise both influence and autonomy (Hirschman 1945; Knorr 1977). Asymmetrical interdependence can not be neglected because, in most interdependent relationships, one side will be more reliant than the other side (Hirschman 1945). For example, Germany and Moldova are economically interdependent, yet Germany is less dependent on Moldova. Berlin can therefore use asymmetrical interdependence to dictate favourable terms for economic agreements and extract political concessions for market access.

States intervene in the market to establish a favourable position in the international economy and use the favourable position in the international economy for political power. Economic interdependence is thus an instrument for power politics, as opposed to the liberal assumption that economic interdependence is a tool for transcending power politics:

> The power to interrupt commercial or financial regulations with any country, considered as an attribute of national sovereignty, is the root cause of the influence or power position which a county acquires in other countries, just as it is the root cause of the "dependence on trade" (Hirschman 1945: 16).

Mercantilism was similarly deemed defensive when protectionism was used to defend national sovereignty (Gilpin 1975: 234–35). Schmoller (1897: 76) opined that political freedom required "shaking off commercial dependence on foreigners which was continually becoming more oppressive." Similarly, while defensive neo-mercantilism entails protection for strategic industries and financial instruments, offensive neo-mercantilism entails using economic and political pressures to open up market access in foreign states (Raza 2007).

Geoeconomics recognises that the international system creates systemic incentives for a "balance of dependence," which mirrors the structural balance of power logic in international relations (Diesen 2017). Realist theory stipulates that the international system naturally gravitates towards a balance of power as states do not constrain themselves. Unconstrained states expand their power in the international system, which exhausts their resources and incentivises other states to balance (Waltz 1979).

A balance of dependence refers to the systemic incentives for skewing the symmetry of dependence to enhance autonomy and influence. Under asymmetrical interdependence, the stronger and less dependent side in a dyad will be able to extract political concessions. The weaker more dependent side consequently has great incentives to reduce dependence on the more power-ful state. The weaker and more dependent state have a greater willingness to accept economic pain to enhance autonomy, while the stronger state will be preoccupied with a multitude of relationships and therefore have less ability to prevent the weaker states from decoupling (Hirschman 1978). Excessive reliance on an asymmetrical interdependent partnership can be mitigated with increased strategic autonomy, diversification of economic partnerships, and establishing geoeconomic regions for collective bargaining power.

The international system therefore naturally gravitates towards a "balance of dependence" or an equilibrium as excessive reliance on a more power-ful state or region undermines political sovereignty. The theory of political realism suggests that peace exists when there is an international balance of power and incentives to preserve the status quo. The geoeconomic equivalent expects that peace is possible under a balance of dependence. In the first half of the 19th century, Friedrich List (1841: 96) posited:

> the ultimate aim of rational politics is. . . the uniting of all nations under a com-mon law of right, an object which is only to be attained through the greatest possible equalisation of the most important nations of the earth in civilisation, prosperity, industry and power, by the conversion of the antipathies and conflicts that now exist between them into sympathy and harmony.

THE GEOECONOMICS OF LIBERAL ECONOMICS

Political realism recognises that temporary stability can also be reached under a benign hegemon. In geoeconomics, hegemonic stability theory manifests itself as liberal economics as a temporary disruption to geoeconomic rivalry. Liberal international economic systems have historically emerged when economic power is concentrated in a hegemon. A skewed balance of depen-dence usually arises after a major war or collapse of a great power, although systemic pressures cause gravitation towards a balance of dependence. The military defeat of Napoleon opened up for British geoeconomic dominance in the 19th century, although the prominent position gradually declined towards the end of the century due to the counter-hegemonic economic nationalist policies of rising powers. Similarly, the devastation caused by the Second World War created the conditions for US geoeconomic primacy. The sub-sequent liberal international economic system was remarkably stable due to the opportune conditions of the Cold War that mitigated geoeconomic rivalry among capitalist allies while the main adversaries were communist states largely decoupled from economic statecraft.

The geoeconomic hegemon has systemic incentives to establish and maintain a liberal international economic system. Once a dominant position has been established over strategic industries, transportation corridors, and financial instruments, the economic hegemon embraces a liberal economic system to cement its competitive advantage. Economic liberalism is thus instrumental to integrate the international economy under the administration of the geoeconomic hegemon:

> If economic capabilities are so concentrated that a hegemon exists, as in the case of Great Britain in the late 19th century and the USA after World War II, an "open" or "liberal" international economic order will come into being. In the organisation of a liberal order, pride of place is given to market rationality. This is not to say that authority is absent from such an order. It is to say that authority relations are constructed in such a way as to give maximum scope to market forces rather than to constrain them (Ruggie 1982: 381).

Geoeconomic hegemons such as Britain in the 19th century and the US in the 20th century rose on economic nationalism, albeit once in a dominant position they embraced free trade to cement core-periphery relations. Liberal economics enables the hegemon's mature industries (high quality, low cost) to compete directly with the infant industries (low quality, high cost) of the rivals, the control over transportation corridors is not contested, and the international system naturally gravitates towards the banks and currency of the hegemon. Friedrich List (1841: 295–96) denounced free trade as the economic strategy of a hegemon by "kicking away the ladder" to economic greatness:

> It is a very common clever device that when anyone has attained the summit of greatness, he kicks away the ladder by which he has climbed up, in order to deprive others of the means of climbing up after him. In this lies the secret of the cosmopolitical doctrine of Adam Smith, and of the cosmopolitical tendencies of his great contemporary William Pitt, and of all his successors in the British Government administrations.

A geoeconomic hegemon can be defined as benign when the dominant position is preserved by providing collective goods for the whole system, as opposed to using its administrative role in the international economy to weaken competitors. While these two actions are contradictory, they must coexist. Sustaining a benign hegemon depends on a delicate balance between facilitating a rules-based international economic system and advancing national interests to perpetuate geoeconomic dominance. The use of economic coercion to advance national interests represents an abuse of the hegemon's administrative role over the international economic system, and rising powers are incentivised to decouple from the hegemon. The use of economic statecraft will always "costs something" (Baldwin 1985: 119). Kindleberger's (1986) hegemonic stability theory posits that the ability to supply collective goods results in voluntary alignment with the hegemon, which reduces the reliance on coercive means to prevent and deter decoupling.

The conditions of a benign hegemon are temporary. The costs of providing collective goods enable the small to exploit the large, and the asymmetries will incrementally even out (Olson 1965; Snidal 1985). Over time, "the differential growth in the power of various states in the system causes a fundamental redistribution of power in the system" (Gilpin 1981: 13). The geoeconomic hegemon faces a dilemma about how to respond to rising powers: Ascending states can be allowed to rise and thus disrupt the international distribution of power that underpins the hegemonic system, or economic coercion can be used against rising power but then forego the status as a benign hegemon. Either way, rising powers will balance the hegemon and rivalry ensues (Layne 1993).

The more rivals are suppressed, the greater incentive the rising powers will have to collectively balance the shared adversary (Huntington 1999). Hence, once economic power disperses away from the hegemon, "the liberal order is expected to unravel and its regimes to become weaker, ultimately being replaced by mercantilist arrangements" in which strategic autonomy and national sovereignty are elevated above market forces (Ruggie 1982: 381).

Geoeconomic regions

Regions are an important geoeconomic instrument that uses collective bargaining power to skew the balance of dependence. Economic regionalism entails a group of states reducing trade barriers among each other, while preserving protective measures against non-members of the region (Hettne 1993; Baldwin 1997; Mansfield and Milner 1999).

Symmetry in an interdependent relationship is achieved by increasing strategic autonomy, diversifying partnership to reduce excessive reliance on any one state or region, and/or seek collective bargaining power with other states. Geoeconomic regions achieve all of the above. Geoeconomic regions are also a natural response to more complex industrial economies as "self-reliance was never viable on the national level" (Hettne 1993: 227). Regions have subsequently become the central pillars of the global political economy (Buzan and Wæver 2003; Acharya 2007).

Much like the incentive for the formation of military alliances, "state A" and "state B" cooperate economically for a collective advantage over "state C." Helmut Schmidt (1974), the former Western German chancellor, predicted that geoeconomic regions would imitate the logic of militarised bloc politics in "the struggle for the world product." However, unlike military alliances, geoeconomic blocs do not need to confront third parties in a zero-sum manner. Instead, geoeconomic blocs can create a more durable format for cooperation with "state C" by improving the symmetry of interdependence and thus reduce unwarranted influence. Case in point, countries such as Russia, Kazakhstan, and Belarus may be more comfortable to deepen economic connectivity with China if they can do so under the format of the Eurasian Economic Union (EAEU) to have more equality in relations—thus reducing fears of excessive Chinese political influence.

Geoeconomic regions multiply as other states must react to the shifting balance of dependence caused by the emergence of new regions. For example, the Europeans pursued collective bargaining power through the EU to improve symmetry in relations with the US; then the US advanced the North American Free-Trade Agreement (NAFTA) in response to the growing competitiveness of the Europeans and Japanese; and next "the East Asian countries in view of the fortresses emerging in Europe and North America must plan for a future with a much stronger regional interdependence" (Hettne 1993: 227). In contrast to the liberal interpretation of regions, economic regionalism in Asia is commonly advocated to shield the region from the intrusive influence of the US (Breslin 2010: 714).

Geoeconomic regions are used both defensively by enhancing symmetry and offensively by increasing asymmetries. Benign and defensive geoeconomic regions can be defined as "inward-looking blocs, where protectionism is predominantly motivated by considerations of domestic welfare and internal political stability" (Buzan 1984: 608). Offensive regions seek to maximize asymmetrical dependence by non-members to establish core-periphery relations. The EU as a geoeconomic region acts pursues both defensive and offensive policies. The EU sought to improve symmetry with US, and also increase asymmetries with its own neighbourhood to dictate the terms of trade and extract political concessions.

External pressure is important to the viability of geoeconomic regions. Non-members have natural incentives to undermine the internal cohesion of a geoeconomic region. Why would any external state support a geoeconomic region organised to skew the balance of dependence? External states have a natural preference for bilateral arrangements with individual states of a region and can even be inclined to employ wedge strategies to weaken the solidarity of a region (Crawford 2011; Wigell and Vihma 2016: 611). Case in point, Brussels frequently accuses Russia of engaging its member states in bilateral agreements, while the EU only engages EAEU members bilaterally and even refuses to establish diplomatic relations.

A geoeconomic region can counter wedge strategies by reducing the porousness of regional borders. A region can centralise power or reduce economic connectivity with non-members by for example imposing economic sanctions. For example, the US fervent accusations of human rights abuses in China and Russia are consistently linked to economic sanctions aimed to reduce their economic footprint in Europe to preserve the economic structures and political loyalties that buttress the trans-Atlantic region. Geoeconomic power is inherently more covert and thus less likely to be balanced (Dzarasov, Lane, and Dadabaev 2017). Geoeconomic regions with economic porous borders, such as the trans-Atlantic region, also have incentives to militarise economic competition with external rivals to harden the external borders and enforce regional cohesion.

A geoeconomic region can remove the incentives for wedge tactics by becoming a benign region, defined as providing benefits for non-member states. This can be material benefits. For example, the Russian-led EAEU provides China with improved access to the region due to common standards, and the development of one custom zone between China's borders and the EU is vital for the competitiveness of Chinese land-based transportation corridors. Non-material benefits include mutual recognition of regions as "engagement of external powers can enhance the legitimacy of a region" (Hettne and Söderbaum 2000: 469). Brussels could increase the legitimacy and value of the EU towards Russia by recognising the legitimacy of the Russian-led EAEU, thus making Moscow a self-interested stakeholder in the preservation of the EU. A region also provides benefits for non-members of the region by becoming a component of a larger region. The EU gains support from the US by positioning itself as a sub-region of the wider trans-Atlantic region, the EAEU obtains legitimacy with China by placing itself as an autonomous region within the larger Greater Eurasian region. The EU could similarly enhance its legitimacy with both Russia and China by positioning itself as a sovereign region within Greater Eurasia.

The internal balance of dependence

Geoeconomics can more aptly be understood as a neoclassical realist approach to political economy. While realist theory outlines the external balance of power, neoclassical realism adds an important layer by assessing decision-making and the internal workings that preoccupied classical realists. Neoclassical realism therefore becomes a more suitable meeting point for regionalist theories and realist theory (Rose 1998; Schweller 1999). Neoclassical realism explores issues affecting internal cohesion as an intervening variable between the international distribution of power and foreign policy. The ability of a state or region to act rationally according to systemic pressures is conditioned on the extent to which it functions as a unitary actor.

Geoeconomic regions are less capable than states to act as unitary actors as the state remains the highest sovereign, and interests among the member states differ. The efficiency and durability of geoeconomic regions are largely dependent on the ability to align national interests. Harmonising the economic interests of members solidifies political loyalties, which is a requirement for maintaining internal cohesion and mobilising resources towards common goals.

Geoeconomic regions liberalise trade internally, yet imposes external protectionism to defend the internal socioeconomic structures (Buzan 1984: 613). The liberalisation of trade within the region is imperative to increase intra-regional economic connectivity and dependence, which translates into political loyalties towards the region. A dilemma presents itself as expanding the geoeconomic region strengthens the collective power and achieve a more favourable external balance of dependence, yet it can disrupt the internal balance of dependence and reduce the ability to preserve exercise socioeconomic stability at the national level.

In a national economy, the state intervenes to establish a balance between market efficiency and social responsibilities. These social responsibilities are defined differently by the political Left and the Political Right, yet they range from redistributing wealth to reduce economic inequality, providing mechanisms for social mobility, and defending traditional values, families and communities from unfettered market forces. Market efficiency is also limited by protecting domestic strategic industries and subsidising infant industries to avoid excessive reliance on foreign powers.

Liberalising economic connectivity within a region with similar and national economies can shield states from wider international economic liberalisation. Although, deepening economic liberalisation within a region can be problematic if the region is widened excessively and including vastly different economies. By enhancing market efficiency within a regional framework, member states are less able to exercise social responsibilities at the national level and support their strategic industries from competition within the region. Members of a region will subsequently need to manage the dilemma between regional solidarity and upholding the social responsibilities of the state.

As productive powers shift within the region and disrupt the internal balance of dependence, disadvantaged member states will have incentives to withdraw from the geoeconomic region. Furthermore, a skewed balance of power within a region enables the dominant actor to undermine the political sovereignty of other member states. Geoeconomic regions are therefore more beneficial and stable when the member states have a similar economic size (Sorhun 2014: 288).

The internal balance of dependence reflects a pragmatic cost-benefit approach by the members of a geoeconomic region, aimed towards maximising sovereignty. Geoeconomic regions are paradoxical as states seek membership to strengthen sovereignty through collective bargaining power, yet geoeconomic regions require the transfer of sovereignty towards the collective. A state like Italy will transfer sovereign powers to the EU with the expectation that the EU's collective geoeconomic bargaining power in the world will enhance its sovereignty. After all, by standing on its own, a country like Italy would easily be trapped in asymmetrical partnerships with more powerful counterparts. An implicit "social contract" thus forms that stipulates the material *benefits* provided by the EU must be greater than the *costs* of transferring sovereignty to Brussels.

The cost-benefit logic of sovereignty maximisation can be managed by improving the balance of dependence within a region. Under a skewed balance of dependence, the dominant state within a geoeconomic region will be able to maximise both its autonomy and influence among other member states. Yet, the concentration of power in a hegemon, one centre of power within the region, also makes it easier to liberalise trade, impose internal cohesion of the region, and limit the porousness of the region's external borders. The dominant powers within regions, such as the US within the trans-Atlantic partnership; Germany within the EU; or Russia within the EAEU, have the incentive to organise their respective geoeconomic regions as a cohesive unitary actor in the international system. Albeit, a skewed balance of dependence within a geoeconomic region and the subsequent loss of political sovereignty among other member states will have to be compensated in the form of delivering more collective goods.

The Europeans pursue collective bargaining power to improve symmetry in relations with the US within the trans-Atlantic region; the Mediterranean states, Eastern Europe, and Britain become more critical of the German-dominated EU; while Belarus and Kazakhstan express caution about the transfer of sovereign powers to a Russian-dominated EAEU unless it is outweighed by geoeconomic benefits. The emergence of powerful external powers enhances the benefit of membership in a geoeconomic region as an instrument to achieve symmetry with more powerful economic actors. Case in point, the rise of China incentivises Central Asian states to align closer with Russia to achieve a more favourable balance of dependence.

The dominant power within a geoeconomic region is confronted with a dilemma between prioritising the internal balance of dependence and the external balance of dependence. For example, the US has incentives to cement its position as a benign hegemon by providing collective benefits in the trans-Atlantic region and the Indo-Pacific region to marginalise rival centres of power such as Russia and China (Blackwill and Harris 2016).

However, the US will not be able to sustain the geoeconomic regions if the transfer of relative economic power to allies is not sustainable. While the NAFTA and the Trans-Pacific Partnership (TPP) were important initiatives to establish US-led geoeconomic regions, they were nonetheless abandoned as the transfer of geoeconomic power to allies undermined the dominant position of the US.

CENTRALISING POWER IN REGIONS

The centralisation of power in regions presents a dilemma between collective strength and internal vitality. Centralisation of power makes a region more capable to act, counteract wedge tactics, and harden geoeconomic borders. Although, with increased uniformity, a region loses its vigour and becomes less capable of reversing a regional decline.

In ancient Greece, the dilemma became evident in terms of the value of smaller political entities versus the impulse to create larger entities of power to confront rivals. The competition between various Greek city-states was the source for a diversity of ideas and a vitality that elevated Greek civilisation above others. Integration into one political system would entail losing the diversity of philosophy, wisdom, and leadership that incentivised experimentation and advancement. Greek city-states initially did not aspire for integration and centralisation of power as it contradicted the Hellenic idea and betrayed Greek civilisation. Yet, the competition with the Persians created incentives for Greek city-states to integrate to obtain collective strength and due to the rise of pan-Greek nationalism in confrontation with an external other. In the absence of a shared enemy, the Greeks then turned on each other, which culminated in the destructive Peloponnesian War.

The founding fathers of the US were greatly influenced by Greek-Roman experiences. The US political system also resembled that of the Greek city-states. Power was decentralised into various states, which limited the powers of federal authorities. The cooperation and competition between states fuelled vitality by enabling experimentation with economic models and governance. Much like the Greek confrontation with the Persians resulting in the concentration of power, so did the US begin centralising power to act more forcefully in the world. The competition resulting from the multitude of rival political entities in Europe also fuelled vitality and destruction. The EU as a geoeconomic region has been able to temper rivalry among members states, yet the push towards uniformity undermines the internal socioeconomic and political vitality.

Operationalising geoeconomics: the three pillars of nation-building and region-building

Geoeconomics is commonly used as an ambiguous and ill-defined concept. By exploring the roots of geoeconomic thinking it is possible to clearly define and operationalise the concept with observable and measurable indicators. Geoeconomics entails state intervention in the market to skew the symmetry of interdependence with the expectation that asymmetrical interdependence enhances political autonomy and influence. Not all market activity creates the same amount of dependence, and geoeconomics can therefore not be reduced to gross domestic product (GDP) and trade. Some economic activity creates more dependence due to the limited possibility for establishing strategic autonomy and diversifying partnerships. There are three geoeconomic levers of power for both nation-building and region-building: strategic industries, transportation corridors, and financial instruments.

Geoeconomics builds on the economic nationalism of the 19th century that recognised political autonomy could not be sufficiently sustained if they were excessively reliant on the British. The economic nationalist policies of Alexander Hamilton that resulted in the American System relied on state intervention in the economy to cement political independence from the British. The three pillars of the American System consisted of a manufacturing base, transportation corridors (roads, rail, and canals), and a national bank. The Germans similarly relied on protectionist policies to develop infant industries, constructed railways for physical connectivity between German states, and a banking revolution in the 1850s to mobilise domestic funds to finance development. The German customs union was a vital instrument for economic integration as a stepping-stone towards the political integration of German states. Russian industrialisation in the second half of the 19th century emulated the economic nationalism of Alexander Hamilton in the US and Friedrich List in Germany. Under the policies of Sergei Witte, Russian protection for infant industries resulted in rapid industrialisation, constructed railways through Central Asia and the trans-Siberian Railway to connect the vast Eurasian territory, and efforts were made to improve domestic financing.

Alexander Hamilton, Henry Clay, Friedrich List, Gustav Schmoller, Sergei Witte, and other economic nationalists of the 19th century did not reject Adam Smith's arguments about the benefits of market efficiency and free trade. Rather, they recognised that state intervention was necessary to limit asymmetrical interdependence as an impediment to political sovereignty. List (1827: 30) opined that liberal economics had to be balanced with the realist structure of the world:

As long as the division of the human race into independent nations exists, political economy will as often be at variance with cosmopolitan principles . . . a nation would act unwisely to endeavour to promote the welfare of the whole human race at the expense of its particular strength, welfare and independence.

The reallocation of funds to develop industry, transportation infrastructure, and financial instruments are considered national investments to skew the balance of dependence with other states in the international system. As "free trade" entailed integration into core-periphery relations with the dominant state, economic nationalists in the 19th century advocated "fair trade" in terms of creating more equitable economic relationships.

The same three pillars of geoeconomics are used to construct regions. Geoeconomics incentives regionalism as regions have more capacity for self-sufficiency and can negotiate with the wider world from a position of collective autonomy and influence. A region, unified economically with strategic industries, transportation corridors, and financial instruments, creates incentives for political loyalties that enable the region to behave as a powerful unitary actor.

In the 19th century, London established a British-led Europe by controlling manufacturing as the strategic industry of its time, dominated the seas as the main transportation corridor, and had the leading trade currency and banks. After the Second World War, Washington advanced a US-led trans-Atlantic region with the leading technologies, taking control over the key sea-lanes and choke points of the world, and asserting its financial leadership with the dominance of the dollar and US control over the International Monetary Fund (IMF) and the World Bank. The European Union (EU) has similarly developed an autonomous European region within the trans-Atlantic region with industrial policies to support strategic industries, developing bimodal transportation corridors, and financial power with the Euro as a trade currency and a regional development bank.

STRATEGIC INDUSTRIES

Strategic industries are defined by scarcity and their importance to socio-economic development, which makes them pivotal to ensure autonomy and create dependencies by others. Natural resources can be considered strategic industries due to the imperative of reliable supply. Innovative and advanced technologies are also strategic industries as tools for an efficient economy and the limited ability to diversify.

Geoeconomic dominance is attained by "develop[ing] exports in articles enjoying a monopolistic position in other countries and direct trade to such countries" (Hirschman 1945: 34). The quasi-monopolistic position of a technological leader results in greater economic gains as competition places downward pressures on profit. The technological leader can also extract significant political concessions from other states due to the inability to develop competitive self-sufficiency or diversify economic partners.

The core-periphery relations in the 19th century was defined by manufactured goods as a strategic industry vis-à-vis agricultural goods that had lower profitability and did not produce the same dependence due to the scope for diversification of partners. List (1841: 269) warned against succumbing to economic colonisation by failing to industrialise the economy:

> The mother nation supplies the colonies with manufactured goods, and obtains in return their surplus produce of agricultural products and raw materials. . . The superior power of the mother country in population, capital, and enterprising spirit, obtains through colonisation an advantageous outlet.

In the digital era, new and smart economies add another layer to industrial growth. States aim to transition from a manufacturing economy and to a smart and innovative economy. The highest stage is difficult to reach due to the middle-income trap. Developing economies that rise rapidly on low-wage manufacturing suddenly stagnate when salaries grow and they are no longer competitive as manufacturers, yet have not developed the capabilities of an innovative smart economy.

The central role of strategic industries is enduring as evident by the US and Russian competition to supply Europe with gas. Similarly, the US and China are competing to supply Europe with digital platforms, such as 5G technology. The EU is subsequently seeking to diversify its energy supplies and pursues ambitious industrial policies to advance "strategic autonomy" due to the assumption that reliance on foreign strategic industries diminishes political sovereignty and influence.

Economic nationalists avoid direct free-trade competition against the economic hegemon as their infant industries (low quality, high cost) could not develop and compete against the mature industries (high quality, low cost) of the dominant power. Economic nationalists therefore use temporary subsidies and tariffs to develop infant industries. Furthermore, wages and the national currency can be suppressed to increase exports and minimise imports. This export-based strategy can be considered an investment in the future as the standard of living is temporarily reduced for its citizens, although it enables the country to accrue productive power and foreign reserves. A state that produces and saves can thus establish temporary interdependence with a state that borrows and consumes.

Competition in the international system for leadership in strategic industries can create instability at the domestic level. Industrialisation, the transition from rural agricultural societies to urban manufacturing societies represented immense socioeconomic disruptions that unleashed instability and revolutions. Similarly, in the digital era, the transition from manufacturing societies to innovative smart economies resulted in creative destruction that collapsed entire communities. Case in point, US digital leadership required trade agreements that offshored manufacturing jobs, which divided the country as some parts thrived and other parts of the country experienced a socioeconomic decline. The subsequent political instability undermines the ability of the state to mobilise resources to compete in the international sphere.

TRANSPORTATION CORRIDORS

Transportation corridors are imperative to physically connect both the national and regional economy. Countries such as Germany, with excellent river systems, have been more capable to develop an efficient and competitive economy. Albeit, without a regional format that offers reliable regional transportation corridors, the economic connectivity with the wider world will be at the mercy of rival powers. States controlling key transportations corridors are more inclined to embrace open markets to enhance economic efficiency as they have less risk to be cut off from the arteries of international trade. Trade-post empires established taxation for access to ports, while also limiting the access of rivals to key markets. The ability to assure or deny freedom of navigation also enables the dominant state to extract political concessions. The dominance over maritime corridors for international trade has therefore made land-powers less willing to gamble on freedom of navigation and instead prioritise autarchy (Hirschman 1945: 8).

Controlling transportation corridors is imperative to construct region as evident by the Swedish-Russian competition in the Baltic Sea in the 17th and 18th centuries; the French-British rivalry over the Suez Canal in the 19th century; the US-Russian competition in the Baltic Sea, Black Sea and the Arctic in the 21st century; and the US-Chinese rivalry over the South China Sea and the Strait of Malacca in the 21st century. Energy corridors, both transportation routes and pipelines, have also remained a consistent focus of great power politics. Case in point, the British Commissioner to South Russia, Halford Mackinder, advocated that the British seize control over the Baku-Batumi energy corridor during the Russian Revolution as an instrumental asset to build an anti-Russian alliance. The post-Cold War effort of NATO states to establish an energy corridor through Georgia and Azerbaijan to gain access to the energy resources of the Caspian Sea and Central Asia follows almost the same route.

While the US established its dominance of strategic transportation corridors after the Second World War, China's multi-trillion dollar bimodal Belt and Road Initiative is challenging US primacy over physical connectivity.

FINANCIAL INSTRUMENTS

States require financial instruments to mobilise capital through national banks and establish a competitive currency for financial autonomy and influence. Germany's banking revolution in the mid-19th century was motivated by the need to assert national sovereignty, yet by the early 20th century, the rise of German financial power represented an existential threat to Italy's financial autonomy and thus political sovereignty (Preziosi 1916).

National currencies can be a source of national independence, regional currencies are central for political integration, and the national control over international trade and reserve currencies is an immense source of global geoeconomic power. Control over payment systems, most notably the dominant position of the Society for Worldwide Interbank Financial Telecommunication (SWIFT), has also been a key coercive instrument for the US to impose extraterritorial sanctions and even cut countries off from access to international banking.

The US developed financial sovereignty under the American System to limit reliance on the British, and then eventually replaced the global financial standing of the British. Valéry Giscard d'Estaing, the former president of France, famously referred to the "exorbitant privilege" of the US dollar in the international economic system, which echoed de Gaulle (Eichengreen 2011: 65). As the Nobel Laureate Robert Mundell (1993) articulated: "Great powers have great currencies." The Euro subsequently became an important instrument to reduce the privilege of the US dollar and to pursue political integration of European states. To decouple from the unipolar order of the US, China and Russia must subsequently also develop strategic financial autonomy.

CONCLUSION

Geoeconomic theory provides valuable insight into the role of economic power to advance political autonomy and influence. The control over strategic industries, transportation corridors, and financial instruments is intrinsically linked to nation-building and region-building. Geoeconomics explains the competition within regions and between regions, and even the occasional outbreak of economic liberalism under a benign geoeconomic hegemon.

The theory on geoeconomic regions is vital to understand why the emergence of a Greater Eurasian region will impact Europe. Geoeconomics abide by the theoretical assumptions of neoclassical realist theory as relative gains are pursued to maximise sovereignty and security. Under militarised geopolitics, the emergence of a Russian-Chinese strategic partnership would harden the external borders of the West and Europe as geopolitical regions. Under geoeconomics, regional borders are more porous and balancing requires a symmetry of interdependence rather than containment and complete autarchy.

2

Eurasia as a Geoeconomic Region

The failure to accommodate major land powers in the oceanic world economy has historically incentivised efforts to reinvent a Eurasian region. The leading theory about the geostrategic rivalry between land powers and maritime powers was most famously developed in the writings by Halford Mackinder in the early 20th century. However, Mackinder was preceded by Russia's efforts since the beginning of the 19th century to revive ancient land corridors as a response to the failure to establish reliable maritime trade corridors. Thereafter, Friedrich List envisioned an Anglo-German Eurasian land corridor in 1846, which was later reimagined as a German-led Eurasian continental bloc through both world wars. In more recent times, Russia and China have begun to collaborate to develop the geoeconomic architecture to integrate Europe and Asia into a Greater Eurasia.

Nomadic civilisations previously ruled over the Eurasian steppes as their mobility endowed them with commercial and military competitiveness. The nomadic Scythians migrated from Central Asia westwards towards southern Russia and Ukraine in the 8th and 7th centuries BC and established an empire centred in Crimea. The Huns similarly emerged from Central Asia through Crimea with their nomadic horsemen skills and attacked the Roman Empire in the 4th and 5th centuries. Yet again, the Mongols invaded Russia in the 13th century as they entered along the same path, through Central Asia and Crimea. The Mongols revived the ancient Silk Road in the 13th and 14th centuries, a trade corridor that had been very active in the 2nd and 3rd centuries. The Mongols were the last custodians of the great land corridors that placed Central Asia at the heart of world trade before European maritime powers reorganised the arteries of global commerce from the early 16th century.

Russian Eurasianism suggests that Russia's geography makes it the natural successor of the Mongol Empire. For most of its history, Russia struggled with establishing an organic path to development as a Eurasian power attempting to modernise as a European maritime power. Russian ambitions to regain its status as a European power has also been resisted by European powers for three centuries. A Eurasian political economy denotes that Russia must embrace its Eurasian geography to obtain economic competitiveness vis-à-vis the oceanic powers of the world.

Establishing a Eurasian geoeconomic region is an ambitious effort to restore the economic connectivity along the Eurasian landmass to revive the competitiveness of land powers. In the era of an oceanic-centric international economy, the economic infrastructure of the land-locked Eurasian space is merely organised to feed maritime trade. Eurasian land powers subsequently are relegated to economically backward regions and their interdependence with maritime powers are organised unfavourably according to core-periphery structures.

The geoeconomics of Eurasia suggests that the nomadic mobility of land powers can be restored in the modern era with railways and various bimodal transportation infrastructure. The objective of a Eurasian region is thus to organise the strategic industries, transportation corridors, and financial instruments from the centre of the Eurasian continent to counter maritime powers attempting to rule Eurasia from the oceanic periphery.

This chapter first explores Russia's incremental path towards establishing Eurasia as a geoeconomic region. Russia aimed for centuries to break free from the economic isolation of Eurasia by expanding towards maritime corridors in Europe. Following the humiliating defeat in the Crimean War in the 1850s, Russia began to modernise and connect the Eurasian landmass with railways. By the end of the 19th century appeared destined to lead one of the two major economic regions of the world. The Bolshevik Revolution derailed the revolutionary economic statecraft, albeit Russian emigres formalised the concept of a conservative Eurasian political economy that should guide Russia's strategic thinking once the Marxist experiment inevitably failed.

Second, the German concept of a Eurasian region is assessed. After decades of seeking to revive a new format of the Napoleonic Continental European, Friedrich List proposed in 1846 to construct an Anglo-German continental bridge from Belgium to India to counter the rapid rise of the US. In the early 20th century, Germany instead began to develop the Berlin-Baghdad railway in a partnership with the Ottoman Empire. General Haushofer similarly advocated, well into the Second World War, that Germany should balance aggressive maritime powers by forming a Eurasian continental bloc with Russia, China, India, and Japan.

Last, the Eurasian theories of the British by Mackinder and the Americans by Spykman focused on preventing the rise of a state or a group of states on the Eurasian continent capable of wrestling geoeconomic control away from the oceanic powers. These theories influenced the Cold War policies of balancing the Soviet Union and then the post-Cold War policies aimed towards cementing the unipolar moment.

It is concluded that incentives for Russia and China to collectively con-struct the geoeconomic foundations for Greater Eurasia is consistent with the efforts through history to develop a Eurasian region.

RUSSIA AS THE CUSTODIAN OF AN
ECONOMICALLY BACKWARD EURASIA

Russia originated as a European power and was exiled into an economically backward Eurasian geography. Economic development and modernisation subsequently entailed returning to Europe. Russia commonly identifies Kievan Rus as its civilisational cradle, a "normal" European maritime power located on the Dnieper River and connected with the arteries of trade. The influence of the Byzantine Empire in the south and the Vikings in the north rooted the Russians in Europe (Quigley 1961: 81). Kievan Rus was inte-grated into the Hanseatic League with European trade networks between Scandinavia and Byzantium. The fragmentation of Kievan Rus resulted in the Russians losing much of their access to maritime corridors and international trade, while the following invasion by the Mongols in the 13th century made Russia largely disappear from the European political map for the next 250 years (Hosking 2001).

The rise of Moscow, located far away from major trade corridors, did not become a major power due to its economic connectivity. Moscow's distance from maritime trade corridors enabled it to recover in the protective embrace of the north-eastern forests. In the mid-15th century, Moscow expanded rapidly to the north, deeper into remote regions to avoid clashes with the Mongols in the south and the east, and Polish-Lithuania in the west. The new territories of Moscow had weak economic potential and the economy transitioned further towards agriculture. The territorial expansion away from international trade further isolated Russia from economic connectivity with the Europeans.

By the late 15th century, Moscow was able to shed the Mongol yoke and continued to unify Russian lands to recover its strength. The Tatars, deemed indistinguishable from the Mongols, continued to linger threatening at the periphery until the Russian victory and conquest of Kazan in 1552. With the Tatar kingdoms defeated along the Volga river, the vast Eurasian steppes were opened for Russian colonisers. For the first time in history, a European power emerged as the possible successor of the Scythians, the Huns, and the Mongols to control Eurasia.

The lesson for Russia following the victory over the Tatars was that it had to adopt a Eurasian strategy for security. The open spaces without naturally defensible borders such as mountain ranges or oceans made Russia vulnerable to invasions from all sides. As a Eurasian power, Russia relied on its vast territory as a buffer zone to absorb invading forces through attrition by cutting off the supply lines of invading forces. Since Ivan the Terrible, expansion became a defensive strategy and Catherine the Great explicitly made the statement that the best way to defend Russian borders were to expand them. Russia consolidated its control over newly acquired territories by further expanding its borders, which resulted in an impulsive expansion. Over three centuries, between 1613 and 1917, Russia expanded an average of 140 square kilometres per day (Heller 2015).

Novgorod thrived by trading with the Europeans through the partnership with the Hanseatic League, while the rest of Russia was still recovering and readjusting from the Mongol invasion. Although, the unification of Russian lands following Mongol occupation led to the brutal massacre of Novgorod in 1570 by Ivan the Terrible to place it under the authority of Moscow. Novgorod did not recover as a trading city, and the economic connectivity of Russians continued to suffer. Arkhangelsk was then founded on the White Sea in 1584 as the principal port to trade with the English. Its location, near the Arctic Circle, made its inhospitable geographical location a natural source of defence.

Russia almost fell under the European yoke in the early 17th century during the Time of Troubles. Poland invaded and seized Moscow and Sweden conquered the trading city of Novgorod, while approximately a third of the Russian population perished under the Time of Troubles. Russia was finally able to expel the Polish invaders and an agreement was reached with Sweden in 1617, the Treaty of Stolbovo, in which Sweden ended its interference within Russia in return for controlling the maritime corridors by depriving Russia's direct and independent access to the Baltic Sea. Although, Sweden failed to obtain control over the port of Arkhangelsk, which was an important objective to completely subjugate Russia.

Russia eventually reasserted itself as a European power under Peter the Great, who sought to modernise Russia by shedding its Eurasian past. The victory over Sweden in the Great Northern War (1700–1721) and the subsequent foundation of St. Petersburg made Russia a maritime power. The victory officially established the Russian Empire in 1721 and ushered in three centuries of Russia's occidental era. Europe was defined by the Russian leadership as a region stretching to the Ural Mountains, which thus included the most populous region of Russia (Neumann 1994).

Peter the Great also launched a divisive cultural revolution to uproot and eviscerate Russia's Muscovite past in Eurasia to become more European. After establishing itself as the dominant force in the Baltic Sea, Russia aimed to modernise its economy and restore itself as a normal European maritime great power.

Although, other European powers have ever since countered Russia by attempting to push the country back into the Eurasian space. As US naval power became more powerful than the British, Spykman (1942: 182) wrote it was the responsibility of the US to take over the historic responsibility of encircling and containing Russia by limiting its access to maritime corridors:

> For two hundred years, since the time of Peter the Great, Russia has attempted to break through the encircling ring of border states and the reach the ocean. Geography and sea power have persistently thwarted her.

Escaping containment by maritime powers became a key challenge for Russia through the next centuries. Russia's confinement as a Eurasian land-power resembles the challenge of Germany since the 19th century as a rising industrial power with the geographical limitations of a land-power at the centre of Europe. Dostoevsky (1997: 891–92) described the historical challenge for

> an enormous giant as Russia to emerge at last from his locked room in which he has already grown to reach the ceiling—to emerge into open spaces where he can breathe the free air of the seas and oceans.

THE BRIEF RUSSIAN-FRENCH
EURASIAN PARTNERSHIP

The concept of a Eurasian region capable of reaching the maritime edges can be traced to an agreement between Tsar Paul I of Russia and Napoleon in the late 18th century. Britain and France had fought throughout the 18th century for dominance over the seas, and Napoleon looked towards consolidating control over continental Europe and land corridors to challenge the British Empire. Russia had allied itself with Britain and other European monarchies against France in the 1790s due to its opposition to the liberal ideology and Jacobin destructiveness of the French Revolution. However, Tsar Paul I switching sides in the conflict.

In an agreement with Napoleon, Tsar Paul I dispatched a Cossack army to march across Central Asia to seize British India (Van der Oye 2015). Collectively, the French and Russians could defeat the British by mastering the Eurasian space and thus possibly assert global primacy. However, Tsar Paul was assassinated in 1801 and the Cossack army was returned to Russia and the vision of Eurasia as a wider geostrategic chessboard was suspended. Napoleon also courted Paul's successor, Alexander I, with the same plan to march on British India, although Alexander I declined (Hopkirk 2001).

Russia, heavily dependent on trade with the British, rejected the European Continental System and Napoleon responded by invading Russia in 1812.

Russian Eurasianism after the Crimean War

The Great Game, the British-Russian rivalry in Central Asia throughout the 19th century, was a clear manifestation of sea power versus land power to dominate Eurasia. Russia's victory in the Russian-Persian War (1826–1828) had appeared to pave the way for future Russian dominance in the southern Eurasian region. The war weakened British influence due to its inability to provide support, and Persia had to look towards Russia as the leading regional power. The risk of a Russian-Persian conquest of British India became a growing concern for Britain, as a possible repetition of the Russian-French initiative at the beginning of the century.

Britain, allied with France and the Ottoman Empire, finally went to war against Russia in the Crimean War (1853–1856). Russia had been expanding along the Black Sea to advance a maritime political economy. Russia would cement its position as a conservative European great power by retaking Constantinople from the Ottomans, a key city in the Christian world and a vital coastal city that would make Russia a leading maritime power in the Mediterranean. Dostoevsky (1997: 900) later opined that retaking Constantinople "contains as well our final collision with Europe and our final uniting with her."

Although, European diplomats had openly argued that the motivation for going to war in Crimea had been to push Russia back into Asia and exclude it from Europe (Kipp and Lincoln 1979: 4). The attack on Russia was deemed to be a great betrayal as narrow power interests were elevated above civilizational ideals for the region. A historical parallel could be drawn as the Fourth Crusade intended to recapture Jerusalem from Muslim control was instead redirected towards pillaging and destroying Constantinople in 1204, the world's largest Christian city.

Russia's humiliating defeat had largely been caused by its failure to industrialise and the absence of railway infrastructure to enhance mobility across Russia's vast geographical expanse (Blackwell 2015: 184). Russia did not have the Eurasian features of a fast-paced nomadic power, while Britain and France had been able to transport supplies and reinforcements faster from the maritime corridor from Gibraltar to Crimea than Russia could reach Crimea from Moscow.

Russia's Great Reforms that followed its humiliating defeat in the Crimean War included physical connectivity with extensive construction of railways. The initial railway lines constructed after the Crimean War had a quasi-colonial design as they were financed by British, French, and German corporations to extract resources from Russia to the West. However, Russia's railways towards the East had the geoeconomic utility of reducing the core-periphery relations with Western Europe by developing the foundations for a Eurasian political economy. Russia's defeat in the Crimean War had slowed down expansion into Central Asia, although supported by railways, Russia pushed into the region again in the 1860s.

The lessons of the Crimean War was that Russia had to physically connect its vast territory. Following the conquest of new territory in the East, Russia consolidated control over its territorial acquisition with railway. By 1879, railways were firmly built into the expansion strategy into Central Asia (Cheshire 1934). The expansion into Central Asia was motivated by security considerations, although the economic benefits also became evident as Russia gained access to cheap cotton and other natural resources.

At the time when Western European maritime powers were dividing the world among each other, Russia was charting a path with a land-based empire through the Eurasian continent until reaching the Hindu Kush mountain range—almost connecting with British India. The Trans-Caspian Railway stretched towards Herat in Afghanistan and revealed ambitions about connecting with India at the southern maritime periphery of the Eurasian super-continent (Cheshire 1934: 96). The British-Russian conflict only came to an end with the Pamir Boundary Commission protocols of 1895, which made Afghanistan a buffer state between the Russian Empire and the British Empire.

However, while Britain had temporarily secured India as its most valued colonial possession, Russia also began to establish connectivity with the Pacific Coast. Following Britain's victory over China in the Opium Wars of the 1850s, Russia also expanded its presence in the region by seizing 1.5 million square kilometres of Chinese territory in the Treaty of Aigun in 1858 and the Treaty of Peking in 1860. The founding of Vladivostok in 1860 on the Pacific Coast gave Russia the ability to challenge the British navy.

Towards the end of the 19th century, Russia had developed robust geoeconomic power. Russia's new Finance Minister in 1892, Sergei Witte, adopted the policies of Friedrich List and even translated some of List's work into a Russian-language pamphlet that was distributed. Russia rose to become the fastest growing economy among all the largest powers in the world. Temporary tariffs and subsidies were used to support infant industries in Russia until they matured. Under Witte, Russia developed railways at an unprecedented rate. Russia had 31,000 km of railway tracks in 1891, 53,000 km in 1900, and 70,000 km by 1913.

Instead of feeding maritime-led trade, the new railways were organised to connect the vast Russian regions and rival maritime powers. Witte (1954: 66) endeavoured to end Russia's role as an exporter of natural resources to the West, which resembled "the relations of colonial countries with their

metropolises." Trade with Asia was aimed to offset Russia's unfavourable economic position in Europe. The reliance on foreign capital was also
aimed to be overcome by mobilising the profits from trade with Asia (Witte
1954: 71).

In 1891, Tsar Alexander III commenced with the construction of the Trans-
Siberian Railway to connect Moscow with Vladivostok to consolidate its control over the north-eastern Pacific Coast. Russia then sought a warm-water
port on the Pacific coast by leasing Port Arthur on the Chinese coast of the
Yellow Sea in 1898, which was to be connected with the Trans-Siberian
Railway. However, Japan went to war against Russia, with material support
from Britain, which led to Russia's humiliating defeat in 1905 that also cancelled the lease of Port Arthur (Towle 1980). The domestic instability caused
by Russia's defeat to Japan also became an important contributing factor to
the Bolshevik Revolution in 1917.

Birth of Russian Eurasianism as a conservative political economy

Eurasianism was first developed as a Russian conservative political movement in the 1920s following the Bolshevik Revolution. Russian conservatives
had previously identified themselves as Slavophiles due to the Slavic and
Eastern European origin of Russia. However, the Eurasianists recognised that
the revolution had fundamentally altered Russia and attempting to turn back
the clock contradicts the conservative ethos of organic change.

The Eurasianists subsequently incorporated Turkic, Ugro-Finnic and other
non-Slavic elements into the collective historical consciousness and identity
of Russia. The invasion of the Mongols in the 13th century and Russia's
annexation of Tatar kingdoms along the Volga River in the mid-16th century
had given Russia a Eurasian character, which had been further cemented
by the Soviet experience. Russia's eastern experience was instead hailed by
the Eurasianists as the Mongols protected the Orthodox Church and Russia
from the spiritual decadence of the Roman-Germanic world (Mirsky 1927).
Eurasianism represented the transformation of the Russian Empire established by Peter the Great that ruled over other peoples, to become a Eurasian
civilization state. The Eurasianists denounced the Soviet Union as a far-Left
Eurasian project, although they advocated it should be replaced with a conservative Eurasian project rather than a neo-Petrine return to Europe.

Savitsky argued that the First World War had largely been caused by
maritime powers compelling Germany to expand eastwards, which would
also set the stage for future conflicts between Germany and Russia. Savitsky
believed, much like Mackinder had feared, that an alliance with Germany
was the best solution to collectively balance the oceanic powers. The maritime powers had a natural proclivity towards destructive divide and conquer

strategies, as the Eurasian continent had to be divided to rule it from the periphery (Savitsky 1921). In contrast, Eurasian powers were strong by cooperating and harmonising their interests. Russia's geographical position made it a natural "Middle Kingdom" that could unify Eurasia and thus end oceanic imperialism (Savitsky 1996).

The great curse of Russia could be diagnosed as a Eurasian power attempting to modernise as a Western European state. The obsession with the West had prevented Russia from advancing an organic path towards change and modernisation, and the Eurasian geography had been treated as a disadvantage rather than an asset that could transform the geoeconomic architecture of the world. The Eurasianist conservative argument suggested that Eurasianism had to be embraced to preserve Russia's cultural distinctiveness and to develop a Eurasian political economy.

Trubetskoi and Savitsky, leading figures within the Eurasianist movement, were profoundly influenced by Mackinder's ideas of Eurasia. The title of Savitsky's (1921) paper "Continent-Ocean" analysed the political economy based on geography and the dichotomy between maritime powers and land powers. Oceanic states were recognised to be more competitive due to the proximity to maritime transportation corridors, while land-locked regions are destined to become the perpetual economic backwater in a core-periphery global economy (Savitsky 1921). No other region in the world is more distanced from the sea than Central Asia.

Rather than attempting to reinvent Russia as a European maritime power, Savitsky argued that Russia should establish a regional land-based economy at the centre of Eurasia. Eurasian economic integration for regional strategic autonomy was deemed imperative to scale back the domination of maritime power and avoid core-periphery economic relationship. The competitiveness of oceanic power could be reversed by developing railways to revive the nomadic character and impulse of former Eurasian civilisations (Savitsky 1997).

German Eurasianism: Friedrich List and vision of an Anglo-German Eurasia

Before the Crimean War, Britain was presented with a proposal for an Anglo-Germanic Eurasia. Friedrich List had for most of his life viewed economic nationalism and the prospect of a new European continental system as a strategy for Germany to counter British geoeconomic dominance. List, therefore, had great sympathy for and supported Hamilton's economic nationalism in the late 18th century and early 19th century as the US shared the challenges of Germany. Yet, towards the end of his life, List recognised that the spectacular rise of the US would soon disrupt the international distribution of power. The US appeared destined to surpass Britain and dominate the sea, which should incentivise Britain to forego its hegemonic strategy and instead develop a partnership with Germany.

List recognised that the invention of the railway enabled states to revive the mobility of old nomadic powers that controlled land corridors. List argued that Britain could enhance its competitiveness vis-à-vis the US if it developed land corridors across the Eurasian continent to complement its maritime power (Henderson 2012: 120). Herein was the foundation of an Anglo-German alliance to resist the emergence of US dominance. List posited that Britain should support German industry, navigation, and trade, while Germany should support the British navy by constructing and controlling the western end of a Eurasian land-corridor. Britain would defend Germany from the French and the Russians, and Germany would protect Britain's transportation corridors through the Balkans and the Middle East (Stråth 2008: 176–77).

In 1846, Friedrich List developed his proposal for a trans-Eurasian continental system in his memorandum on "The Railway Line from Ostend to Bombay." Ostend is a harbour on the Belgium coast, and the railway line would run through the Balkans and Baghdad before reaching Bombay. List presented his document "On the Value and Conditions of an Alliance between Great Britain and Germany" to leading English statesmen in 1846, which stipulated that Britain could only preserve its existing role in the world by engaging in an alliance with the Germans (List 1846).

The rise of America and Russia was making the case for an Anglo-German partnership (Henderson 1983: 117). Collectively, Britain and Germany could dominate Eurasia by controlling both the land and sea. With striking similarities to the French-Russian plan to collectively dominate the world by taking British India, the German proposal suggested that Britain required Germany to keep its empire. The English rejected the idea of List and continued along the status-quo of ruling the world by controlling the sea.

List aptly predicted the US future incursion into the Pacific. More than half a century later, President Roosevelt was greatly influenced by Brooks Adams' *America's Economic Supremacy* and Alfred Thayer Mahan's *The Problem of Asia*, as the US set forth an ambitious strategy to control the maritime corridors of the Pacific Ocean. Both Adams and Mahan recognised the growing future role of Asia in the international economy, and both voiced deep concerns about Russian expansionism.

Half a century later, the ideas of List were revived in the 1890s as the Pan-German League proposed the Berlin-Baghdad Railway in cooperation with the declining Ottoman Empire. The initiative was pushed during the same decade Russia was constructing the Trans-Siberian Railway to connect Moscow with the Pacific Ocean by land. The Berlin-Baghdad Railway was constructed between 1903 and 1940, which was aimed to be connected with German seaports on the Persian Gulf. The British were consequently concerned that Germany would use its land corridors to take over British oil fields in Iraq and Iran (Ireland 1941). The Russian Empire and French Empire were also threatened by Berlin-Baghdad railway, as it would facilitate German control over the Balkans and access to the natural resources in the Middle East. The heightened geostrategic significance of the Balkans subsequently contributed greatly to the First World War.

GERMANY'S EURASIAN CONTINENTAL BLOC

Friedrich Ratzel (2019), influenced by Alfred Thayer Mahan, wrote *Politische Geographie* in 1897 about the industrialisation of Germany and the rivalry with Britain. Ratzel's concept of the "law of the growing spaces" made him look towards the Pacific shores as the greatest potential for growth and power. Ratzel viewed the giant space as the "dawn of the Pacific age, the successor to the ageing Atlantic, the over-age of Mediterranean and the European era" (Weigert 1942: 735). Ratzel's view of the future importance of the Pacific Ocean was shared by the Americans and expressed explicitly by Theodor Roosevelt.

Ratzel's ideas of Eurasia were developed further by Rudolf Kjellén, who coined the term geopolitics. Russia's victory over Sweden in the Great Northern War (1700–1721), followed by Sweden's loss of Finland in 1809, had compelled Sweden to choose between East and West, and Sweden positioned itself as a western maritime power. By conceptualising Europe and Asia as a single Eurasian continent, Kjellén (1900: 179) compared the location of Sweden with Korea as Sweden must "always be looked at in the context of the larger organic whole" of Eurasia. The rise of Russia challenged Sweden in the same way as it challenged Korea in the early 1900s, as Russia could absorb Scandinavia to improve its access to the Atlantic (Kjellén 1900: 58).

The German General Karl Haushofer, inspired by the writings of Mackinder, Ratzel and Kjellén, developed the ideas of German territorial expansion to facilitate industrial rise. Haushofer recognised the division between sea and land powers and considered it necessary to control both sea and land to overcome this rivalry. Also recognising the shifting balance of power in the world, Haushofer was against a war between England and Germany as it would devastate Europe and thus leave the Pacific to be ruled by the Americans and the Japanese. Haushofer (1924) believed that Germany had to shift its focus to the Pacific as the land-powers of Eurasia shared a common cause against the oppressive rule by the maritime powers. Haushofer envisioned a partnership with the Asians as the Europeans had excluded Germany from maritime-based regions:

By a dreadful decision, with consequences of utmost gravity for those who made it, the ocean-embracing cultural and economic powers of our own race have expelled us from their midst. They have left us in no doubt about the fact that only their destruction and decomposition will create another life for us who are now mutilated and enslaved. Thus they have forced us to search for comrades of destiny who are in a similar situation. We see such companions of disaster in the 900 million southeast Asiatics (quoted in Weigert 1942: 736).

General Haushofer advocated that Hitler seek reconciliation with Russia to establish an alliance as a successful strategy required a clear choice in the dilemma between maritime powers or Eurasian land-powers. In 1925, Haushofer wrote that Germany had to decide: "does she want to be a satellite of the Anglo-Saxon powers and their super-capitalism, which are united with the other European nations against Russia, or will she be an ally of the Pan Asiatic union against Europe and America?" (quoted in Weigert 1942: 740). Haushofer (1924: 142–43) envisioned a "Eurasian continental organization from the Rhine to the Amur and Yangtze," and argued that Germany and Russia were destined to complement each other.

Haushofer thus considered the Molotov-Ribbentrop non-aggression pact of 1939 to be a great triumph. Russia was deemed to be an indispensable partner to construct a German-Russian-Chinese-Japanese transcontinental Eurasian block. Haushofer also encouraged the communists in Moscow to overcome Marxist ideology and align themselves with (non-communist) China as "the geopolitical future will belong to the Russian-Chinese bloc," which is why Germany and Japan would need to make their peace with Russia and China (quoted in Weigert 1942: 741).

General Haushofer's ambitions for Germany to expand its *lebensraum* (living space) was incorporated by the national socialists, although the strategic thinking was corrupted by anti-Bolshevism, radical race theory, and hegemonic solutions. Haushofer seemingly had different ambitions for Germany as he desired an alliance with Russia, India, China, and Japan. However, Hitler's decision to attack the Soviet Union effectively destroyed the dream of the Eurasian Continental Bloc. Haushofer, seemingly disappointed, argued that the Eurasian goal could still be achieved, but it would then have to be under German dominance (Herwig 2016: 186).

Hitler frequently referred to America's westward expansion as a model to be emulated, which was a key motivation for German expansion to the East. The territorial expansion of the US in the 19th century had few precedents in history, and the establishment of a continental-sized state dwarfed the competitiveness of European states. Much like the Americans had displaced the Native Americans, so did Hitler believe he could merely push aside inferior races to clear the path for the Germans to exploit the vast economic possibilities in the East. Hitler, looking to the East argued: "In the East a similar process will repeat itself for a second time as in the conquest of America" (Beorn 2018: 61). Germany failed to make a strategic choice towards a Eurasian Continental System to balance the growing power of maritime states, and the aspiration for hegemony culminated in the invasion of the Soviet Union and the subsequent downfall of Germany.

The Anglo-American containment of Eurasia

Maritime powers such as the UK and US have historically pursued an offshore strategy aimed to prevent a hegemon from emerging in Eurasia (Mearsheimer and Walt 2016). Island-states preserve their strength due to the lack of need for a large standing army. The expensive and antagonistic balancing is left to land powers, as the threat to major island-states is only threatened by the emergence of a hegemon.

The offshore strategy stipulates that the island-state only enter Eurasian land wars at a later stage when the major powers have exhausted their resources and manpower. The offshore balancer enters the war with the limited objective of ensuring an outcome with a balance of power, before withdrawing from the Eurasian continent. The pragmatic balance of power designs for Eurasia was articulated by Harry Truman in 1941 when Nazi Germany invaded the Soviet Union: "If we see that Germany is winning the war we ought to help Russia, and if Russia is winning, we ought to help Germany and in that way let them kill as many as possible" (Gaddis 2005: 4). If the offshore balancer establishes a permanent presence, it drains resources and becomes a target to be balanced (Mearsheimer and Walt 2016).

The prospect of Russia controlling the Eurasian landmass from the centre gave birth to Halford Mackinder's "heartland theory," which postulated that whoever would control the Eurasian heartland would control the world. At the turn of the 20th century, Mackinder challenged Alfred Thayer Mahan's argument of maritime superiority. Mackinder presented ideas similar to that of List, suggesting that the emergence of transcontinental railways would undermine the ability to control Eurasia by sea. Mackinder noted that "railways acted chiefly as feeders to ocean-going commerce," although transcontinental railways across the Eurasian continent could instead replace maritime transportation corridors:

A generation ago steam and the Suez canal appeared to have increased the mobility of sea power relatively to land-power. Railways acted chiefly as feeders to ocean-going commerce. But trans-continental railways are now transmuting the conditions of land-power, and nowhere can they have such effect as in the closed heartland of Euro-Asia, in vast areas of which neither timber nor accessible stone was available for road-making (Mackinder 1904: 434).

Mackinder argued that the world is divided into two naturally antagonistic spheres—sea and land (Mackinder 1919: 150). Eurasian connectivity by land was incrementally reducing the advantage of maritime powers and "the Russian army in Manchuria is as significant evidence of mobile land-power as the British army in South Africa was of sea power" (Mackinder 1904: 434).

The heartland theory stipulated that whoever controlled the Eurasian heartland could control the Eurasian supercontinent, and eventually the world: "The heartland is the region to which under modern conditions, sea power can be refused access" (Mackinder 1919: 86). The great fear of Mackinder was the prospect of a German-Russian alliance for control over Eurasia, which made it a key priority for the British to preserve a division between these two European powers and ensure their interests were organised in a zero-sum game. Preventing a Eurasian hegemon was therefore reliant on maintaining division in Europe:

> The oversetting of the balance of power in favour of the pivot state, resulting in its expansion over the marginal lands of Euro-Asia, would permit of the use of vast continental resources for fleet-building, and the empire of the world would then be in sight. This might happen if Germany were to ally herself with Russia (Mackinder 1904: 436).

Spykman (1942), an influential American scholar, built on Mackinder's theory with his Rimland Theory. The crux of the theory was that the US had to control the periphery of the Eurasian continent. The US would need to establish partnerships with the UK to control the western periphery of Eurasia, and "adopt a similar protective policy toward Japan" on the eastern periphery of Eurasia (Spykman 1942: 470). The influential ideas put forward by Spykman was seen to be put into official US strategy after the Second World War as the containment strategy against the Soviet Union was commonly referred to as the "Spykman-Kennan thesis of containment" (Parker 1985). The architect of the containment policy, George Kennan, argued in favour of containing the industrial potential of the Soviet Union with a "Eurasian balance of power" by ensuring that the German and Japanese power vacuum would not be filled by a power that would "threaten the interests of the maritime world of the West" (Gaddis 1982: 38). Instead, Germany and Japan were cultivated as a US frontline against Eurasian powers.

Henry Kissinger's geopolitics and policy of decoupling China from the Soviet Union, mimicking the dividing lines between Germany and Russia, were also influenced by Mackinder's ideas of Eurasia. Kissinger (1994:

50–51) reflected on the divide and conquer strategies of oceanic powers on the Eurasian continent:

> For three centuries, British leaders had operated from the assumption that, if Europe's resources were marshaled by a single dominant power, that country would then have the resources to challenge Great Britain's command of the seas, and thus threaten its independence. Geopolitically, the United States, also an island off the shores of Eurasia, should, by the same reasoning, have felt obliged to resist the domination of Europe or Asia by any one power and, even more, the control of *both* continents by the same power.

The militarised dividing lines of the Cold War precluded any partnership between Germany and the Soviet Union to control Eurasia, although Kissinger reimagined the threat in a Soviet-Chinese partnership. The efforts to normalise relations and "open up" China in the 1970s was therefore instrumental to decouple the partnership that could have produced collective rule over Eurasia.

US National Security Council reports from 1948 and onwards referred to the Eurasian containment policies in the language of Mackinder's heartland theory (Gaddis 1982: 57–58). As outlined in the US National Security Strategy of 1988:

> The United States' most basic national security interests would be endangered if a hostile state or group of states were to dominate the Eurasian landmass-that area of the globe often referred to as the world's heartland. We fought two world wars to prevent this from occurring (White House 1988: 1).

PENETRATING EURASIA AFTER THE COLD WAR

The US strategy to advance and sustain the unipolar moment instructed its Eurasian policy after the Cold War. The US sought to absorb Eurasia into a US-led international system, which represented a clear departure from its historical offshore strategy. The risk of a hegemonic strategy for Eurasia was that the US would become the target of collective balancing by Eurasian powers.

Less than two months after the collapse of the Soviet Union, the US developed the Wolfowitz doctrine of global dominance. The leaked draft of the Defense Planning Guidance (DPG) of February 1992 argued that the durability of US primacy depended on the ability to prevent future rivals from emerging in Eurasia. In the language of Mackinder, the DPG document recognised that "It is improbable that a global conventional challenge to US and Western security will re-emerge from the Eurasian heartland for many years to come" (DPG 1992). However, ensuring unipolar peace meant that the "first objective is to prevent the re-emergence of a new rival," which included preventing allies and frontline states such as Germany and Japan from rearming. Furthermore, a geoeconomic assessment was evident as the DPG specified in "the non-defense areas, we must account sufficiently for the interests of the advanced industrial nations to discourage them from challenging our leadership or seeking to overturn the established political and economic order" (DPG 1992). It was also advocated that the US "must seek to prevent the emergence of European-only security arrangements which would undermine NATO."

Zbigniew Brzezinski outlined the Mackinderian post-Cold War policies of the US to sustain global hegemony. Brzezinksi had been the advisor of both Lyndon Johnson and Jimmy Carter, and had a central role in arming the Muhajeen in Afghanistan during the 1980s. Brzezinski (1997a: 30) argued that "America's global primacy is directly dependent on how long and how effectively its preponderance on the Eurasian continent is sustained." The strategy of preserving US dominance was defined as: "prevent collusion and maintain security dependence among the vassals, to keep tributaries pliant and protected, and keep the barbarians from coming together" (Brzezinski 1997a: 40).

Brzezinski identified Russia as a potential future rival due to its central position in the Eurasian heartland. Yet, the unipolar moment presented an immense opportunity for the US to penetrate Eurasia. The West was "Russia's only choice—even if tactical—thus provided the West with a strategic opportunity. It created the preconditions for the progressive geopolitical expansion of the Western community deeper and deeper into Eurasia" (Brzezinski 2009: 102).

If Russia would resist American efforts, the US could use its maritime dominance to strangle the Russian economy. It was therefore argued that the West should communicate that in the event of a conflict "Russia must know that there would be a massive blockade of Russia's maritime access to the West" (Brzezinski 2017). To permanently weaken Russian control over Eurasia, Brzezinski argued that the collapse of the Soviet Union should ideally be followed by the disintegration of Russia into a "loosely confederated Russia—composed of a European Russia, a Siberian Republic, and a Far Eastern Republic" (Brzezinski 1997b: 56). The economic rise of Asia organised in an oceanic-centred international economy seemingly destined Russia, at the centre of Eurasia, to become geostrategic "black hole" at the dual periphery of Europe and Asia (Brzezinski 1997a: 87).

Washington developed its Silk Road concept in the 1990s, which envisioned the integration of Central Asia into the US-led international economy by feeding ocean-based trade and US allies on the maritime periphery of

Eurasia. The US Silk Road concept became more explicit in 2011 when US Secretary of State Hillary Clinton (2011a) announced the new Silk Road idea in India:

> Let's work together to create a new Silk Road. Not a single thoroughfare like its namesake, but an international web and network of economic and transit connections. That means building more rail lines, highways, energy infrastructure, like the proposed pipeline to run from Turkmenistan, through Afghanistan, through Pakistan into India.

The underpinning logic of the US Silk Road concept was not to integrate Europe and Asia into one Eurasian supercontinent, but rather to use economic connectivity to sever the relations between Russia and Central Asian states (Mankoff 2013). The US Silk Road therefore balances the geopolitical strategies of Brzezinski with practical considerations (Laruelle 2015: 371).

The EU and the US launched their respective initiatives to connect with former Soviet republics in Central Asia to marginalise the role of Russia in the region. Both the US and the EU support the Transport Corridor Europe-Caucasus-Asia (TRACECA) project, a transport corridor connecting Europe with Central Asia that bypasses Russia, which was launched in 1993. The EU also launched INOGATE in 1996, an international energy cooperation program that included every former Soviet republic, except Russia.

Energy pipelines constructed had the explicit purpose of skirting Russia by transiting through the energy corridor of Georgia and Azerbaijan to reach the Caspian Sea and Central Asia. The Eurasian heartland was also to be penetrated from the south with the TAPI (Turkmenistan, Afghanistan, Pakistan, India) pipeline, although it was stalled due to the conflict with the Taliban government. The TAPI project was revived in December 2002 after the US invasion of Afghanistan.

The US engagement with the Commonwealth of Independent States (CIS) was informed by the overarching objective of marginalising Russia in the post-Soviet space. The EU's Eastern Partnership similarly engaged all of its Eastern Neighbours, except Russia, in a multilateral framework to restructure the region's transportation corridors, pipelines, and industries away from Russia. Efforts were also made by the EU and US to establish and support anti-Russian regional framework such as the GUAM (Georgia-Ukraine-Armenia-Moldova) initiative.

The EU refuses to establish diplomatic ties with the Russian-led Eurasian Economic Union, while the US has suggested it is seeking to sabotage the Eurasian Economic Union. Russian Foreign Minister, Sergey Lavrov (2013) opined that "some of our European partners are now inventing new dividing lines, begin trying to artificially divide integration projects into 'good' and 'bad,' 'friendly' and 'alien.'"

NEW CENTRES OF POWER EMERGE AT THE
PERIPHERY OF THE UNIPOLAR ORDER

The Soviet Union did not exercise noteworthy economic statecraft to reorganise Asia. However, Karaganov (2020) posits that the Soviet Union provided the space for new independent centres of power to emerge in Asia and subsequent set the conditions for a return to global multipolarity. The world had been multipolar until the 16th century until European military superiority served as the foundation for political-economic dominance. Armed with nuclear weapons, the Soviet Union midwifed the rise of Asia by constraining Western military superiority for the first time since the early 16th century (Karaganov 2020). Yet, the Soviet Union similarly advanced a hegemonic project in Asia as the liberalisation of the colonised world was to be organised under Moscow's leadership.

With the rise of China, an Asian power is returning to the central actor of developing the Eurasian region. More than a century ago, Mackinder (1904: 437) entertained the possibility of Eurasian dominance by an Asian power:

> Were the Chinese, for instance, organized by the Japanese, to overthrow the Russian Empire and conquer its territory, they might constitute the yellow peril to the world's freedom just because they would add an oceanic frontage to the resources of the great continent, an advantage as yet denied to the Russian tenant of the pivot region.

In the post-Cold War era, China has the leading geoeconomic strength to challenge the US-centric international order and efforts to control Eurasia. Rather than conquering Russian territory, Beijing is finding Moscow to be an important ally to construct Greater Eurasia.

Russia's post-Soviet Eurasianism is markedly different from the past as the capability and intention for hegemony is absent. Yet, Russia's exclusion from the oceanic-centric unipolar international system incentivises Russia to pursue a partnership with China to construct a multipolar Eurasia where Russia has a seat at the table. By positioning itself as a Eurasian power, the restoration of the political subjectivity of Asia can also be extended to Russia. By connecting the Greater Eurasian space, Russia also develops connectivity between its own regions and with the wider world (Lukin and Yakunin 2018). Russia connects European Russia with Pacific Russia, while China connects its prosperous coastal regions with the underdeveloped regions in the Western part of the country. For Russia, the Eurasian political economy assists in completing its historical conversion from a European/Slavic empire to a Eurasian civilisation state.

CONCLUSION: EURASIANISM AS A REACTION TO MARITIME DOMINANCE

The concept of a Eurasian geoeconomic region implies reviving the mobility of nomadic civilisations with transportation infrastructure to connect the space between Europe and Asia. In a more modern sense, it also entails connecting a Greater Eurasian region with strategic industries and financial instruments. While it appears unlikely that land powers can completely replace maritime powers with land corridors, bimodal connectivity is a form of diversification that can skew the balance of dependence.

The history of Eurasianism demonstrates that bold ambitions to unify Europe and Asia emerge when the oceanic-centric economic system becomes untenable. Oceanic powers have a natural proclivity to assert leadership and core-periphery relations. Although, when the ambition of leadership is expressed as dominance, the ability to deliver collective good diminishes and the land powers have great incentives to construct a Eurasian region. The Germans, Russians, and Chinese were all placed in situations where their possibility for development has been restricted. The American unipolar strategy after the Cold War has set in place powerful systemic incentives that are creating a common cause between large powers on the supercontinent that includes Russia, China, Iran, and other Eurasian states.

3

The Dominance of the West
as a Maritime Region

European history has to a great extent been defined by a struggle between maritime powers and land powers to organise the European continent. The trans-Atlantic partnership, commonly referred to colloquially as the West, is a wider geoeconomic region shaped by the supremacy of maritime geography. The formation of the trans-Atlantic region is a natural development as European civilisation is largely a tale about human interactions with the sea. However, the peaceful coexistence and internal cohesion of the West as a region is a historical abnormality based on a unique and waning geoeconomic configuration.

Ancient Greece demonstrated that control over the seas was imperative to exercise commercial and military power. The lesson of the Peloponnesian War (431–404 BC), the defining conflict among city-states in Ancient Greece, was that sea power enables mobility and determines leadership. The war between Athens as a sea power and Sparta as a land power resulted in the victory of Sparta only when it developed naval power. The following history of Rome, the Vikings, and the Hanseatic League similarly revealed that control over the seas was imperative for economic power and military strength. From the early 16th century, during the age of discovery, Western European maritime powers established trade-post empires across the globe and in the process discovered America as an extension of the West. Voyagers such as Columbus, Magellan, and Da Gama unleashed a revolution of geography by uniting the waters of the world. Europe was no longer a continent closed along its western maritime periphery.

Maritime power was instrumental to Europe's dominance for centuries due to commercial and military mobility, although the oceanic character of the continent also made it an open system where a hegemon could not establish itself:

If Europe had been a closed system, some great power would eventually have succeeded in establishing absolute supremacy over the other states in the region. But the system was never entirely closed. Immediately before a would-be continental hegemon could unify the European region by coercion, counterweights on the eastern and/or western wings of the continent emerged to deny a hegemonic victory by introducing new, extraregional resources into the struggle for regional supremacy. The eastern wing supplied brute land force commanded by some form of "oriental despotism." The western wing specialized in sea power, which was closely associated with its assumption of the principal commercial intermediary role between Europe and Asia and America (Thompson 1992: 129).

Britain and the US as island-states enjoyed natural competitive advantages to organise Europe as a region, although their respective positions for geoeconomic leadership has been reliant on dividing Europe to prevent the rise of continental challengers.

The history of Europe and the West demonstrates that geoeconomics is used for both nation-building and region-building. Geoeconomic instruments of power and geoeconomic regions used to reduce excessive reliance on a hegemon are also used to establish hegemonic control. Geoeconomic hegemons are capable of constructing somewhat stable regions by liberalising trade and delivering collective goods such as safe passage through transportation corridors.

This chapter first explores the rise of British geoeconomic dominance in Europe, and its subsequent hegemonic position that cemented with free trade policies. The Napoleonic Continental System aimed to marginalise a British-led Europe by organising a European region among land powers under French leadership. The principal weakness of the Continental System was the excessive reliance on coercion due to the insufficient geoeconomic incentives.

Second, the remarkable industrial rise of Germany created a new challenger for a British-led Europe. Germany aimed to restore the structures of the Continental System, which supported by industrial might and railways, was expected to create a gravitational pull that first unified Germany in 1871 and then a wider European region. Bismarck's focus on Germany's "peaceful rise" after unification aimed to unify and strengthen German lands without provoking conflicts with the great powers. By the time Wilhelm II became Kaiser, Germany had outgrown the geoeconomics of nation-building and began to reorganise Europe. The failure to develop a new Continental System adapting to a changing international distribution of power resulted in a Germanic hegemonic project in Europe that contributed to sparking two world wars.

Third, the rise of the US was similar to that of Germany. The US initially advanced economic nationalist policies to reduce dependence on British dominance, before using the same geoeconomic instruments of power to construct a greater region in the Americas and the Pacific. Without a balancer in North America, the US could assert hegemony and eventually surpass British power. The devastation of Europe and East Asia in the Second World War, and the emergence of an unbalanced Soviet Union, enabled the US to organise the former rival geoeconomic regions under a US-led geoeconomic region.

Last, the post-Cold War era became a paradox for the West as a region. The unipolar moment revitalised US power and, in a partnership with a rising EU, established collective hegemony over the pan-European region and beyond. However, the foundations for a unified West soon diminished. The US became too reliant on military power to extend its influence; the geoeconomic rivalry among allies was no longer tempered by the Cold War; and the former adversaries, China and Russia, are incentivised to advance geoeconomic strategies to reduce reliance on the West.

It is concluded that the foundation for a cohesive Western maritime region is weakening due to overextension in the unipolar era.

BRITAIN'S OCEANIC EUROPE VERSUS NAPOLEON'S CONTINENTAL EUROPE

Island-states relying on maritime power enjoy crucial benefits for claiming leadership in Europe, as the seas become natural barriers to protect from invaders. It is thus no accident that Western civilisation has its origins from ancient Crete and Athens. Land-powers such as Germany and Russia were exposed to invaders due to the lack of natural barriers, while Britain as an island-state enjoyed the protection of the sea. The US also falls within the category of an island-state due to the absence of challengers in the Americas.

Island states did not need large standing armies during peace times, which meant that the authorities could not rely on military power to subdue their own populations, at least not to the same extent as continental land powers. Subsequently, the governments of island-states were under greater pressure to accept limitations on power, which laid the foundation for liberal and democratic governance. Alexander Hamilton (1857: 37) wrote that Britain would not have been in the position to advance liberty if it had been positioned on the European continent, and would probably have become "a victim to the absolute power of a single man." The power of the British Parliament vis-à-vis the Monarch was instrumental to advance land rights and enclosures, which intensified the efficiency of the agricultural industry and eventually the industrial revolution. Soon, British control over maritime transportation corridors was complemented with the two other pillars of geoeconomic power—strategic industries due to technological leadership and financial instruments as British banks and currencies financed development.

The competition for European primacy between Britain and France throughout the 18th century manifested in a competition over colonial possessions. Furthermore, Britain cultivated allies and fought to prevent the French from establishing hegemony on the European continent. British policies towards continental Europe was primarily aimed towards preserving divisions and a balance of power to prevent the emergence of hegemony by one state or a group of states in Europe that could threaten the primacy of Britain. In continental Europe, there were efforts to construct a region to sever dependence on British industries, sea corridors, and banks.

In the early 19th century, revolutionary France sought to organise Europe as a region ruled from the continent. The Napoleonic Continental System aimed to shift the balance of dependence vis-à-vis Britain with a blockade by continental Europe. The Continental System can be conceptualised as an early geoeconomic region, defined by political intervention to shift economic dependencies with new industries, transportation corridors, and financial instruments. By enhancing economic connectivity among European states, the British would be unable to rule the continent from the maritime periphery.

Napoleon was the first major European leader to express interest in conquering Europe to develop "the United States of Europe" (Riley 2013: 30). Napoleon wrote: "I wish to found a European system, a European Code of Laws, a European judiciary; there would be but one people in Europe" (Ingram 1998: 49). The Continental System, issued by decree in Berlin by Napoleon in 1806, was a reaction to British dominance that rested on industrial leadership, sea power, and banking power. The Continental System developed Europe as a geoeconomic region to restrict market access and "strangling British trade with the continent" (Heckscher 1922: 98).

The geoeconomics of the Continental System was perhaps accidental, but effective nonetheless. Continental industries emerged as infant industries developed through import substitution. Transportation corridors in Europe also changed significantly. British control over the seas created blockades and maritime restrictions that severed France from its colonial vassals, which therefore incentives new transportation corridors on continental Europe to redirect trade within the European market (Heckscher 1922: 93). Napoleon claimed that the Civil Code was a greater victory than what he had achieved on the battlefield (Lyons 1994: 94). Within France, more than 300 different legal systems were abolished and reforms were implemented such as property rights, the abolition of privileges, and equality under the law. These Civil codes were also exported to conquered states in Europe. Britain similarly restructured its trade network with the wider world and thus developed "global Britain" (Gates 1997: 161).

However, geoeconomic regions must deliver economic benefits to member states to incentivise solidarity. The Continental System offered reforms and innovation, although it relied heavily on subordination and exploitation to sustain French leadership. The Continental System did not provide Russia with the necessary economic connectivity and its economy suffered greatly under the blockade of Britain. Furthermore, Russia grew increasingly uncomfortable with the extensive territorial control France demanded across Europe to uphold the system, and the ideological mission of the French revolutionaries (Broers, Hicks, and Guimera 2012). In the absence of economic incentives, the geoeconomic region had to be held together through coercion. Russia withdrew from the Continental System in 1810, and Napoleon responded with the disastrous invasion of Russia. Russia's victory over Napoleon resulted in Europe's first collective security institution, the Concert of Europe, which lasted from 1815 to 1914.

However, Russia's victory over France also ended the British-French rivalry that had perpetuated throughout the 18th century. The subsequent primacy of Britain enabled more focus and cooperation with France to marginalise Russia in Europe. This phenomenon would later repeat itself as the Soviet Union defeated Nazi Germany, which resulted in the Germans being absorbed into a US-led Europe.

Britain organised Europe as a region throughout the Victorian era in the 19th century when British industrial leadership and maritime dominance placed European trade under its geoeconomic control. The new Europe was subsequently administered from the maritime periphery. The head start in the industrial revolution, supported by state intervention, enabled Britain to establish core-periphery relations with continental Europe. Britain became the dominant world trader, shipper, and banker (Hobsbawm 1968).

The concentration of geoeconomic power in Britain incentivised liberal economics to construct a European region under London's administration. Free trade was instrumental to sustain Britain's technological leadership. Mature British industries, defined by low costs and high quality, were competing against the infant industries on continental Europe, defined by high costs and low quality. Under a system of free trade, Britain could saturate the markets of manufactured goods in Europe and thus prevent the continent from industrialising. The repeal of the Corn Laws in 1846 had the explicit purpose of creating an international division of labour, with Britain producing manufactured goods and continental Europe producing agricultural goods.

London feared that, without free trade, states such as Germany and the US would develop national manufacturing industries and thus weaken Britain's comparative advantage (Hilton 1977: 280; Irwin 1989). David Ricardo (1821:

139) explained that his concept of *comparative advantage* is the "principle which determines that wine shall be made in France and Portugal, that corn shall be grown in America and Poland, and that hardware and other goods shall be manufactured in England." Free trade became a hegemonic policy, and as it was stated in the British parliament, with free trade "foreign nations would become valuable Colonies to us, without imposing on us the responsibility of governing them" (Semmel 1970: 8). Thus, Britain's ability to saturate foreign markets with industrial goods depended on free-trade, which subsequently made it necessary for the US and Germany to repudiate free trade and instead make the case for "fair trade" (Klug 2001: 221).

GERMANY'S EUROPE AS A REGION

Germany emerged as a contender for developing a European geoeconomic region. The dense concentration of navigable rivers on German territory provided cost-effective transportation of goods as a competitive advantage in trade. Germany unified in 1871 and the spectacular industrial rise that followed could not be confined within national borders, which meant that nation-building was intimately linked to region-building. Without a regional framework, Germany was challenged with a powerful France to the west, Russia to the east, and the British and American controlling the seas to the north.

German nation-building and region-building largely followed the lessons from the Napoleonic System and the three-pillared geoeconomic principles outlined in the American System. Germany protected its infant industry from British exports and avoided dependence on a British-dominated international system. The Napoleonic Continental System had benefitted Germans by enhancing connectivity between German states and wider Europe. As the former German Chancellor Helmut Kohl famously remarked, German integration and European integration represent two sides of the same coin.

The collapse of Napoleon's Continental System caused economic decline as the ports opened and British goods flooded the German market to the extent German industries could not develop and mature (Henderson 1983: 143). List (1841: 421) mourned the abolition of the Continental System, yet he was very critical that it had merely replaced British dominance with French dominance.

German states thus aimed to recreate the regional structure of the Napoleonic Continental System with the Zollverein, the German Customs Union, which lasted from 1834 to 1919. Friedrich List famously referred to railways and the customs union as the "Siamese twins" of German state-building (Earle 1943: 442). Germany's physical infrastructure consisted of railways and river systems, and the Zollverein laid the foundation for both German unification and European regionalism. Friedrich List's views on the European customs union was inspired by the American experience that the nation-state imposed excessive limitations on economic activity (Brechtefeld 1996: 16). The prolific philosopher, Johann Gottfried Herder, similarly argued German nation-building was intimately linked to the construction of a central European region (Brechtefeld, 1996: 14). Europe would be German-centric and without Napoleon's reliance on coercion. The economic benefits of the Customs Union were expected to create a geoeconomic gravitational pull as the Swiss, Dutch, and other regions of Europe would integrate with a unified Germany out of self-interest.

German financial instruments of power were also developed, modelled after the French experience. France had augmented its financial instruments with the establishment of Crédit Mobilier in 1852, which mobilised the savings from the middle class to develop industry, railways, and other infrastructure. France reduced its dependence on British finance and its investments abroad resulted in greater access to resources and the establishment of core-periphery relations with underdeveloped states such as Russia (Henderson 1975: 125). Germany's banking revolution in the 1850s aimed to emulate the accomplishments of Crédit Mobilier and rid the Germans of irresponsible reliance on foreign banks (Henderson 1975: 123).

Germany had resisted tariffs on industrial goods in the 1850s and 1860s as they feared the British would retaliate with tariffs on German grain (Pflanze 2014: 311). The constraints on economic nationalist policies diminished as grain prices dropped and swift industrialisation became a necessity. Improved railways and shipping enabled bulk-cargo and thus increased grain imports from both the US and Russia. The downward pressures on grain prices incentivised the Germans to abandon agriculture and migrate to the cities in search of industrial jobs.

Temporary subsidies and tariffs were subsequently used to aid the development of Germany's infant industries. It was recognised that infant industries could not develop under free trade as Germany's high-price and low-quality goods could not mature in direct competition with British low-cost and high-quality goods. Otto von Bismarck, much like Alexander Hamilton, aptly argued that free-trade was the policy of the strong, and Bismarck subsequently established tariffs in 1879 (Mackinder 1919: 100).

When Germany unified in 1871, Britain produced twice as much steel as Germany, with steel being a good measure of industrial power at that time. By 1893, German steel production surpassed British production, and by 1914, German steel production was twice that of British production. With its spectacular rise in industrial power, the German state began assisting an offensive geoeconomic policy by subsidising new shipping lanes and penetrating foreign markets with German banks.

Growing tensions from competition between rising industrial states incentivised the calls for creating a European geoeconomic region. In 1871, the same year of German unification, the French National Assembly proposition to establish a "United States of Europe."

For two decades thereafter, Otto Von Bismarck as the German Chancellor prioritised "peaceful rise" that would not attract unwanted attention and balancing by the great powers. Bismarck was initially also sceptical about partaking in the "scramble for Africa" as it would create tensions with the British.

Yet, Wilhelm II, who replaced Bismarck in 1890, believed that Germany had outgrown its territorial limitations and its further military and economic expansion made it necessary to challenge the position of Britain, France, and Russia. Max Weber, the prolific German sociologist, argued in 1895 during his inaugural lecture in Freiburg that the industrial prowess achieved during unification had to be supported with imperial expansion. Weber (1980: 438) opined that "the world-wide economic community is only another form of the struggle of the nations." The industrial and economic success of Germany also relied on "the amount of elbow-room we conquer" and it was of immense importance to the economy "when the German flag waves on the surrounding coasts" (Weber 1980: 436; 445).

Kaiser Wilhelm II envisioned a new Continental System to assert the collective strength of Europe and rebuke the American efforts to seize control over international trade. In September 1896, Kaiser Wilhelm II approached Tsar Nicholas II to include Russia in a new European Continental System against America, and possibly include England as well (Röhl 2017: 59; 215). Russia desired a Continental System, although Russia was reluctant as it prioritised good relations with the Americans (Yarmolinsky 1921: 408). Although, the Russian Finance Minister Sergei Witte agreed that Europe eventually had to unify to remain relevant instead of wasting money on endless conflicts that divided the continent. Witte argued in favour of a Greater Europe:

> To achieve this ideal we must seek to create a solid union of Russia, Germany, and France. Once these countries are firmly united, all the States of the European continent will, no doubt, join the central alliance and thus form an all-embracing continental confederation (Yarmolinsky 1921: 409).

Without a regional solution to the geoeconomic rivalry, rising and European industrial societies began drifting towards war. Adam Brooks recognised the limitations on German industrial growth: "the Germans cannot increase their velocity because they cannot extend their base, and augment their mass"

(Wiebe 1967: 234). Germany could not increase its productive power by engaging in more international trade as dependence on maritime corridors under British control would subject German economic survival to the British navy (List 1841: 295–296).

Germany's "hunger" for markets became "one of the most terrible realities of the world," which meant that the Slavs had to be subjugated to supply agricultural goods and to buy Germany's manufactured goods (Mackinder 1919: 102). After Hitler seized power in Germany in 1933, Trotsky (1934: 397) succinctly recognised that Europe went to war in 1914 to construct a geoeconomic region:

> The basic tendency of our century is the growing contradiction between the nation and economic life. In Europe this contradiction has become intolerably acute. . . One of the main causes of the World War was the striving of German capital to break through into a wider arena. Hitler fought as a corporal in 1914–1918 not to unite the German nation but in the name of a supranational imperialistic program that expressed itself in the famous formula "to organize Europe". . . But Germany was no exception. She only expressed in a more intense and aggressive form the tendency of every other national capitalist economy.

The inability to limit the economic activity of growing industrial societies within national borders fuelled the expectation that the world would be organised into geoeconomic regions. Friedrich Naumann's (1915) famous book, *Mitteleuropa*, published in 1915 during the war, called for the formation of a German cultural and economic empire in Central and Eastern Europe. Naumann, much like Tocqueville, expected that the world after the war would be divided into two economic super-regions: the Anglo-American maritime region against a Russian-Asiatic region. Germany's leading objective should thus be to establish an independent German-led region.

A European federation would have to be unified voluntarily to avoid reliance on coercive means, which would be achieved through geoeconomics by integrating Europe through internal free trade and economic protection to erect external borders. The German-Russian Brest-Litovsk agreement of March 1918 that outlined the conditions of Russia's surrender included the "liberation" of Eastern European lands that would instead become vassals of Germany. Winston Churchill argued that the Treaty of Brest-Litovsk endowed Germany with "the granaries of the Ukraine and Siberia, the oil of the Caspian, all the resources of a vast continent." Although, Germany's defeat in the war prevented the construction of a wider geoeconomic region.

Following the First World War, the efforts to construct a European region by diplomacy continued to avert the military solution. French Prime Minister,

Aristide Briand, called for the establishment of a United States of Europe during a speech in 1929 at the League of Nations. French politician and financier Joseph Caillaux proposed a treaty limiting industrial development to mitigate the growing economic tensions. Yet, the limitations on industrial output had already been imposed on Germany in the Treaty of Versailles, which attempted to maintain peace by merely perpetuating German weakness and thus sowing the seeds of political extremism.

The national socialists thus added militarism, radical race theories, and anti-Bolshevism to the construction of a German-led region. The regional division of labour would thus be structured by race as the Slavs would be used for hard labour, while the Germanic peoples of Germany, Scandinavia, Netherlands, and Belgium would be responsible for the high-value commercial activities (Du Bois 1941).

AMERICAN GEOECONOMICS: FROM NATION-BUILDING TO REGION-BUILDING

The US also opposed British primacy by contesting the principle of free trade. Alexander Hamilton's policies sought to cement political independence with economic independence. The subsequent three-pillared American System pursued national independence in all three branches of geoeconomic power: a manufacturing base, railways, and a national bank.

The ability to rapidly industrialise prevented Britain from converting the American mid-West and Central America into dependencies (Gallagher and Robinson 1953: 10). The ideological commitment to free trade after the Second World War neglects that the US rose to power for a century, from 1815 to 1914, based on protectionist policies (Hudson 2010). Much like its British counterpart, the US only began to embrace and advocate free trade once a dominant position had been established.

In 1827, during the early years of American development, Friedrich List contrasted belligerent English geoeconomics of seeking hegemony with benign American geoeconomics aimed to develop national sovereignty: "English national economy is predominant; American national economy aspires only to become independent" (List 1827: 12). Although, much like in Germany, the geoeconomic of nation-building was soon thereafter used for region-building. In 1841, List argued that the spectacular rise of America would change Europe as a region:

> Thus in a not very distant future the natural necessity which now imposes on the French and Germans the necessity of establishing a Continental alliance against the British supremacy, will impose on the British the necessity of establishing a

European coalition against the supremacy of America. Then will Great Britain be compelled to seek and to find in the leadership of the united powers of Europe protection, security, and compensation against the predominance of America, an equivalent for her lost supremacy (List 1841: 111).

List (1841: 111) therefore encouraged Britain to forego its hegemonic ambitions in favour of a European regional partnership and "should accustom herself betimes to the idea of being only the first among equals."

US unrestrained territorial expansion continued swiftly with the annexation of Texas in 1845 and then California in 1848, although expansionism then slowed down due to the American Civil War. Britain leaned cautiously towards the Confederate South to take advantage of the rupture in the American Union, yet did not intervene to avoid war. However, the incentive and interest were to establish a similar balance of power in North America as existed in Europe to restrain its challenge to Britain. The Russian Ambassador to London wrote in 1861:

> The English Government, at the bottom of its heart, desires the separation of North American into two republics, which will watch each other jealously and counterbalance one the other. Then England, on terms of peace and commerce with both, would have nothing to fear from either; for she would dominate them, restraining them by their rival ambitions (Adams 2019: 45).

Following geoeconomics for successful nation-building, the US used its strategic industries, transportation corridors, and financial instruments to construct new regions. Towards the end of the 19th century, the US began developing a maritime empire. The peaceful rise of the US had come to an end due to its growing industrial output, accompanied by new transportation corridors for its industrial output and finance. The US aimed to establish hegemony over the Americas and East Asia as the Europeans had cemented control over Africa and the Middle East (Wiebe 1967: 239). US Senator, Albert Beveridge, argued that the increased industrial output demanded an imperial posture:

> American factories are making more than the American people can use; American soil is producing more than they can consume. Fate has written our policy for us; the trade of the world must and shall be ours . . . We will establish trading-posts throughout the world as distributing points for American products. We will cover the ocean with our merchant marine. Great colonies governing themselves, flying our flag and trading with us, will grow about our posts of trade (Bowers 1932: 67).

The American imperial rule over Latin America had originated rhetorically as anti-imperial with the Monroe Doctrine of 1823 calling for the Americas to be free from European empires. However, the Monroe Doctrine was formulated as regional hegemony by US Secretary of State Richard Olney in 1895: "the United States is practically sovereign on this continent, and its fiat is law upon the subjects to which it confines its interposition" (Smith 1984). Germany strengthened its economic influence in Eastern Europe during the first half of the 1930s to increase its political sway (Kaiser 2015).

The US began to assert its control over maritime transportation corridors at the turn of the 20th century according to the strategic thinking of Alfred Thayer Mahan, a US naval officer. Mahan (1890) conceptualised the US as a continental-sized island state that should replace the British Empire and dominate international commerce. Although, a partnership with Britain was instrumental to contain the maritime edges of the Eurasian continent and prevent land powers such as Germany and Russia from challenging US leadership. Mahan (1892) also acknowledged that controlling oceanic trade corridors was instrumental to win wars.

The US went to war against Spain in 1898 largely to secure its commercial interests abroad. President McKinley requested the US Congress for authorizing the use of military power in Cuba where "our people have such trade and business relations; when the lives and liberties of our citizens are in constant danger, and their property destroyed and themselves ruined; where our trading vessels are liable to seizure" (Arnold and Wiener 2016: 297). The victory in the American-Spanish War in 1898 awarded the US colonial acquisitions as the spoils of war and the US began to resemble the European empires. The US was able to establish control over strategic sea-lanes by annexing Hawaii, the Philippines, Guam, Puerto Rico, Wake Island, American Samoa, and the Virgin Islands.

The new colonies in the Pacific provided the US with reliable refuelling stations to gain a foothold in China. In the effort to maintain its access to the Chinese market, under the Open Door policy, the US deployed US Marines in 1900 to crush the Chinese anti-imperial Boxer Rebellion to maintain commercial access to China. The US also connected the Atlantic with the Pacific by coercing Panama's secession from Colombia in 1903, where the Panama Canal was constructed and claimed as US sovereign territory.

Following the First World War, it was evident that the rising productive power of the US would translate into a more active role in the world. Trotsky (1934: 401–402) predicted imperial expansion as "sooner or later American capitalism must open up ways for itself throughout the length and breadth of our entire planet":

> The relative equilibrium of its internal and seemingly inexhaustible market assured the United States a decided technical and economic preponderance over Europe. But its intervention in the World War was really an expression of the

fact that its internal equilibrium was already disrupted. The changes introduced by the war into the American structure have in turn made entry into the world arena a life and death question for American capitalism. There is ample evidence that this entry must assume extremely dramatic forms.

REGIONALISATION IN THE INTER-WAR PERIOD:

The international economic system gradually opened up towards a more liberal format following the First World War before retreating towards empires / geoeconomic regions in the 1930s. The five main geoeconomic regions that emerged were organised as the British Empire, French Empire, Germany and Eastern Europe, the US and Latin America, and Japan and Eastern Asia. Each of the five regions attempted a certain degree of protectionism from free trade on a global scale to preserve the regional power structures.

All five regions had an imperial structure resting on military power where the authority of the leading state could not be challenged, as opposed to obtaining voluntary participation with a flatter power structure based on a regional balance of power. The British and French empires were overt in their imperial organisation and the US imperial posture also was becoming increasingly evident. Japan emerged as a rival in the Pacific Ocean with its "Greater East Asia co-prosperity sphere" that endeavoured to develop an economically self-sufficient bloc of Asian nations under the imperial leadership of Japan (Yellen 2019).

The lack of cooperation between the blocs, or inter-regionalism, fuelled tensions that were increasingly difficult to control. Even the leading maritime powers were seemingly heading towards confrontations. In the interwar period, a war between the US and Britain over naval dominance became a real possibility. Woodrow Wilson wrote in 1920:

> It is evident to me that we are on the eve of a commercial war of the severest sort, and I am afraid that Great Britain will prove capable of as great commercial savagery as Germany has displayed for so many years in her competitive methods (Baer 1996: 85).

On the other side of the Atlantic, the British Vice-Admiral Sir Osmond Brock stipulated that "The late war has removed Germany as a possible enemy, but the other effect of the war has been that the United States has become our rival for the carrying trade of the world" (Bell 2000: 51). Efforts were made to preserve benign rhetoric, although Winston Churchill argued in 1927 that although it was "quite right in the interests of peace to go on talking about war with the United States being 'unthinkable,' everyone knows that this is not true" (Bell 1997: 790). A future British-American war was expected to be fought over the primacy over the seas. The US aimed to control the maritime periphery of the North American Continent with its "War Plan Red" in the late 1920s, which envisioned a US invasion of Canada to prevent Canadian ports from being used by the British.

EUROPE AS A US-LED REGION AFTER
THE SECOND WORLD WAR

During the Second World War, the US efforts to preserve an equilibrium in Europe and Asia was threatened by the expansionism of Nazi Germany and Imperial Japan. Yet, after their defeat, the balance of power was severely skewed and the Soviet Union could aspire for hegemony across the Eurasian landmass and possibly the world. Washington concluded that it could not rely on a self-regulated balance of power emerging organically on the Eurasian continent without US assistance.

A new regional formation of a unified West emerged under American leadership following the Second World War. The US sought to incorporate former geoeconomic regional leaders under its leadership - Britain, France, Germany, and Japan (Nierop and De Vos 1988). Former economic rivals were key nodes in establishing a unified capitalist world under US hegemony. While the adversaries of the US were communist states decoupled from international markets, the geoeconomic competition among allies was mitigated by security dependence on the US due to the Cold War.

The first instinct towards the end of the war was to impose an even more draconian "Treaty of Versailles 2.0." to permanently neutralise Germany as a future rival on the European continent. The US was intent on dismantling German industrial power, as outlined in the Morgenthau Plan, also known as US Directive JSC 1067. The US president, Herbert Hoover, estimated that the de-industrialisation of Germany would "exterminate or move 25,000,000 people out of it [Germany]" (Chang 2003: 455).

The victory of the Soviet Union in the war had left Europe without a balance of power. The Soviet adversary created strong incentives for the US to develop Europe as a collaborative region as opposed to the US ruling as a victor. Thus, both the US and the UK recognised that Germany had to be allowed to rebuild its industrial might so Western Europe would be capable of balancing the Soviet Union. Without an industrialised Germany, Western Europe would not be able to rebuild and the ideological lure of communism would prevail. Churchill (1994: 6) argued in September 1946, six months after his Iron Curtain speech, that "a kind of United States of Europe" that included Germany was required.

Germany was therefore brought into the trans-Atlantic region under US leadership. The communist adversary, the Soviet Union, was largely decoupled from international markets and the US had to rapidly convert its economic prowess into military power. Western Europe's geoeconomic reliance on the US was subsequently complemented with security dependence. The first Secretary-General of NATO, in no uncertain terms, defined the purpose of the military alliance as "to keep the Americans in, the Russians out, and the Germans down."

The devastation of the Second World War made Western Europe and East Asia porous regions that were penetrated by the US. Yet, core-periphery relations were made benign as the Soviet Union as a new centre of power had emerged. The US was also prepared to grant its allies access to its domestic market on more favourable terms to strengthen trade and the ability of allies to remain the "free world." This contradicted the American tradition of economic nationalism and asymmetrical interdependence. Washington provided material benefits as a common good and security guarantees. The organisation of a benign trans-Atlantic region, united by common interests, earned the US the description of an "empire by invitation" (Lundestad 1986) and an "empire by consent" (Risse-Kappen 1995: 6). The ability of US leadership to negate geoeconomic rivalry among the Europeans attributed to the concept of hegemonic stability theory (Kindleberger 1986).

The concentration of economic power in the world enabled the US to use free trade to construct a US-led international economic system (Baldwin 1985: 46). The Marshal Plan financed the reconstruction of Western Europe in return for removing protectionist measures obstructing US exports. The pressure on the Europeans to decolonise meant that these markets would naturally gravitate towards the US. The principal challenge came from the Soviet Union, also an active supporter of decolonisation, yet defining human freedom as liberation from the capitalist system.

American strategic industries had grown immensely powerful as the US become the factory of the world. American wartime industry was converted into commercial production and its productive infrastructure was intact due to the absence of combat on its own continental soil. Furthermore, technological innovations and the emergence of big business created a profound advantage vis-à-vis its capitalist allies that had been ravaged by war. Natural resources also fell under US control as its European allies decolonised. The Chief of the Near Eastern Division, Gordon Merriam, wrote in a 1945 memorandum draft to the US president: "Saudi Arabia, where the oil resources constitute a stupendous source of strategic power, and one of the greatest material prizes in world history, a concession covering this oil is nominally in American control" (US State Department 1945).

The US also seized control over the maritime corridors of the world. The pressure on Europe to decolonise placed key transportation corridors and markets under US control. The fierce response by the US to the British-French-Israeli invasion of the Suez Channel in 1956 demonstrated US supremacy in the postwar era.

Financial instruments were also important to construct a larger Western region under US control. The economic system established at Bretton Woods established the US dollar as the international trade and reserve currency, while the US-led IMF and World Bank became the leading financial institutions. After the Cold War, the US Trade Representative of President Bill Clinton referred to the IMF as "a battering ram" to open Asian markets to the US (Subramanian 2011: 66). With the international payment system SWIFT under US control and the use of dollars in transactions, Washington has been able to impose extraterritorial sanctions as their legal reach goes beyond US territory.

The US struggled throughout the Cold War to manage an internal balance of dependence within the West and a balance of power vis-à-vis the communist world. This dilemma between the internal and external balance of power created a conflicted relationship with the European Community, the predecessor of the EU. The US enjoyed the collective strength of the Western Europeans as an ally, yet this diminished the ability to maximise asymmetrical interdependence by engaging its member states in bilateral formats. France was not comfortable with the domineering presence of the US: Charles de Gaulle opined that European regionalism was vital to scale back US dominance and the "exorbitant privilege" of its currency on the European continent (Hurrell 1995: 340).

Germany prospered under the dual region of the West and Europe. Under the patronage of the dominant maritime power, Germany was able to advance its industrial development. The ability to integrate with other European powers in the European Community provided Germany with a regional format it had lacked since the Napoleonic Continental System and Zollverein. During the Cold War, Western Europe was able to construct its own market and strategic autonomy behind tariff walls. Chancellor Helmut Schmidt argued at a Bundesbank Council meeting in 1978 that the peaceful rise Germany, by not provoking the great powers, demanded that Germany grew within existing structures:

> German foreign policy rests on two great pillars: the European Community and the North Atlantic Alliance. . . It is all the more necessary for us to clothe ourselves in this European mantle. We need this mantle not only to cover our

foreign policy nakednesses, like Berlin or Auschwitz, but we need it also to cover these ever-increasing relative strengths, economic, political, military, of the German Federal Republic within the West. The more they come into view, the harder it becomes to secure our room for manoeuvre. The more desirable it is that we are able to lean on these two pillars which are simultaneously here a mantle for us, in which we can conceal our strength a bit (Bundesbank 1978).

By the 1980s, it was deemed necessary to re-organise relations with its allies to skew the symmetry of dependence. The Western Europeans employed economic nationalist policies by supporting its infant airline industry with temporary subsidies to mature and outcompete the American competitors (Luttwak 2010: 34). The Germans applied the same aggressive industrial policy to the car industry.

ASIA AS A WESTERN-LED OCEANIC REGION

China's centuries-long tributary system in East Asia was a unique geoeconomic region. The tributary system largely came into force due to asymmetrical power, which enabled the Chinese to establish what resembled a benign hegemon facilitating trade and diplomacy. Other states paid tribute and affirmed China's primacy within the hierarchical structure, and China reciprocated with reassurances that East Asian nations could remain autonomous and independent.

China's first encounter with the Romans was first recorded in Chinese history in 100 BC, although the first meeting between the two civilisations was not established before AD 166 when the Roman King, Marcus Aurelius Antoninus Augustus, sent his envoys to Luoyang (Morris 2014: 164). During the ancient Silk Road, an asymmetrical economic partnership developed between the Roman Empire and China. China primarily exported silk as manufactured/processed goods, yet it imported mostly gold and silver due to a great degree of self-sufficiency. The interdependent partnership was thus not sustainable due to the huge outflow of gold from the Roman Empire, resulting in the rise of China's relative power. China protected the industrial secrets of silk production to preserve its strategic industry, while the Roman Senate made formidable efforts to decouple from the partnership by resisting the use of silk and limiting trade.

Trade through the Indian Ocean developed over the centuries, under the control of regional actors. Between the 11th and 13th centuries, Indian Ocean trade networks weakened as the Mongols facilitated reliable and economically competitive trade corridors by land. In the 14th and 15th centuries, after the disintegration of the Mongol Empire and the loss of the nomad land-corridors, maritime trade networks began to emerge again in the Indian Ocean from Africa, the Middle East, India, and China. The Islamic world controlled and administered these maritime trade networks, and economic dependence was followed by socio-cultural influences. Subsequently, the developing economic centres across the Indian Ocean region were increasingly influenced by the Islamic faith and culture. Even Zheng He was a Muslim, the admiral of China's maritime Silk Road in the 15th century.

The growing military prowess and maritime capabilities of the Europeans in the early 16th century paved the entry of the Europeans into the Indian Ocean, which would be the start of 500 years of Western dominance. The initial shift in power was spearheaded by Portugal, which under Vasco da Gama began asserting its influence over the Indian Ocean with the establishment of a trading post empire. Yet, the reliance on coercion contributed to Portugal's failure to dominate the region.

The Dutch had greater success in seizing control over trade in Asia. The mercantilism of the Dutch East India Company (1602–1798), an early forerunner of geoeconomics, made it the most powerful company in world history. The logic of the Dutch East India Company was rooted in a market economy as the consolidation into a large corporation mitigated the volatility of investments in high-risk/high-reward trading companies that often lost ships. Yet, geoeconomic logic dictates its structure as the powerful Dutch East India Company was placed under the patronage of the Dutch government to enhance competitiveness in the market, offer military support, lower interest rates, and ensure the economic interests of the company was aligned with national interests. The establishment of a powerful and reliable corporation also lent support to a superior financial system. The company enabled the government to mobilise domestic financial resources as the Dutch could invest their savings in the Dutch East India Company. Monopolisation was an important source of power and the economics of vertical integration and controlling the seas was instrumental to pursue the foreign policy goal of decoupling from excessive reliance on the Spanish.

Mercantilism emerged in the period before the industrial revolution when trade was more of a zero-sum game due to the scarcity of productive power, which resulted in economic rivalry being fought by maximising exports and minimising imports. The positive trade gap made it possible to make huge investments towards constructing a powerful navy to strengthen control over foreign markets. Yet, the reliance on coercion to maintain a dominant position involved great costs that eventually led to the bankruptcy of the Dutch East Indies Company.

The British copied much of the centralised corporate and financial structures of the Dutch East Indies Company. The industrial revolution is often argued to have transformed the logic of economics, as wealth became a positive-sum game as new technologies enhanced productive power that enabled a market economy to maximise efficiency. However, the underpinning logic of relative gain to survive in an anarchic international system merely reformed mercantilism towards neo-mercantilism and geoeconomics. With a powerful manufacturing base, dominance over maritime transport corridors, and a formidable financial system, the British could rely more on free trade to cement their comparative advantage and impose asymmetrical core-periphery dependencies.

Britain's growing geoeconomic power in Asia in the 19th century was stifled by Chinese autarchy. Britain became dependent on Chinese silk, tea, and ceramics, while China's self-sufficiency resulted in only demanding gold and precious metals. The British thus relied on the illegal export of opium to China to restore a trade balance (Wong 2002).

The powerful British navy was used in the Opium Wars (1839–1842 and 1856–1860) to impose the conditions of trade and extract commercial privileges such as favourable tariffs, exemptions from local laws, and acquisition of strategic territory for trade. The defeat of China resulted in the economic giant crashing and ushering what has become known as the "Century of Humiliation," which lasted from the defeat in the First Opium War in 1842 to the Communist Revolution in 1949.

Japan embraced economic nationalist policies to survive among Western Empires. Initially, during the West's Age of Exploration, Japan isolated itself from Western European powers as asymmetrical power was resulting in European cultural and political influence penetrating Japan. The Sakoku Edict of 1635 removed foreign influence in Japan that was deemed harmful to national security. Albeit, the seclusion from international trade and cultural engagement was primarily a reaction to the domineering presence of the West in Asia (Toby 1977). Under the threat of US warships, Japan was eventually compelled to open its markets with the Convention of Kanagawa in 1854. China was at the time between the two Opium Wars, and the Japanese recognised the dilemma between opening their markets voluntary or being forced to do so by the US navy. Gunboat diplomacy had established an irrefutable link between controlling the sea and economic policy.

Japan advanced economic nationalist policies to avoid falling under core-periphery relations and colonial control. Tokyo sought to acquire technologies to pursue a vigorous industrial policy and strengthen its maritime power. The ideas of Alexander Hamilton and Friedrich List were brought directly to Japan by E. Peshine Smith, a second-generation economic nationalist and advocate of the American System. Peshine Smith served as an advisor to the Japanese Emperor in the 1870s following the Meiji restoration. Among other foreign economic advisors, Peshine Smith sought to bring the "American System of Manufacturers" to Japan (Reinert and Daastøl 2007:

38). As a strong Japanophil, Pershine Smith advised Japan to increase productive power to safeguard national sovereignty (Hudson 2010). The economic nationalist policies of Japan, emulating the American and German experience, resulted in Japan becoming an equal to Western empires. Japan grew rapidly and surprised the world by defeating the Russian Empire in 1905. The expanding Japanese empire was to be transformed into a formal geoeconomic region with the so-called "Greater East Asia co-prosperity sphere" that would place Northeast Asia and Southeast Asia in a Japanese-led region to counter the imperial expansion of European powers and the US.

Following Japan's defeat in the Second World War, the island-state became an important junior partner and a frontline of the US to contain Eurasian land powers. US Secretary of State, John Foster Dulles (1952: 181–82), argued that Japan was a key ally and indispensable participant of America's dual island-chains of the eastern periphery of the Eurasian continent to limit the access of the Soviet Union and China to the Pacific Ocean. A decade earlier, Spykman (1942: 470) had argued that the US-British partnership in Europe had to be replicated with Japan in the Far East to rule the eastern periphery or "rimland" of the Eurasian continent:

> Twice in one generation we have come to the aid of Great Britain in order that the small off-shore island might not have to face a single gigantic military state in control of the opposite coast of the mainland. If the balance of power in the Far East is to be preserved in the future as well as in the present, the United States will have to adopt a similar protective policy toward Japan. The present inconsistency in American policy will have to be removed. It is illogical to insist that Japan accept a Chinese empire from Vladivostok to Canton and at the same time support Great Britain in her wars for the preservation of buffer states across the North Sea.

Japan re-industrialised rapidly after the Second World War with renewed economic nationalist policies and under the patronage of the US. Washington also sabotaged Japan's peaceful settlement of territorial disputes with the Soviet Union in 1956 by threatening to annex Okinawa if Japan gave up the Southern Kuril Islands to the Soviets. By maintaining the territorial dispute between Japan and the Soviet Union, the US ensured that Japan's geoeconomic ambitions and foreign policy autonomy were limited by dependence on US security guarantees (Clark 2005; Brown 2016). Thus, the European security architecture was replicated in East Asia as Soviet-Japanese relations would be hostage to Soviet-US relations.

Japan's industrial policies were successfully pushed through its Zaibatsu system, in which the government and large enterprises cooperated towards investment in high-value activities and development of technological platforms owned by domestic corporations (Lazonick 2009: 166). New financial instruments were constructed that replicated the European arrangements, such as the US-Japanese dominated Asia Development Bank. However, Japan gradually became bolder by challenging US technological leadership and strategic industries in electric consumables, cars, and semiconductors from the 1970s. Washington was concerned that Japan could overtake the US, which could incentivise regional ambitions that entailed decoupling from US geoeconomic leadership. In a series of economic attacks on Japan in the 1980s, the US imposed a 100 percent tariff on Japanese semiconductors, banned the export of several products to the US, and the Japanese were compelled to open their semiconductor patents to the US. Toshiba was a leading producer of semiconductors until the US banned its products in 1987 for three years, among other punitive actions to diminish its competitiveness. Toshiba never fully recovered.

By the 1990s, Japan's geoeconomic rise came to an abrupt end. Its strategic industries failed to establish leadership, the economic bubble burst, stagnation ensured, and the island-state entered its lost decade. While the US had been concerned that its ally was becoming too powerful and thus disrupting the internal balance of dependence with the Asia-Pacific region, China was able to displace Japan as the leading power in East Asia.

THE UNIPOLAR REGION AFTER THE COLD WAR

The 1990s provided new impetus for American leadership in the world. In the 1980s there had been concerns about a rapidly rising Japan and West Germany also strengthening its industrial might in direct competition to the US. Washington also had concerns about the consequences of the collapse of the gold standard in 1971.

Yet, by the 1990s, Japan entered its lost decade and Germany was preoccupied with the costly affair of unification. The Soviet Union collapsed in 1991 and the principal foreign policy objective of a diminished Russia was to align itself with the West. The continued opening of both China and India provided the US with ample foreign markets.

The US reorganised its economy according to the neoliberal ideology of the 1980s to cement unipolarity by asserting the centre of a globalised economy. Neoliberalism manifested itself in international supply chains based on a radical international division of labour. The US government supported the establishment of a liberal economic system based on free trade and extended intellectual property rights to construct a new international division of labour (Prechel 2000; Baruch 2001; Shadlen 2005). The US and the wider West began restructuring the international economy to ensure post-Cold War globalization became a Westernisation project. Large mergers and acquisitions to take the high-position in international value-chains (Hopkins and Lazonick 2014). The focus was shifted towards intangible assets such as property rights, while less valuable tangible assets were outsourced (Baruch 2001). Western states pursued international trade agreements that opened their industries for international competition while extending and enforcing trade-related intellectual property rights (Sell 2003). Following the logic of the British repeal of the Corn Laws in 1846, the US saturated global markets with digital technologies in return for opening its manufacturing industry to low-wage markets. The unipolar moment was born and a global Monroe doctrine was constructed.

The opening of Eurasian economies, in particular the post-Soviet space, China and India in the 1990s, made it necessary for the US to strengthen the inter-regional partnership. Inter-regional formats were instrumental to strengthen and cement the unipolar moment. The US developed "system-dominance" by supporting regional powers in return for adherence to the US-centric system (Schweller 1999: 41; Katzenstein 2005: 57; Buzan 2005). Germany and Japan became the main nodes in Europe and East Asia to preserve US control over the other two major economic regions of the world (Bretherton and Vogler 1999: 66–67). Ensuring that the US is responsible for delivering energy security to Europe and East Asia is imperative to sustain US leadership and strengthening these regions against Russia and China (Blackwill and Harris 2016).

Yet, the US also had to manage the balance of dependence within the West. The EU came into force in 1993, which aimed to reduce asymmetries between the US and Europe. The EU also became a vehicle for collective hegemony in the pan-European space (Hyde-Price 2006: 227). The US thus continued to support the EU as it empowered the EU as a partner to contain Russian influence in Europe (Katzenstein 2005: 50). Yet, cautions about the shifting balance of dependence, the US established the North American Free Trade Agreement (NAFTA) in response to the growing strength of Europe and Japan (Hurrell 1995: 341). The primacy of NATO as a European security institution was also imperative to preserve European security dependence to sustain the trans-Atlantic region.

The EU was commonly defined as the most successful geoeconomic project (Hettne 1993). Integration was based on the sound objective of improving the symmetry between the US and Europe, while also extending collective hegemony over the pan-European space. The EU also enjoyed internal cohesion due to the balance of dependence within the bloc, as power was dispersed between the UK, France, Germany and Italy. The EU rapidly developed as a geoeconomic region with its shared industrial policy, new transportation corridors, and financial instruments that includes the European Central Bank (ECB) and a common currency.

The EU's strength derives primarily from two major achievements—the Single Market that eliminated barriers for goods and the Schengen agreement that removed border control. The Single Market and Schengen agreement represented regional liberalisation between somewhat similar economies, which therefore limited socioeconomic disruptions. Strong economic interdependence between member states translated into political loyalties and voluntary transfer of sovereign powers to Brussels. The EU uses collective bargaining power to establish asymmetrical interdependence with non-members whereas the EU can protect the strategic industries of member states and open the markets of non-member states (Raza 2007).

The EU converted its collective economic strength into political power as a regulatory power, by conditioning favourable trade on adapting to its regulatory framework. The EU's approach to its neighbourhood demonstrates that "bilateralism is clearly predominant over regionalism" to maximize asymmetrical interdependence, and thus extract political concessions in the form of abiding by EU standards and laws (Smith 2005a: 360). The collective economic power of the EU was converted into political power by establishing conditionality for market access—thus making the EU a "regulatory power" as (Eberlein and Grande 2005) the Brussels effect meant that the EU could enhance its influence beyond its borders by merely regulating its own market, and the international markets would subsequently adapt for market access (Bradford 2012).

The EU's "peaceful rise" entailed not aggravating the US by the excessive challenge to its geoeconomics instruments of power. The French, in Gaullist tradition, sought to develop more encompassing financial institutions that would not include the US, while other European powers wanted to include the US to avoid advancing the EU at the expense of the wider Western region (Smith 2002: 653). Britain, with a privileged position in the trans-Atlantic region, has been cautious to advance Europe at the expense of the West. The US also set clear conditions for its continued development of the EU. US Secretary of State, Madeleine Albright (1998), cautioned that Washington would only support the EU's development of military capabilities if Brussels followed the "three Ds": no duplication of NATO capabilities, no decoupling from NATO, and no discrimination of NATO members that are not members of the EU.

The EU's support for other geoeconomic regions reflected systemic incentives to maximise its own position in the world. The EU established inter-regional frameworks with other regions in the world, depending on its geostrategic ambitions. In Asia and Africa, Brussels sought to tie the regions to the EU, while in the Gulf region the EU sought to counterbalance the

US and China (Meissner 2017: 360). In the post-Soviet space, the EU has been reluctant to support or cooperate with regional frameworks that include Russia (Smith 2005b).

The US has demonstrated greater capability and preparedness than the Europeans to use military power to organise geoeconomic regions. Yet, supporting geoeconomics with military power is also evident in Europe. Horst Köhler, the German President, resigned in 2010 after arguing that the German military had to be prepared to use force to safeguard transportation corridors and advance geoeconomic interests:

> a country of our size, with such an export orientation, that in an emergency, military deployments are necessary in order to protect our interests, for example, securing free trade routes or preventing regional instabilities, which would definitely negatively influence out trade, jobs, and incomes (quoted in Szabo 2015: 7).

The following year, German strategic documents stipulated that competition to control trade corridors would be a key focus for the military:

> Free trade routes and a secure supply of raw materials are crucial for the future of Germany and Europe. Around the globe, changes are taking place in markets, channels of distribution, and the ways in which natural resources are developed, secured, and accessed. The scarcity of energy sources and other commodities required for highly developed products will have implications for the international community. Restricted access can trigger conflicts. Disruptions of transport routes and the flow of raw materials and commodities, e.g., by piracy or the sabotage of air transport, pose a threat to security and prosperity. This is why transport and energy security and related issues will play an increasingly important role for our security (German Ministry of Defence 2011: 3).

CONCLUSION

The modern history of Europe can be summarised as the effort to establish a geoeconomic region to manage the growing industrial potential. Island-states such as Britain and the US enjoy a competitive advantage due to the primacy of maritime powers. A stable European region has been facilitated under a geoeconomic hegemon, which cements its control over strategic industries, transportation corridors, and financial instruments with free-trade in a liberal economic system under the patronage of the hegemon.

Yet, the ability to exercise benign leadership by proving collective goods and accommodating the geoeconomic rise of allies is limited. Once new centres of power emerge within the geoeconomic region, the hegemon must restore its dominant position vis-à-vis allies that undermines the benevolence of leadership and replaces liberal economics with economic nationalism.

A unified and cohesive West and Europe only emerged under extremely unique historical conditions. The Second World War had devastated Europe and East Asia, which enabled the US to establish leadership over former competing geoeconomic regions. The militarized rivalry of the Cold War and subsequent security dependencies necessitated solidarity, which mitigates geoeconomic competition within regions. Europe only emerged as a cohesive geoeconomic subregion region under the patronage of the US as the result of negotiations based on collective gain. While geoeconomic borders are porous, the main adversaries of the West had less ability to use economic statecraft in its foreign policy due to their communist character.

The reorganisation of the trans-Atlantic region and Europe after the Cold War to establish geoeconomic primacy resulted in overextension. The US reliance on military instruments of power resembles traditional imperial overstretch that prevented a return to geoeconomics. Yet, there is also evidence of geoeconomic overstretch. Strengthening geoeconomic regions to wield greater influence in the wider world has diminished the internal balance of dependence with the West and Europe as regions.

4

Restoring Political Subjectivity in Greater Eurasia

In the unipolar order, the three main economic regions of the world - North America, Europe, and East Asia, were organised under US geoeconomic and military leadership. Europe was integrated into the wider trans-Atlantic region and Asia was integrated into the larger Asia-Pacific region that was later reconceptualised as the Indo-Pacific region.

Integrating China and Russia into the US-led international system was imperative for the stability and durability of the post-Cold War international order. China and Russia are the largest states in Asia and Europe, and the world's most powerful states after the US. A dilemma is evident as integrating these former Cold War adversaries into a US-led international system dilutes the relative power of the US and diminishes the security dependencies of a bloc-based international system, while failing to make Russia and China stakeholders in the existing order converts them into rivals and opponents of the unipolar order.

Did the US accommodate China and Russia in the post-Cold War international order? This is possibly the most important question in contemporary international relations. Since Nixon "opened China" in the 1970s, every American president argued that China was accommodated in the international political and economic order. Similarly, since an independent Russia emerged in 1991, every US president has claimed to have reached out to Russia.

Yet, both Beijing and Moscow have consistently castigated US policies as being aimed towards containment. This has profound consequences. When the Cold War came to an end, the US and its allies enjoyed abundant political legitimacy and the leading foreign policy of both Beijing and Moscow was to cultivate benign relations with Washington. Less than two and a half decades later, China and Russia commenced a strategic partnership to decouple from the US and restore their political subjectivity with collective geoeconomic power.

The usual response from the US and its European partners is to dismiss the position of Beijing and Moscow as paranoia, fear of democracy, insecurity, and an unacceptable unwavering longing for empire. The global ambitions and domestic authoritarianism of Xi Jinping supposedly derailed US-Chinese relations. Similarly, the dominant narrative about Russia inaccurately suggests the US and Russia were forming a partnership until it was disrupted by Putin's effort to restore the Soviet empire (Cohen 2018).

Inclusion in the international system is an ambiguous concept, although it can be observed and measured by the extent to which an actor has a voice to influence decision-making. At the extremes, the international system can be divided into political subjects and political objects, with the former being the states that do something and the latter have something done to them.

Washington's effort to integrate China and Russia into the US-led international system never entailed accepting the restoration of political subjectivity—a seat at the table. Subject-object partnerships were cultivated, in which cooperation between the teacher and a student implies that the latter falls in line. The unipolar era was subsequently always untenable for China and Russia, and their growing power enabled greater resistance. Russia had incentives to punch above its weight to balance an expansionist NATO and EU, while China enjoyed more stability and could bide its time to grow in strength without attracting unwanted attention. A geoeconomic partnership for Greater Eurasia came to fruition when China outgrew the US-centric regional framework and Russia lost faith in the prospect of future inclusion in a Greater European region.

This chapter first explores the West's ideological project of liberal hegemony to balance between engagement and containment of Russia and China. Building and maintaining an international system based on global hegemony demands that the largest states in Asia and Europe are contained, yet concurrently accommodated to the extent they accept the role as political objects.

Second, Moscow's principal post-Cold War security concerns derive from the efforts by Western powers to demote Russia into a civilizational. A new Europe was constructed without and thus inevitably against Russia, while Russia was presented with the dilemma of either accepting the role as an eternal apprentice of the West or a threat to be contained.

Third, China's struggle towards restoring its political subjectivity has focused consistently on geoeconomic means. China's "peaceful rise" entailed implicit consent to the role as a political objectivity by pursuing internal development without making its presence felt in the international system to avoid unwanted attention from the great powers. The strategy was, however, always temporary as China's economy would eventually outgrow the format of a US-dominated Asia. Thereafter, Beijing has begun demanding political subjectivity and a regional leadership role.

It is concluded that the failure to accommodate China and Russia as political subjects in the posttCold War international system inevitably led to the collective repudiation of US leadership and instead pursue a strategic partnership for Greater Eurasia.

BETWEEN CONTAINMENT AND ENGAGEMENT

The post-Cold War international order was structured around the notion that global hegemony would ensure durable stability. The security strategy builds on hegemonic stability theory, which has enjoyed great support among both American scholars and politicians (Kindleberger 1986; Krauthammer 1990–1991; Mastanduno 1997; Wohlforth 1999).

The leaked draft of the US Defence Planning Guidance in February 1992 recognised that the US had to expand rather than withdraw its military presence as US strategy for global primacy relied on preventing the emergence of future rivals (DPG 1992). Rather than enjoying the peace dividend, the Defence Planning Guide called for military superiority. This required the unravelling of key agreements for strategic stability such as the Anti-Ballistic Missile Treaty as the DPG advocated for an "early introduction" of a global anti-missile system as a part of a wider initiative to counter possible future threats from Russia. A month before, in January 1992, President Bush had in his State of the Union address also called for developing missile defence and assert global leadership. The US Security Strategy in 2002 explicitly argued for global dominance as a security strategy: To "dissuade future military competition" it was imperative to build and maintain "the unparalleled strength of the United States armed forces, and their forward presence" (NSS 2002). The US also demanded unquestionable loyalty from the world after the September 11 attacks as President Bush announced: "everyone must choose; you're either with the civilized world, or you're with the terrorists."

The liberal international order became an ideological project aligning the monolithic domination by the West with the advancement of liberal democracy. Former Secretary of State Condoleezza Rice (2003) linked global hegemony to liberal peace, which was contrasted with multipolarity:

> The reality is that "multipolarity" was never a unifying idea, or a vision. It was a necessary evil that sustained the absence of war but it did not promote the triumph of peace. Multipolarity is a theory of rivalry; of competing interests--and at its worst--competing values.

States aspiring for global hegemony have systemic incentives to embrace ideologies that endow them with the right to defend other peoples and advance human freedoms. The French National Convention declared in 1792 that France would "come to the aid of all peoples who are seeking to recover their liberty," and the Bolsheviks proclaimed in 1917 "the duty to render assistance, armed, if necessary, to the fighting proletariat of the other countries" (Herz 1950). The US similarly called for security through global dominance under the guise of the liberal international order, which professed the right and responsibility of the West to advance and defend the liberal democratic values in other countries. The liberal international order implies hegemony through sovereignty inequality as, for example, US interference in the domestic affairs of Russia advances democracy, while Russian interference in the domestic affairs of the US is an attack on democracy.

Herz (1950: 165) cautioned that democracies are especially likely to resist the democratisation of the international system because democracies "assert their weight, influence, and indispensability, in order to defend themselves against control by the people." Half a century later, Waltz (2000: 11) similarly cautioned against ideological fundamentalism as "democratic states tend to think of their countries as good, aside from what they do, simply because they are democratic" while considering "undemocratic states as bad, aside from what they do, simply because they are undemocratic" (Waltz 2000: 11).

European integration and the subsequent military, political, and economic structures after the Cold War were organised along what can be referred to as "inter-democratic security institutions" (Diesen 2015). In Asia, the US vigorously sought to reconceptualise the Asia-Pacific Region to the Indo-Pacific Region as a regional construct to limit the influence of China.

The legitimacy of the UN has sought to be reformed or sidelined as it provides excessive representation to Russia and China as rival powers that are not liberal democracies, which constrains the West. In 1999, NATO launched a "humanitarian interventionism" against Yugoslavia without a mandate from the UN, which was justified by questioning the legitimacy of Russian and Chinese veto powers as they were not liberal democracies that sufficiently embraced human rights. Regime change wars subsequently became the prerogative of Western democracies ever since.

After the illegal invasion of Iraq, Daalder and Lindsay (2004) advocated for an "alliance of democracies" to buttress the legitimacy of US foreign policy instead of relying solely on the UN. This idea was reformed and reconceptualised as a "Concert of Democracies," which "could become an alternative forum for the approval of the use of force in cases where the use of the veto at the Security Council prevented free nations from keeping faith with the aims of the U.N. Charter" (Ikenberry and Slaughter 2006: 26). During the US presidential campaign in 2008, the Republican presidential candidate, Senator John McCain, similarly promised to establish a "League of Democracies" to reduce the constraints on Western democracies under US leadership (Geis 2013).

The principal argument behind inter-democratic security institutions was that democracy is an intrinsic part of security, which legitimised the West's self-assigned role as the guardian of liberalism and the rules-based system. However, the concept of a rules-based liberal international order under the collective leadership of the West becomes a contradiction in terms. The requirement for solidarity among Western powers must take precedence over the consistent application of international law and rules. In Kosovo self-determination was prioritised above territorial integrity, and in Crimea territorial integrity was prioritised above self-determination. Subsequently, in the Western-led rules-based international order based on solidarity, Western states would always be in the right when disputes arise with Russia and China.

Assumptions about the perpetuity of the unipolar era were deeply flawed as the need to marginalise rising powers would only incentivise further balancing of the US (Waltz 2000). Putin argued: "sometimes it seems to me that America does not need allies, it needs vassals" (Wingard 2011). While the statement may appear crude, it aptly acknowledges that Washington recognises no equals. US leadership largely depends on preserving the Cold War dividing lines in Europe and Asia as it marginalises Russia and China while upholding the security dependencies of allies.

The US embraced the concept of being a "benevolent hegemon" to distinguish itself from the historical counterparts seeking dominance through coercion. What made the US benevolent? The loyalty of strategic allies was greatly dependent on maintaining Cold War dividing lines and threat perceptions. In Europe, NATO began expanding towards Russian borders rather than disbanding or converting itself into an inclusive security institution.

Hence, the power structures inherited from the Cold War, dependent on continued animosity, continued to fuel distrust. Beijing is adamant that the US military must the expelled from the Western Pacific, while Russia has become more forceful in upholding red lines against further NATO and EU expansionism towards its borders.

MARGINALISING RUSSIA IN EUROPE

Russia's historical tensions with Europe has been the result of attempting to establish its political subjectivity and gain a seat at the table in Europe. After shedding the Mongol Yoke, Russia believed it had cemented a European identity due to its central role in defending Christian civilisation as the "Third Rome" after the fall of Constantinople (Neumann and Pouliot 2011: 135). Although, the Europeans did not recognise Russia as a member of the

European family. Neumann (2013: 13) suggests that since the late 15th cen-tury Russia has been engaged in a "500-year-long struggle for recognition as a European power" and "Russia's major problem in Europe in the years to come is not, first and foremost, a security problem but a general political problem that has repercussions for security policy."

The West had always deemed Russia to be inferior and barbaric due to its Asiatic ethnicity, culture, and political legacy. The Asiatic component remained an overt explanation for the divisions in Europe into the Cold War. US General Patton opined:

> The difficulty in understanding the Russian is that we do not take cognizance of the fact that he is not a European but an Asiatic and therefore thinks deviously. We can no more understand a Russian than a Chinaman or a Japanese and, from what I have seen of them, I have no particular desire to understand them except to ascertain how much lead or iron it takes to kill them (Province 1983: 99).

POST-COLD WAR EUROPE

The Helsinki Act of 1975 had sowed the seed for ending the European secu-rity dilemma by advocating for the concept of "indivisibility of security in Europe." Gorbachev further developed the principle of indivisible security to overcome the zero-sum bloc politics of Europe by constructing a "Common European Home." Gorbachev's vision entailed dismantling NATO and the Warsaw Pact as confrontational alliances, and instead strengthen inclusive security institutions such as the OSCE and the UN (Tsygankov 2016: 458). Following Russia's independence from the Soviet Union, both Yeltsin and Putin argued that Russia could join NATO if this would be the main security institution in Europe (Flanagan 1992; Kupchan 2010: 112).

The US countered Gorbachev's Common European Home with the con-cept of a "Europe Whole and Free" in 1989. This appears to be a similar concept, albeit it denoted that Europe would be governed by liberal democ-racy (Hoagland 1989). Translated into power, this entailed that the US as the champion of liberalism, would be endowed with leadership and the East-West divisions in Europe would be reorganised by a subject-objective divide and given the role of teachers and students. This unresolved issue remained when Bush and Gorbachev declared the end of the Cold War in December 1989 in Malta. Bush had been adamant that the negotiated end of the Cold War meant "there were no losers, only winners" (Cohen 2009: 160).

However, the collapse of the Soviet Union in 1991 severely skewed the bal-ance of power, which inevitably influenced how Europe would be organised as a region. One month after the Soviet Union seized to exist, President Bush (1992) triumphantly declared at the State of the Union address: "By the grace of God, America won the Cold War . . . the Cold War didn't end, it was won . . . we are the United States of America, the leader of the West that has become the leader of the world."

Herein lies the source of the subject-object contentions in Europe. If the Cold War ended in 1991 due to the collapse of the Soviet Union, the subsequent new security architecture of Europe should be organised around the victorious power. A key function of the security architecture should be to deter revisionist efforts by the defeated power to challenge the outcome. In contrast, if the Cold War ended in 1989 through mutual compromise, the post-Cold War architecture in Europe is interpreted as a betrayal. From this perspective, Moscow voluntary walked away from an empire to overcome the Cold War legacy of rival military blocs. NATO and EU expansionism thus represent revisionism to the negotiated end of the Cold War.

Russia resents the narrative of US victory in the Cold War as it legitimised denying Russia political subjectivity in the new Europe and instead treat it as a defeated power (Sakwa 2017: 16). Instead of unifying Europe under an inclusive security architecture based on the OSCE, the dividing lines were merely moved to the East as the West expanded its Cold War institutions (Kupchan 1994). The alleged "victory" over Russia in the Cold War resembles the defeat in the Crimean War in 1856 as the terms of surrender were motivated by the objective of pushing Russia out of Europe and into Asia.

Jack Matlock (2010: 3), the last US ambassador to the Soviet Union, cautioned that the benign rhetoric regarding a negotiated end of the Cold War was reversed as "mythmaking began almost as soon as the Soviet Union fell." Matlock (2010: x) cautions that "too many American politicians looked at the end of the Cold War as if it were a quasi-military victory rather than a negotiated outcome that benefitted both sides." The consequence is an American political culture that believes durable peace is achieved through victory and military might rather than compromise and diplomacy (Matlock 2010). George Kennan, author of the *Long Telegram in 1946*, expressed his disdain over continuing his original containment strategy by expanding NATO:

> I think it is the beginning of a new cold war . . . There was no reason for this whatsoever. No one was threatening anybody else. This expansion would make the Founding Fathers of this country turn over in their graves . . . Of course there is going to be a bad reaction from Russia, and then [the NATO expanders] will say that we always told you that is how the Russians are--but this is just wrong (Friedman 1998).

Opposition to NATO expansionism was a bipartisan issue in the US before it became *fait accompli*. Even hawks such as Richard Pipes signed a statement as the Coalition Against NATO Expansion (CANE), which stipulated that:

> By its nature, a military alliance is directed against someone. The geography of NATO expansion makes its target clear: Russia . . . The proposal to expand NATO tosses it away by telling Russia in unmistakable terms that it remains excluded from the community of Western nations . . . [Russia] will remember, and ultimately, she will react, either from a position of renewed strength or out of desperation. The last great unfinished business of the 20th century is the reintegration of Russia with the West. With the proposal to expand NATO, we have turned our back on it (CENA 1998).

Former US Secretary of State, James Baker (2002: 100), also cautioned against using NATO as a security guarantee against possible future conflicts with Russia as this would become a self-fulfilling prophecy: "the best way to find an enemy is to look for one, and I worry that that is what we are doing when we try to isolate Russia."

When the First World War was unleashed, James Fairgrieve (1915) famously defined Central and Eastern Europe as the "crush zone," a region that had throughout history been crushed by the unforgiving power competition between Germany and Russia. The strategic interest of the UK was to maintain divisions in Europe as the alternative to the conflict, a partnership between Russia and Germany, would be an intolerable threat to Britain. Integrating Central and Eastern Europe into the EU and NATO represents continuity rather than change as the US and UK are now allied with Germany in competition for power in the "crush zone."

In 1999, NATO began its conversion from a defensive alliance into an instrument to preserve the unipolar moment. On the 12th of March 1999, NATO began to expand the alliance without including Russia, which meant that bloc politics would not be replaced with an inclusive European security architecture. In following expansions, NATO began increasing its control over the Baltic Sea and the Black Sea, in what Russia interpreted as the historical continuity of pushing Russia back into Asia. On the 24th of March 1999, NATO attacked Yugoslavia without a UN mandate, whilst using liberal arguments to sideline the UN. Kissinger (1999) even denounced the Rambouillet text presented to Yugoslavia as "an excuse to start bombing." The development of "energy security" as a key responsibility for NATO demonstrated that the alliance was no longer solely a defensive alliance. The efforts to use the military bloc to assert control over energy resources was also evident as, for example, the former CEO of Royal Dutch Shell co-chaired the draft of NATO's new Security Concept in 2009 (Ercolani and Sciascia 2011).

President Putin later diagnosed the reason for the collapse in relations with the West:

From the beginning, we failed to overcome Europe's division. Twenty-five years ago, the Berlin Wall fell, but invisible walls were moved to the East of Europe. This has led to mutual misunderstandings and assignment of guilt. They are the cause of all crises ever since (Bertrand 2016).

ASYMMETRICAL INTERDEPENDENCE TO MAINTAIN RUSSIA'S POLITICAL OBJECTIVITY

The calculation in the West appeared to be that perpetuating unipolarity required a weakened Russia relegated to the periphery of Europe, as opposed to accepting a Russia inside Europe that would upset the internal balance of power. By organising Europe under an expanding NATO and EU, Russia was marginalised from the main institutions and relations were organised in a core-periphery relationship.

The EU conceptualises Europe by concentric circles that signifies the level of integration with European institutions. The primary objective of the EU is to keep its "core intact, ensuring there is one centre rather than several" and ensure the neighbourhood gravitates towards this core (Wæver 1997: 68). By its sheer size, Russia is a problematic neighbour as it is too large to be included, and it becomes a rival when excluded.

Organising relations with Europe's largest state required the maximisation of asymmetrical interdependence. Collective bargaining power is maximised with NATO+1 and EU+1 relationships. Both the EU and NATO assign themselves a pedagogic role to socialise Russia, and the relationship is commonly conceptualised as a teacher-student relationship (Neumann 1999: 107–9; Browning 2003: 58; Zürn and Checkel 2005: 1056; Gheciu 2005). Implicit in the teacher-student format is the assumption that cooperation entails that Russia as a political object accepts one-sided adjustments and unilateral concessions.

By conflating values with national interests, Russia can be included to the extent it abides by the decisions of the West, thus making Russia responsible for its own exclusion if it does not embrace its role as a political object (Möller 2003: 316). The teacher-student format even penetrates the language to the extent that the West no longer discusses national interests and policy references, rather the word "policy" is replaced with "behaviour." Instead of cooperating to harmonise interests to align policies, the paternal or pedagogic role of the West is to punish "bad behaviour" and reward "good behaviour."

A certain degree of political radicalism is subsequently evident as peace does not derive from mutual understanding and compromise, rather understanding and compromise represents a betrayal of indispensable values. Peace precludes "rewarding bad behaviour" and instead a winner-takes-all approach is embraced as peace prevails when good values defeat bad values. Aron (1966: 584) opines:

> Idealistic diplomacy slips too often into fanaticism; it divides states into good and evil, into peace-loving and bellicose. It envisions a permanent peace by the punishment of the latter and the triumph of the former.

The West has historically considered itself to have a civilizing mission in the barbaric East, which includes Russia (Lehti 1999: 28; Browning 2003). In the 1990s, the EU continued along this tradition by embarking on a "civilising mission" to tame its eastern regions (Zielonka 2013). Case in point, EU Commission President, Romano Prodi (2000), argued: "Europe needs to project its model of society into the wider world. We are not simply here to defend our own interests: we have a unique historic experience to offer." This subject-object mentality was also evident in Washington. US Deputy Secretary of State, Strobe Talbott (2007: 201), recalled a conversation with Bill Clinton in 1996 in which the US president outlined what cooperation with Russia entailed: "We keep telling ol' Boris, 'O.K., now, here's what you've got to do next—here's some more shit for your face.'"

The civilising mission of the EU resulted in several paradoxes in Europe. For example, the EU's "Common Strategy of the European Union on Russia" in 1999 argued for multilateralism, yet the document did not present a joint framework and instead outlined a vast number of tasks that Russia must implement (Lynch 2003). Institutions were not used to harmonise competing interests and stimulate benign competition, instead, the extent of engagement in institutions and diplomatic engagement is used as a tool to reward good behaviour or punish bad behaviour.

The West's ability to enforce the subject-object dynamics can be augmented by increasing the asymmetry by expanding to the East and establishing unilateral partnerships with the shared neighbourhood for collective influence against Russia. Thus, the failure to include Russia in European institutions resulted in "European integration" becoming a zero-sum process where the shared neighbourhood would have to choose between the West or Russia.

Even Russian liberals, who had desired to Westernise Russia and make it "more European," largely reject the notion that Russia should submit to the EU's rules and legislation (Lukyanov 2021). Yeltsin's liberal and pro-Western foreign minister, Andrey Kozyrev, cautioned in 1994 that Russia's European future was in danger and Russia was "doomed to be a great power" because "some people in the West have succumbed to the fantasy that a partnership can be built with Russia on the principle of 'if the Russians are good guys now, they should follow us in every way'" (Pouliot 2010: 178).

Former US Secretary of Defence, Robert Gates (2014: 162), acknowledged the failure of treating Russia as a political subject with national security interest:

> When Russia was weak in the 1990s and beyond, we did not take Russian interests seriously. We did a poor job of seeing the world from their point of view, and of managing the relationship for the long term . . . The relationship with Russia had been badly mismanaged after Bush 41 left office in 1993. Getting Gorbachev to acquiesce to a unified Germany as a member of NATO had been a huge accomplishment. But moving so quickly after the collapse of the Soviet Union to incorporate so many of its formerly subjugated states into NATO was a mistake . . . Trying to bring Georgia and Ukraine into NATO was truly overreaching.

Kissinger had hoped to integrate Russia as a secondary power, yet member, of the Western-centric international economic system. Kissinger cautioned that Russia had "come under a kind of colonial tutelage" and the subject-object organisation of relations would only fuel resentment (Smh 1999: 19). After the Western-backed coup in Ukraine in 2014 and ensuing fighting in Donbas, Kissinger criticised US policies towards Russia as "breaking Russia has become an objective; the long-range purpose should be to integrate it" (Kissinger 2015).

Rand Corporation, the think tank linked intimately with US intelligence services since the 1940s, published in 2019 a strategy for extending and weakening Moscow. The report advocates hybrid warfare against Russia by creating a quagmire more Russia in Syria, instigate regime change in Belarus, inciting tensions in the South Caucasus, pushing Russia out of Moldova, reducing Russian influence in Central Asia, limit Russian gas exports to Europe, using sanctions, and undermine regime legitimacy by partnering with actors inside Russia that can instigate protests and revolt (Rand 2019).

Restoring Russian political subjectivity was never an option. Russia can accept the role as an eternal apprentice to the West or be chastised as a counter-civilizational adversary that must be contained or confronted (Williams and Neumann 2000: 361; Browning 2003).

4

FROM GREATER EUROPE TO GREATER EURASIA

Yeltsin was partly to blame for the subject-object relationship between the West and Russia. By dedicating Russia to integrate into the West by adopting capitalism and liberal democracy, he implicitly accepted unilateral concessions and the role of an apprentice seeking to return to Europe. Furthermore, Russia diminished its negotiation power by committing solely to the integration into the West. Russia's "leaning-to-one-side" policy resulted in reduced engagement with former Soviet republics and even avoiding meetings with Chinese officials (Tsygankov 2016: 58). The West became Russia's only option (Straus 2003: 229; Brzezinski 2009: 102), which allowed the West to dictate the terms of cooperation.

The consequence of Russia turning to the East had widely predicted by leading scholars who argued that NATO expansionism would compel Russia to turn to China to counter an expansionist West (Russett and Stam 1998; Waltz 2000: 22). Yeltsin had recognised the need for Russia to diversify its economic connectivity to reduce the excessive dependence on the West. Furthermore, Yeltsin argued that relations with the West "had to be balanced. After all, we are a Eurasian state" (Tsygankov 2016: 71).

Yeltsin argued in 1997 that a Russian-Chinese partnership was required to adjust to the new world created by NATO expansionism:

> We shall do everything to minimize the consequences of NATO expansion for Russia's security . . . We shall continue to deepen integration within the Commonwealth of Independent States, especially with Belarus. We shall strengthen cooperation with neighbouring countries, first of all with China (quoted in Carpenter and Conry 1998: 136).

Russian and Chinese leaders agreed in June 1997 to "promote a multipolar world and the establishment of a new international order," albeit at the time the duo lacked sufficient geoeconomic instruments of power. The subsequent efforts by Russian Prime Minister, Yevgeny Primakov, to establish a Eurasian partnership with China and India in the late 1990s was premature as the potential partners had the capacity or willingness to directly challenge the West. However, in 2006, the feasibility for a Eurasian partnership was tested with a China, Russia, India trilateral process, which Chinese President Hu Jintao promoted as a strategic partnership for regional peace (Xinhua 2006).

Once the West began constructing a Europe without Russia by expanding NATO, Yeltsin's pro-Western liberal platform collapsed and Yeltsin stepped down to let his Prime Minister, Vladimir Putin, take over and reorganise relations with the West. Russian Foreign Minister Sergey Lavrov (2012) argued that Russia aspires to construct a Greater Europe, "but this should not be Russia's incorporation into the West, but genuinely equitable rapprochement." Recognising Yeltsin's liberal platform had collapsed, Putin continued to pursue the Greater Europe initiative by negotiating from a position of strength.

In 2008, Russia proposed the development of a new inclusive European Security Architecture, which was largely ignored by the Western powers (Diesen and Wood 2012). In 2010, Moscow proposed an EU-Russian Union to create a common economic space from Lisbon to Vladivostok, which was also met with a cold shoulder by the EU.

After the Georgian War in August 2008, President Medvedev demanded recognition for a "sphere of privileged interests." The terminology represents a departure from the concept of spheres of influence, which denotes exclusive interests. The concept of spheres of interests signifies that Russian interests must be taken into account along its periphery. Moscow will thus reject efforts by Western powers to pursue zero-sum initiatives and exclusive influence. This represented another effort to restore Russia's political subjectivity by arguing that Russia should be included in consultations, as what occurs in its neighbourhood will affect Russia (Trenin 2009).

The Western support for the 2014 coup in Ukraine became the final straw for Moscow (Mearsheimer 2014). Western efforts to draw Ukraine into the Western sphere and evict Russia from the Crimean peninsula were deemed to be an existential threat. The Crimean peninsula is the most important region in the Black Sea and all major powers of the past ranging from the Scythians, Greeks, Romans, Huns, Mongols, Turks, and Cossacks have all laid claim to Crimea. Russia conquered Crimea in 1783 and it has since been a cornerstone of its power. Crimea has been a key source of Russia's connection with the world economy. The Black Sea Fleet is stationed in Sevastopol in Crimea and maintaining a military presence there prevents the Black Sea from being converted into a NATO lake.

Putin (2014) opined that Russia had been left with no alternatives than to push back against the West: "They must have really lacked political instinct and common sense not to foresee all the consequences of their actions. Russia found itself in a position it could not retreat from." Any lingering illusions about the prospect of incremental integration with Europe had been shed, which ended the decades-long Greater Europe initiative. Vladislav Surkov, a leading intellectual in the Russian presidential administration, argued it was time to end the "repeated and fruitless attempts to become part of Western civilization" and instead recognise that Russia needs to chart its own path.

Russia subsequently began embracing a strategic partnership with China to construct a Greater Eurasia. The renewed efforts to push Russia back into Asia was different in 2014 in the past as Russia could partner with another centre of power. After approximately 500 years, the global domination of the West has come to an end due to the spectacular rise of China. Moscow therefore looks towards Beijing as an indispensable partner to collectively restore their political subjectivity in the Greater Eurasian region. In 2013, President Putin had already recognised the need to become a continental power: "Eurasian integration is a chance for the entire post-Soviet expanse to become an independent centre of global development, rather than remaining on the outskirts of Europe and Asia" (Putin 2013a).

Demoting Russia to the only non-European country in Europe has increasingly been internalised by Russians as well. A Levada poll in 2021 indicated that only 29 percent of Russians consider Russia to be a European country. In comparison, Levada polled in 2008 that 52 percent of Russians deemed Russia to be a European country. This trend is even stronger among younger Russians, with only 23 percent who believe in 2021 that Russia is European. The findings contradict common expectation in the West that the post-Soviet generation would grow up with a greater affinity towards the West and a stronger European identity. Having grown up with NATO expansionism and interventionism, young Russians are deeply sceptical of the US and distrust NATO more than any other international organisation, while 42 percent believe that relations with the West "will always be marked by mistrust" (Friedrich-Ebert-Stiftung 2020). The next generation is thus less committed to a European future for Russia.

China's "peaceful rise" and return to the world stage

China's recovery of political subjectivity has gone through various stages, each lasting approximately three decades. China's "Century of Humiliation," which had lasted since the Opium Wars, ended with the Communist Revolution in 1949. Mao Zedong proclaimed that the revolution meant that "the Chinese people have stood up." Under the leadership of Mao's leadership over the next three decades, Beijing restored sovereign control over China, although with what can only be described as disastrous economic mismanagement.

Responding to these failures, China began to embrace market reforms in 1978 under the guidance of Deng Xiaoping. For the next three decades, China pursued domestic economic reforms that were linked to nation-building. Deng Xiaoping committed his nation to a "peaceful rise," which implied that China would temporarily forego political subjectivity in international relations. China pursued rapid domestic development without a significant presence in international affairs that would attract unwanted attention by the great powers. In Deng Xiaoping's own words, peaceful rise meant that China's objective was to "bide our time and hide our capabilities." Three decades later, by the time of the Global Financial Crisis of 2008–2009, China began pursuing political subjectivity and the return to global leadership.

In 1990, Deng Xiaoping had told members of the Central Committee that the world was moving towards multipolarity:

> The situation in which the United States and the Soviet Union dominated all international affairs is changing. Nevertheless, in the future when the world becomes three-polar, four-polar or five-polar, the Soviet Union, no matter how weakened it may be and even if some of its republics withdraw from it, will still be one pole. In the so-called multipolar world, China too will be a pole. We should not belittle our own importance: one way or another, China will be counted as a pole. Our foreign policies remain the same: first, opposing hegemonism and power politics and safeguarding world peace; and second, working to establish a new international political order and a new international economic order (Deng 1990).

The US advancement and consolidation of unipolarity was deemed to be regrettable. China recognised immediately after the Cold War that the complexity of the new world required multilateral solutions, and multilateralism required multipolarity (Kuik 2005). Multipolarity also required China to seek cooperation and integration with regional frameworks to dissuade neighbouring states from aligning with Washington in the future against China (Hughes 2005).

Chinese economic nationalist policies aimed to acquire the productive power of the world. Economic reforms were supported by wage suppression and currency manipulation to complement its low-wage competitiveness, which enabled China to advance the neo-mercantilist objective of maximising exports and minimising imports. China produced and saved to establish interdependence with nations that consumed and borrowed - primarily the US. The subsequent lower standard of living was deemed to be an investment into future greatness, as China acquired productive power, climbed up global value chains, and amassed wealth. In other words, China emulated the economic nationalist policies of the Asian Tigers.

The principal difference has been China's seemingly endless supply of labour from an unproductive agricultural sector (Subramanian 2011). Furthermore, the desire by foreign powers to gain access to the vast consumer base in China enabled Beijing to set strategic conditions for market access. For example, access to the domestic market required production in partnership with domestic companies, which facilitated the transfer of technologies and know-how. China incrementally climbed up global value chains by developing more technologically advanced products and establishing domestic brands and platforms.

The positive trade gap produced vast amounts of foreign reserves, which could be investments into US Treasury bonds. An interdependent partnership between China that produced and lent money was established with the US that consumed and borrowed. This model supported the "peaceful rise" model as the growing dependency of the US on China mitigated Washington's willingness to engage in hostilities towards a rising China. However, the interdependence was always unsustainable as it enabled the US to amass increasingly unsustainable debt, which made both Beijing and Washington increasingly uncomfortable.

China's format for "peaceful rise" was inevitably temporary as nation-building was eventually replaced by region-building. Much like German nation-building between 1871 and 1890 created an industrial potential that could not be accommodated by the regional framework controlled by rival Britain, so did China need to establish a favourable geoeconomic region to accommodate its growing industrial power. The rapidly shifting balance of power increasingly attracted the suspicion and resentment of the US (Kaplan 2012: 200). Future security demands reforming the US-dominated East Asian security architecture. To be truly secure, Beijing aims to push the US back and dismantle the island-chains designed to contain China (Kaplan 2012: 215).

In 2000, The Chinese government defined its Going Global Strategy, which entailed international expansion and outbound investments by Chinese businesses that had matured through activity in the domestic market and thus become competitive in international markets. The growing size and strength of the Chinese economy required affordable and reliable supplies of natural resources and unchallenged access to international markets for exports, which translated into forceful economic inroads into Africa, Central Asia, and other regions of the world (Holslag 2006). Adversaries of Washington, such as Iran and Sudan, became attractive markets due to the lack of US influence and their need for China as an alternative. The government incentivised Chinese companies to acquire strategic industries (technology and natural resources) and transportation assets (Ziegler and Menon 2014). From 2004, the terminology, "string of pearls," was used in reference to China's efforts to establish maritime infrastructure across the Indian Ocean periphery. The efforts to establish maritime corridors under Chinese control emulated the US expansion of ports in the Pacific Ocean at the end of the 19th century.

Washington grew increasingly concerned as China's peaceful rise was defined as lacking a footprint in international affairs as opposed to integrating under the required consensus culture of the unipolar era. The US would have preferred that China demonstrated its intentions to channel its influence within the Western-centric international system and it did not contest the US-dominated security architecture in the Western Pacific. Unlike Russia that had to assert itself to counter the revisionism of NATO expansionism, China enjoyed a temporarily tolerable status-quo that allowed it to gain strength before asserting political subjectivity.

The former Prime Minister of Australia, Kevin Rudd (2012), aptly identified China's future trajectory as the most important development in international politics:

> Very soon we will find ourselves at a point in history when, for the first time since George III, a non-Western, non-democratic state will be the largest economy in the world. If this is the case, how will China exercise its power in the future international order? Will it accept the culture, norms and structure of the postwar order? Or will China seek to change it? I believe this is the single core question for the first half of the twenty-first century, not just for Asia, but for the world."

THE US FAILURE TO REFORM AND ACCOMMODATE CHINESE POLITICAL SUBJECTIVITY

China has been vastly successful with an economic rise unparalleled in human history. This spectacular rise occurred in Asia as a region under US guardianship, so why would Beijing challenge the US-led international order? The simple answer is the temporary and unsustainable format of the subject-object relationship.

Washington's limited accommodation of China was intended to cultivate a place for a political object at the lower end of global value chains. Secretary of State Albright set the tone from Washington when she argued that China had to be engaged and accommodated as a "responsible participant" in the US-led international economic order (Albright 1997). Although, equating the concept of "responsible stakeholder" to accepting perpetual US dominance implies that the US was only able to integrate weak and dependent states rather than equals. US-Chinese relations were remarkably benign in the 1990s, except for the crisis over Taiwan in 1997 and the US bombing of the Chinese embassy in Belgrade in 1999 after Bejing repeatedly criticised the illegality of the war and war crimes.1

It was argued that China would not need to challenge US leadership as it "faces a Western-centered system that is open, integrated, and rule-based" (Ikenberry 2008: 24). However, the US ability to act as a responsible administrator of an open and rules-based order would be compromised by the need

---

1[] The US has claimed the bombing of the Chinese embassy was an accident.

to contain China to ensure the system remains Western-centered. Liberal economics is conditioned on the concentration of economic power in a hegemon, and when a rival emerges, the open economic system predictably unravels.

A renegotiation of the Asia-Pacific region was necessary as China outgrew its marginal role in the US-led system. The continued "peaceful rise" of China as it moved from nation-building to region-building requires a dual process as China must adapt to the existing structures of the international order, while the US as the dominant state must reform the regional framework to accommodate China (Buzan 2010: 5).

The US remained suspicious of Chinese companies expanding across the world, and was reluctant to accept reforms that would elevate China's position in the world. There was no willingness in Washington to reconsider the security architecture of the South China Sea based on US naval primacy. China was accommodated as a member of the IMF and World Bank since 1980, and then joined the WTO in 2001. However, Washington was reluctant to relinquish its domineering role to accommodate an adequate leadership role for China in financial institutions that reflected the changing international distribution of power. Beijing subsequently complained in vain about the failure to acquire a leading position in key economic institutions like the IMF, World Bank, and Asian Development Bank (Hilpert and Wacker 2015: 2).

Without sufficient representation in the regional economic architecture, China began to develop alternative and parallel regional institutions (Paradise 2016). China presented Washington with a dilemma as it could either reform the existing institutions in a power-sharing scheme, or China would decouple from US-led institutions by creating alternatives that are firmly under Chinese leadership and control (Wang 2015).

ALTERING THE ENGAGEMENT/CONTAINMENT BALANCE TOWARDS CHINA

China eventually had to abandon its "peaceful rise," defined by not stoking concerns among the major powers. The status-quo began to unravel with the global financial crisis in 2008 as the worsening global imbalances could no longer be sustained and required adjustments (Wang and Chin 2013). The US was faced with the dilemma between accepting reforms that included greater fiscal discipline and accept a less domineering position in the world, or extend unipolarity by continuing to borrow and spend more. The US national debt in 2008 was 9 trillion, which has surpassed 27 trillion by the end of 2020. As John Maynard Keynes succinctly put it: "If you owe your bank a hundred pounds, you have a problem. But if you owe your bank a million pounds, it has . . ." (Zloch-Christy 1987: 134). The popular sentiment among Chinese decision-makers was that the US-made Global Financial Crisis had created an opportunity to assert Chinese leadership in the world (Ren 2017).

China subsequently altered the concept of "peaceful rise" from a low-profile concept to one of win-win and positive-sum gain (Yan 2014). China's "peaceful rise" has been redefined to fit its new ambitions for leadership. The new format for "peaceful rise" entails China establishing benign geoeconomic leadership based on ambiguous concepts of "win-win" cooperation and the "Silk Road spirit," while less focus is devoted to the relative gain in China's favour. China's ambition to revive its position as the Middle Kingdom as an economic locomotive developing asymmetrical, yet mutually beneficial, economic relationship (Eisemann, Heginbotham, and Mitchell 2015). The effort to align win-win economic cooperation and the conservative idea that "each civilization is distinct and none is superior to others" is codified into the "Shanghai Spirit" of the Shanghai Cooperation Organisation (Xi 2020).

CONTAINING CHINA

Washington subsequently communicated its intentions to contain China. Washington had not reformed the Cold War divisions in the Western Pacific as the US needed an insurance policy against future conflicts with China. Obama defined himself as "America's first Pacific president" and announced the "pivot to Asia" that consisted of strengthening military alliances and military capabilities in East Asia. US Secretary of State Hillary Clinton (2011) added that the US will build a security and economic "architecture and pay dividends for continued American century, just as our post-World War II commitment to building a comprehensive and lasting transatlantic network of institutions and relationships has paid off many times over—and continues to do so." Further militarizing the island-chains and also setting up a military partnership with countries such as Vietnam meant that China would get the same treatment as Russia was receiving in Europe. Yet, China geoeconomic rise has created economic dependence by the US, which implies great costs when the US attempts to decouple and contain China (Zhao 2013).

Yet, geoeconomic balancing did occur. Washington refused China's invitation to join the Chinese-led Asian Infrastructure Investment Bank (AIIB), an alternative to the IMF and World Bank, and even objected to allies joining. Obama (2016) expressed his intention to create the Trans-Pacific Partnership (TPP) to marginalise China's role in East Asia: "The world has changed. The rules are changing with it. The United States, not countries like China, should write them."

Yet, the competition to shape East Asia as a geoeconomic region has shifted in China's favour. The Trump administration abandoned the TPP due to the fear that the balance of dependence within the region would shift from the US to its partners. Thus, the main rival of the US-led TPP, the Chinese-led Regional Comprehensive Economic Partnership (RCEP), prevailed as the main arrangement to reshape the region. In November 2020, the RCEP was signed and became the largest free-trade area in the world by covering almost a third of the global economy. Instead of being marginalised as a political object in its own region, China became the leading power to write the rules and establish the standards of free-trade.

The Trump administration was even more brazen in walking back the four-decade-old One-China policy. After winning the presidential election, Donald Trump suggested the One-China policy would be used as a bargaining chip in a future trade deal when he stated: "I don't know why we have to be bound by a 'One China' policy unless we make a deal with China having to do with other things, including trade" (Panda 2016). Washington opened for diplomatic visits to Taiwan with the Taiwan Travel Act in March 2018. The increased weapons sales to Taiwan and sailing US warships through the Taiwan Strait contributes further to embolden the more hawkish independence hardliners in Taipei. In November 2020, the US appeared to move even closer to officially cancelling its One-China policy as the US Secretary of State, Mike Pompeo, bombastically argued: "Taiwan has not been a part of China." Concurrently, the US began interfering to a greater extent in Hong Kong and referring to the human rights issues in Xinjian as "genocide" to rally support for anti-Chinese sanctions from European allies.

The economic war with China focuses primarily on stunting Chinese technological advancements as the source of dominant strategic industries. As the world enters a fourth industrial revolution where the digital space can manipulate the physical world, the US sought to weaken its Chinese rivals by disrupting supply chains. Most crucially, the US targets China's leading company advancing 5G technology as the arteries of technologies such as the Internet of Things and AI.

The US first began to levy tariffs against China. Then, the US began targeting the Chinese tech sector to weaken its strategic industries akin to the economic sanctions against Japan's tech sector in the 1980s. Washington requested the arrest of Huawei's Chief Financial Officer of Huawei in Canada in 2018; prohibited US tech companies from selling computer chips to Huawei; pressured Google to suspend its Android license to Huawei; increased restrictions on technology transfers to China.

While Trump's character can be assigned some responsibility for the intensified containment of China, these policies will to some extent be followed by the Biden administration. After Biden's election victory in November 2020, Hillary Clinton (2020) penned an article stipulating the need for a vigorous industrial policy with government support. Previously, Hillary Clinton had suggested some limitations on the free market by proclaiming: "I don't want my grandchildren to live in a world dominated by the Chinese" (Goldberg 2016). Echoing Clinton's sentiments, the US Secretary of State under Trump, Mike Pompeo (2020), argued that the failure to confront China will create a future where "our children's children may be at the mercy of the Chinese Communist Party." Historical continuity thus appears evident as a hegemon can rarely be surpassed by a challenger without conflict in what is known as Thucydides trap (Gilpin 1981; Kennedy 1987).

MILITARISING THE GEOECONOMIC CONFLICT

The first sentence in the foreword of the US Naval Strategy of 2020 proclaims: "Our actions in this decade will shape the maritime balance of power for the rest of this century," which is later followed by identifying China and Russia as the main rivals in the global competition for influence (US Department of Defence 2020: 1).

On the 5th of January 2021, the US declassified and released its 2019 Indo-Pacific Strategy Report. The first sentence of the declassified Indo-Pacific strategy states: "how to maintain US strategic primacy" (White House 2021). The ensuing focus on maintaining primacy as an objective rather than a means to an end is deeply problematic as power maximisation is equated to security maximisation. Although, as primacy is upheld by continued dividing lines to marginalise adversaries and maintain security dependence on allies, the system becomes inherently confrontational. Case in point, US security planners cynically view the tensions in the Himalayas as an opportunity to pull India towards a US security arrangement and to distract China from the South China Sea" (Goldstein 2021). By comparison, NATO's relentless expansion towards Russian borders instigates conflicts that create a demand for NATO. The hegemonic structure subsequently reproduces itself by responding to conflicts caused by its own existence.

The US aims to construct new security regions in the East to marginalise and counter China. The US has worked towards replacing Asia-Pacific as a regional concept with the Indo-Pacific, which conceptually beings together with the Indian Ocean and the Pacific Ocean (Medcalf 2017). The Indo-Pacific region is more conducive towards containing China are preserve US leadership as US allies in the Asia-Pacific region has been more apprehensive about forming an anti-Chinese alliance.

Pompeo (2018) sought to clearly define the concept of a "free and open" Indo-Pacific Region by specifying that "free" refers to the commitment to good governance and "open" entails access to the seas. This conceptualisation of the Indo-Pacific Region has striking similarities to the concept of a

"Europe Whole and Free" advanced by President Bush in 1989 to counter Gorbachev's concept of a Common European Home. A "free" Europe and Indo-Pacific both repudiate the notion of collective leadership by endowing Washington with unilateral leadership and denying Moscow and Beijing political subjectivity.

The US endeavours to connect with Japan, India, and Australia as the "Quad." The development of the Quad collapsed in 2007 as India and Australia were apprehensive about joining an anti-Chinese grouping. Australia was determined not to choose between the US as its main security provider and China as its main trading partner. India was apprehensive about losing its status as a cornerstone of the nonaligned movement and wary about provoking China, which could respond by seeking closer alignment with Pakistan. A decade later with growing apprehensions about a more assertive China, the Quad is experiencing a rebirth.

US Deputy Secretary of State, Stephen Biegun, argued in favour of organising a NATO of the East in the Indo-Pacific region. Biegun argued that NATO only began with 12 member states as many European countries desired to maintain neutrality, although the Quad could establish the foundation before expanding (Biegun 2020). Such an overt and confrontational stance would, however, likely be a step too far for both Australia and India.

US Secretary of State, Mike Pompeo (2019), affirmed the Quad's intentions of containing China as the grouping will work towards "ensuring that China retains only its proper place in the world." As tensions rise between India and China, Pompeo also suggested that India should develop a greater military partnership with the US as India "absolutely need the United States to be their ally and partner in this fight" (The Hindu 2020).

China has been highly critical of the Indo-Pacific concept as it is seen as an anti-Chinese construct (He and Li 2020). Russia supports China's sentiments and Russian Foreign Minister Sergey Lavrov denounced it as a ploy to restore the unipolar world order:

> India is currently an object of the Western countries' persistent, aggressive and devious policy as they are trying to engage it in anti-China games by promoting Indo-Pacific strategies, the so-called Quad while at the same time the West is attempting to undermine our close partnership and privileged relations with India (Roy 2020).

US allies are apprehensive about China's relative power increasing vis-à-vis the US, although they also take into account the absolute gain from economic connectivity. China is the main locomotive for global growth in the years to come, and decoupling from China will severely weaken India, Japan, and Australia.

Japan is concerned about China's growing military power, yet is apprehensive about defining economic relations with China in zero-sum terms (Kireeva 2020). India is leaning towards the concept of the Indo-Pacific Region, yet is apprehensive about the Quad due to its overt anti-Chinese purpose.

The US efforts to recreate militarised Cold War institutions in Asia to counter China fails to appreciate that modern China is not comparable to the Soviet Union. Former Indian ambassador, Bhadrakumar (2020), argues that the US and China are competing in the same global society: "Look at the sheer spread of the US-China battlefields—global governance, geoeconomics, trade, investment, finance, currency usage, supply chain management, technology standards and systems, scientific collaboration and so on" (Bhadrakumar 2020). Furthermore, the eagerness to recreate an ideological framework for the new great power rivalry has a weak foundation: "China has no messianic ideology to export and prefers to set a model by virtue of its performance. It is not in the business of instigating regime change in other countries, and actually gets along rather well with democracies" (Bhadrakumar 2020).

NATO AGAINST CHINA

The US aims to use the Russia-China geoeconomic partnership to sow divisions between the EU and China. Benefitting from the militarised dividing lines in Europe, the US advocates expanding existing military structures to confront China. The US Congress subsequently advised:

> Congress direct the Administration to discuss in its engagements with the EU and NATO the implications of China's increasingly close military ties with Russia and growing importance to transatlantic security interests. Such discussions would include how Europe and NATO can promote the exchange of information on common defense and other challenges posed by China and Russia, including both countries' influence operations (US Congress 2018: 305–6).

The US is also moving towards militarising Europe's economic disputes with China, which hardens the regional borders of the West by incentivising greater solidarity. NATO has become increasingly vocal against China as the US-Chinese economic war intensified. NATO, the world largest military bloc and a relic from the Cold War, is an opportune organisation to militarise the geoeconomic rivalry. NATO Secretary-General, Jens Stoltenberg, cautioned against "fundamental shift in the global balance of power" and proclaimed: "One thing is clear: China is coming ever closer to Europe's doorstep . . . NATO allies must face this challenge together" (DW 2020). In March 2021,

NATO Secretary-General Jens Stoltenberg argued that the tensions with China present "a unique opportunity to open a new chapter in the relationship between North America—the United States—and Europe" (DW 2021).

In November 2020, NATO released an analysis and recommendation paper, arguing against both economic and military power:

> China will likely also challenge NATO's ability to build collective resilience, safeguard critical infrastructure, address new and emerging technologies such as 5G, and protect sensitive sectors of the economy including supply chains. Longer term, China is increasingly likely to project military power globally, including potentially in the Euro-Atlantic area (NATO 2020: 17).

Efforts to strengthen internal solidarity and harden regional borders have also been pushed by depicting the geoeconomic rivalry through the lens of a zero-sum ideological conflict. NATO opines that "The scale of Chinese power and global reach poses acute challenges to open and democratic societies" (NATO 2020: 27). Recasting the familiar military-ideological binary division of the Cold War, US Secretary of State, Mike Pompeo (2020) argued: "I grew up and served my time in the Army during the Cold War. And if there is one thing I learned, communists almost always lie. The biggest lie that they tell is to think that they speak for 1.4 billion people who are surveilled, oppressed, and scared to speak out."

CONCLUSION

After the Cold War, both Russia and China were confronted with the dilemma of accepting the enduring and untenable role as political objects in the US-led international order, or be contained as enemies of the liberal international order. Neither Russia nor China could initially challenge the unilateralism embedded in the unipolar system.

The West mistakenly interpreted the temporary weakness of Russia and China as durable stability of the unipolar order. Eventually, Russia would consider it necessary to balance further Western expansionism towards its borders by enforcing its red lines, while China had outgrown the US-led regional framework. The Europeans have played a major role in constructing a Europe without Russia, and a minor role in supporting the construction of the Indo-Pacific region that marginalises China. The effort by Russia and China to restore political subjectivity in Europe and Asia has culminated in US containment policies that are more overt and intense.

Both Russia and China subsequently have systemic incentives to restore the political subjectivity of Eurasia to create an alternative and parallel geoeconomic infrastructure. The geoeconomics of Greater Eurasia entails diversifying economic connectivity to establish new regions based on other strategic industries, transportation corridors, and financial instruments of power. While Russia and China have different visions for Greater Eurasia, these differences are mitigated by their mutual dependence to lay the geoeconomic foundations of a Greater Eurasian region.

5

The Chinese-Russian Partnership
for Greater Eurasia

Western observers commonly dismiss the burgeoning Chinese-Russian partnership as a narrow and provisional "marriage of convenience." This perspective assumes the relationship is excessively reliant on common opposition to
the US, which masks deep-seated distrust and suspicion caused by historical grievances, asymmetrical power, and competing interests. The Chinese
became apprehensive to be the little brother of the Soviets during the Cold
War, and the Russians will likewise find it intolerable to be the little brother
of China. These arguments have a solid foundation and represent key challenges, although they neglect the mutual geoeconomic interest in creating a
multipolar Greater Eurasian region.

Both China and Russia consider it imperative to integrate the Greater
Eurasian region to obtain a more favourable position in the world. While
Beijing and Moscow advance different formats for Greater Eurasia, the commonality is that both formats for the superregion rely on a Chinese-Russian
partnership.

The compatibility of interests and the scope for compromise will deter-
mine the future of the Sino-Russian strategic partnership. Mutual dependence
incentivises the harmonisation of their respective integration initiatives.
Furthermore, the Cold War analogy of the Soviet-Sino relationship is not
suitable as Chinese hegemony in Greater Eurasia is unlikely. Instead, the
supercontinent will likely be defined by multipolarity. Efforts to undermine
Russian political autonomy can thus be countered by skewing the balance of
dependence with increased economic connectivity with other regions.

China and Russia represent the core of Greater Eurasia as they remained
the sole independent poles of power after the Cold War. The Sino-Russian
partnership aims to reorganise the geoeconomic architecture of the international system by drawing in other states. Efforts by Beijing and Moscow to
detach from and replace the Bretton Woods system is referred to by Burrows

and Manning (2015: 3) as "Kissinger's worst nightmare" by reversing the decoupling achieved by the US in the 1970s.

Yet, the asymmetrical interdependence between China and Russia must be mitigated to ensure Greater Eurasia remains a multipolar region and thus guarantees the political sovereignty of Russia. Moscow pursues this objective by developing strategic industries, diversifying economic connectivity in Greater Eurasia, and pursuing collective bargaining power within the Eurasian Economic Union. Russia has made its peace with China's geoeconomic leadership in Asia as the first among equals, but Moscow will reject Chinese dominance as political sovereignty remains sacred to the Russian Federation and multipolarity is thus a necessity.

This chapter first explores the efforts to harmonise the competing formats for Eurasian integration. China and Russia are coordinating their three geoeconomic levers of power: strategic industries are aligned in an energy partnership and a tech-partnership committed to both national and regional technological sovereignty; transportation corridors are both competing and complementary, although they all enhance physical connectivity on the Eurasian supercontinent; the financial instruments indicate a common strategy for establishing new development banks, payments systems, trade/reserve currencies, and hoarding of gold as initiatives for de-dollarisation.

The second part of this chapter explores the efforts to draw in other states in the Greater Eurasian region from the Atlantic to the Pacific. While the bilateral partnership between China and Russia is asymmetrical in terms of geoeconomic strength, these differences can be mitigated with the diversification of relations by engaging the wider Eurasian continent. Russia is discovering that the balance of dependence is creating systemic incentives towards a Eurasian equilibrium. Moscow can benefit from not being the most powerful state in Eurasia as Central Asia, East Asia, South Asia, and Europe share the interest in enhancing economic connectivity with Russia, which is imperative to prevent Russia from becoming excessively reliant on China to the point it infringes on the autonomy of Moscow's foreign policy.

It is concluded that the Chinese-Russian partnership creates the core of an alternative multipolar geoeconomic region with a significant gravitational pull that will unavoidably influence the western peninsula of Greater Eurasia—Europe.

SINO-RUSSIAN EURASIAN GEOECONOMIC LEVERS OF POWER

Regions are constructed on the three-pillared geoeconomic foundation of strategic industries, transportation corridors, and financial instruments. China is spearheading the development of new geoeconomic levers of power, while Russia aims to secure its position as an interdependent pole of power within a multipolar Greater Eurasia.

Strategic industries

Both Russia and China fell behind on the First Industrial Revolution, which had a profound impact on their future. Russia's technological backwardness was the reason for its humiliating defeat in the Crimean War (1853–1856) to the British-French offensive, which undermined its maritime power and changed to course of Russian history. Similarly, the British assault on China in the First Opium War (1839–1842) and the British-French attack on China in the Second Opium War (1856–1860) resulted in the Chinese being forced to make painful commercial, legal, and territorial concessions, which marked the beginning of the Century of Humiliation.

US dominance over strategic industries has been a key feature of the unipolar era as it creates asymmetrical dependency. Technological leadership positioned the US at the top of global supply chains, while also seeking to control access to the world's energy/natural resources.

History is currently at a critical crossroads as Russia and China aim to chart a very different future. The competition for technological sovereignty and leadership is occurring as the world enters the Fourth Industrial Revolution. This industrial revolution is defined by the digital technologies integrating with the physical world and thus revolutionising production, transportation, agriculture, medicine, finance, energy, and other industries across the board. Artificial intelligence, robotics, and automation are alone enabling digital giants to expand across all sectors of the economy.

The aim to develop technological sovereignty has resulted in a cooperative Chinese-Russian framework that aims to develop two distinctive digital ecosystems that cooperate, as opposed to integrating under Chinese-dominated platforms. Both Russia and China are nationalising the digital space and thus converting the internet into the "splinternet." Embracing the principle of sovereignty in internet governance is collectively advocated by Russia and China in the Shanghai Cooperation Organisation and the UN. Russia and China are collaborating on key technologies within artificial intelligence, communications, e-commerce, and the Internet of Things. While Germany used to be Russia's main source for high-tech imports, the Greater Eurasian has rewired the tech partnerships and by the end of 2019 Russia imported almost 2.5 times more from China than Germany (Gabuev 2020). Furthermore, agreements have been signed for joint high-tech research centres, Academies of Sciences, and other collaborative initiatives.

The technological partnership has also culminated in a partnership for space exploration. Russia's Roscosmos (Russian State Corporation for Space Activities) is gravitating towards China and thus being less vulnerable to the US and the Europeans. On 9 March 2021, the Russian Space Agency Roscosmos and the China National Space Administration (CNSA) signed a Memorandum of Understanding to build a moon base. Russia has thus opted out of the US-led Artemis lunar program as it is deemed to be too US-centric and instead sees a partnership with China being favourable.

CHINA'S PATH TO TECHNOLOGICAL LEADERSHIP

China's ability to challenge the technological leadership of the US can make Chinese tech-platforms and strategic industries leaders in the world. Technological leadership is beneficial as it enables the dominant power to set the standards and it creates dependencies due to the inability to diversify supplier. China has for a long time sought to export its standards around the world to circumvent US cyberinfrastructure and reduce Chinese reliance on foreign patents and licenses (Heilmann et al. 2014).

In 2015, the Chinese government launched *Made in China 2025*, a state-led industrial policy to make China the world leader in the main high-tech industries. This strategy is complemented with the China Standards 2035 plan to set the global standards for the next-generation of technologies. The vast amount of reserves are used to subsidise technological development is not directed towards catching up with the West, but to surpass. The assertive industrial policy was largely modelled after the geoeconomics of Germany's industrial policy *Industry 4.0*.

Key Chinese tech-giants such as Baidu, Didi, Alibaba, Tencent, JD, and Taobao have developed a complex digital ecosystem that marginalises its US counterparts within China. Concurrently, import substitution and subsidies to achieve technological sovereignty are imperative for critical areas in the supply chain where China is vulnerable due to excessive reliance on the US. For example, dependence on processing and memory chips from Intel, Broadcom, Qualcomm, Micron, Western Digital, and ARM makes China vulnerable to US pressures.

China's so-called Digital Silk Road initiative is a region-building initiative based on exporting these Chinese strategic industries. China's 5G technology has already obtained a leadership position, which is the digital nervous system for the Internet of Things, self-driving cars, and other technologies of the Fourth Industrial Revolution. As automation is "reshoring" manufacturing by undermining low-wage labour as a competitive advantage, the Chinese technological leadership will contribute to maintain its manufacturing leadership and transcend the middle-income trap.

RUSSIA'S STRATEGY OF TECHNOLOGICAL PREPAREDNESS

Russia cannot realistically compete directly against the US and China for technological leadership in the foreseeable future. Yet, Russia does not have to be the leading state to achieve technological sovereignty and remain an independent pole of power in a multipolar Greater Eurasia. Russia is seemingly pursuing a prudent strategy of "technological preparedness," which entails developing the technological skills and domestic technological platforms required to rapidly absorb new technologies and launch domestic spin-offs into the domestic technological ecosystem (Diesen 2021a). The strategy of technological preparedness can be advantageous as the follower does not bear the heavy costs of research and development as the market leader, and these resources can instead be directed towards capital-intensive investments as barriers for market entry (Gerschenkron 1963). This strategy benefits from a multipolar distribution of power as it encourages the diffusion of technologies at a faster rate and thus limits the first-mover advantage of the lead innovator.

The Russian National Technology Initiative from 2014 aimed to enhance technological advancements and fund the necessary infrastructure. In 2018, $26 billion was allocated for 2019–2024 to further develop Russia's digital economy development national program. These are efforts to intensify the existing development of a domestic digital ecosystem, which has been a necessity due to the hostile relations with the US. The largest search engine is Yandex, not Google; the main Russian social media site is VKontakte instead of Facebook; and it hosts a variety of domestic e-commerce platforms. Following the censorship on Twitter in early 2021, the Russian messaging app Telegram surpassed 500 million users. Yandex follows the Chinese model of digital giants conquering industries previously belonging to the physical world. Yandex develops self-driving cars and has become a domestic Uber by taking over much of the taxi industry and become the largest food delivery company. In 2014, Yandex developed firmware to replace Google's Android apps and by 2018 Russia had replaced Google as the top search engine on mobile phones. By the end of 2018, Yandex also released its first smartphone. International partnerships for modernisation is also pursued to the extent Russia has a controlling share—for example, the development of e-commerce with China or cloud serves with South Korea.

Technological modernisation can be subsidised indirectly with technology-transfers from the military, as military technologies are developed with public funds. States have traditionally been concerned about rival powers using civilian technologies for military purposes, albeit in the era of geoeconomics, governments transfer military technologies for commercial competitiveness (Luttwak 2010: 65). Russia has sophisticated space technology and satellite systems, and the Russian military has developed advanced AI technology and hypersonic weapons with commercial application.

Russia is commonly associated with the export of energy rather than high-tech industries. Russia de-industrialised rapidly following the collapse of the Soviet Union as protected Soviet uncompetitive industries were ill-prepared to be exposed to competition in the international market. Furthermore, the energy curse of exporting natural resources in return for manufactured goods returned Russia to the core-periphery economic relations that Russia has sought to escape in the 19th century. The former energy curse is systematically reversed by using energy revenues to fund subsidies as investments in technological advancements. Temporary tariffs and subsidies are instrumental to support infant industries until they become mature and competitive in international markets. These policies have been successful to make Russia a leading agricultural superpower, and the same policies are pursued to develop capital-intensive innovation-based industries.

In 2009, Russia inaugurated the Eastern Siberian-Pacific Ocean (ESPO) that supplies oil to the East Asian market. The ESPO pipeline made Russia an oil swing supplier as oil that was previously destined to Europe could be directed to East Asian states. The immediate consequence was a China-Japan competition for reliable and affordable Russian oil. In 2013, Russia and China signed what Putin called an "unprecedented" oil deal worth $270 billion, which gave Russia an even greater portion of the Chinese market. Putin argued that this initiative was part of a wider strategy to reduce its traditional reliance on Europe as an export market. It was also part of a wider geoeconomic partnership, as Putin argued:

> Essentially, this is a new era of cooperation which means that in our cooperation with our strategic partners we shift from purely raw supplies to full-fledged cooperation in the engineering and manufacturing sphere (Koreneva 2013).

Shortly after Russian annexed/unified with Crimea and the anti-Russian sanctions ensued, Moscow and Beijing signed the historic $400 billion agreement to construct the Power of Siberia pipeline to supply China with gas. The Power of Siberia began supplying China with gas in 2019, and the Power of Siberia 2 pipeline is now also advancing. However, a lingering fear in Russia is that the Chinese are only interested in Russia as a supplier of natural resources, which results in a reluctance to invest in its modern industries. In 2020, China Petroleum & Chemical Corporation (Sinopec) bought a 40 percent share in the Amur gas processing plant among other Chinese investments in the Russian energy sector.

Transportation corridors

The physical connectivity of transportation corridors is indispensable for efficient and reliable economies. Transportation corridors are the arteries of the world economy, and US global primacy has been bolstered by controlling the main maritime transportation corridors and choke points.

Transportation corridors were imperative to Eurasian powers of the past, which were organised by the nomadic empires of the Scythians, Huns, and Mongols. The critical moment for Eurasian powers is when their transportation corridors reach the maritime periphery of the supercontinent. The regional autonomy of Greater Eurasia therefore requires developing both land corridors and maritime corridors by Eurasian powers.

China and Russia pursue a different path for transportation corridors. Case in point, Russia prefers East-West corridors to transits through the Russian Far East, while China prefers to go through its own underdeveloped western regions and Central Asia. Yet, these are not mutually exclusive routes, diversification is a strength, and both formats are beneficial to Russia and China.

ALL ROADS LEAD TO CHINA

China initially began pursuing greater control over transportation corridors for reliable access to resources and markets. China feared key chokepoints under US control, such as the Strait of Malacca, which could be used to strangle the Chinese economy. Furthermore, the two US Island-Chains established to contain Chinese maritime access was untenable, as Washington grows increasingly wary of China's rise.

The Chinese economy also became increasingly outward-looking. Chinese construction giants had matured after building in China, and were tasked to develop infrastructure in the rest of the world. China subsequently began investing in infrastructure projects abroad such as railways, ports, energy projects, highways, bridges, buildings, and other infrastructure projects. Transportation corridors by both sea and land are to be placed under Chinese control and administration.

The multi-trillion-dollar Belt and Road Initiative aims to connect the world physically with China through land corridors (Belt) and maritime corridors (Road). The Belt and Road Initiative is conceptualised as a regional economic integration initiative (Zeng 2021). Some observers have presented the Belt and Road Initiative as a merely Marshall Plan with Chinese features (Chen 2014). Much like the Marshall Plan, the Chinese financing of infrastructure projects is intended as a "win-win" format that simultaneously reorganises the world towards Chinese leadership.

The land-based Silk Road initiative was first announced by President Xi in Kazakhstan in September 2013, and the maritime-based Silk Road was first broadcasted by President Xi at the Indonesian Parliament in October 2013. The State Oceanic Administration, the main institution developing China's maritime economic policy, later defined the current century as "the century of oceans: the status of oceans in national development dominates more than in any other period of human history" (SOA 2016: 239).

China's East-West transportation corridors aim to connect with all sub-regions of Greater Eurasia, and the subsequent diversification avoids excessive reliance on any one state or region. Land corridors with Russia include direct access into the Russian Far East, through Mongolia and towards Irkutsk and Novosibirsk, and through Central Asia before reaching Kazan in European Russia. Land corridors through Central Asia are also connected with Pakistan (China–Pakistan Economic Corridor) with a further extension to Iran, and directly from Central Asia into Iran and extending to Turkey. Southern corridors are connecting with South East Asia, with the possible inclusion of India, although apprehensions in New Delhi have made the future of the Bangladesh-China-India-Myanmar (BCIM) Economic corridor uncertain. Maritime corridors go south through the South China Sea and are supported by the Port of Gwadar in Pakistan to choke points from the Malacca Strait and with the possibility of India further militarizing the Andaman and Nicobar Islands archipelago in partnership with the US. An East-West maritime corridor is also intended to go north through the Russian arctic. The bimodal maritime corridor and land corridor are also connected in key regions such as the port of Gwadar in Pakistan and the port of Piraeus in Greece. Thus, a shipping container in Greece is connected to China by both an oceanic and a land corridor.

Nation-building and region-building initiatives are harmonised as Eurasian land corridors support the economic connectivity and development of China's western regions, while the maritime-based corridors are complemented by China's affirmation of sovereignty over the South China Sea per the nine-dash line.

Traditional geopolitics plays an intricate part as a military power and territorial control is pivotal to secure reliable maritime transportation corridors. China's immediate waters include the South China Sea, which has been under US dominance since the end of the Second World War through its island-chain containment strategy. China is also countering the intrusively close presence of the US by constructing a blue-water navy, asserting control over the regional airspace and building artificial islands in the South China Sea (Erickson and Wuthnow 2016).

RUSSIA'S EAST-WEST AND NORTH-SOUTH TRANSPORTATION CORRIDORS

Russia has fewer economic resources than China to fund Eurasian transportation corridors, although Russia has the most extensive Eurasian geography in the world with borders from Norway to North Korea. Russia aims to improve the symmetry in relations with China by using the collective bargaining power of the Russian-led Eurasian Economic Union, which aspires to implement a transportation partnership with the Chinese-led Belt and Road Initiative (EEC 2018). Russia also pursued a bimodal initiative of enhancing both land corridors and maritime corridors, and the Chinese-dominated East-West corridor is balanced with a North-South corridor.

The East-West transportation corridor entails an upgrade of the trans-Siberian railroad and the Baikal-Amur railway. This corridor initially sparked the concerns of Halford Mackinder in the early 20th century as Russia connected the Eurasian continent by land. New ports and supporting cargo infrastructure are developed along the Russian Pacific Coast in the East, and in the Baltic Sea, the Black Sea, and the Barents Sea in the West. In East Asia, new roads, railways, and bridges are connecting Russia closer to China, as the initial infrastructure was developed with military considerations rather than economic connectivity (Lukin 2016: 574). Yet, Russia also aims to diversify its physical connectivity in the wider East Asian region with electric grids and modernised free ports with LNG terminals along the Pacific Coast that are connected with the transportation infrastructure. Russia's Eurasian geographical expanse provides Moscow with a natural competitive advantage to position itself as an energy provider in North-East Asia and a Eurasian transportation corridor (Scholvin and Wigell, 2018).

The Russian Northern Sea Route along the Arctic represents an entirely new transportation corridor, which is faster and cheaper than the alternative maritime routes. The Barents Sea, the European entry point to the Arctic, was named after the 16th-century Dutch explorer who reached Novaya Zemlya in the search for an Arctic corridor trade with China. These ambitions have been revived by Russia as the melting of the Arctic opens up the region to extract energy resources and establishes a new transportation corridor.

Murmansk is expected to become an Arctic transport hub and bridgehead into Europe with enhanced railway connections into Finland and southwards into the continent. China released its first White Paper on the Arctic in January 2018, which conceptually integrated the Arctic into the Belt and Road Initiative by referring to the "Polar Silk Road." The Arctic corridor also represents an opportune format for cooperating with China due to symmetry in relations. China needs to fund much of the infrastructure and provide the traffic, yet as it transverses along with Russian sovereign territory the partnership will be more equal. New legislation in Russia since February 2018 reserves the Northern Sea Route to Russian-flagged vessels (Gunnarsson 2021). However, this also represents a challenge in negotiations. China expects some territorial control to safeguard its investments, as it achieved at the Port of Gwadar in Pakistan. However, territorial sovereignty is sacred for Russia and a compromise must therefore be found to ensure Chinese investments moves beyond merely energy extraction.

The International North-South Transportation Corridor (INSTC) between Russia, Iran, and India seeks to diversify away from excessive reliance on the East-West corridor, and thus make the continent less China-centric (Kazmin 2016). This corridor revives memories of the 19th-century rivalry between the British Empire and the Russian Empire for access to India in what became known as "the Great Game" (Hopkirk 2001).

The INSTC has been gradually gaining momentum in the shadow of the Chinese-led East-West corridor. The transportation corridor through India, Iran, and Russia was initially agreed to be developed in 2000, yet a decade passed without significant progress. From Russia's perspective, the corridor would also enhance the physical connectivity between Russia and South East Asia (Muraviev 2011: 207). The INSTC initiative was finally brought back in 2012 and the first dry run occurred in March 2014 (Lee and Gill 2015: 114). Moscow is open to accommodate India's economic incursion into Central Asia as Russia does not aim to dominate Central Asia, merely be the "first among equals" (Lee and Gill 2015: 111). There are fewer apprehensions about the INSTC among its participants as, unlike the Chinese-led East-West corridor, it has a more even distribution of power.

The INSTC is also a bimodal transportation network connecting Russia and Iran through the Caspian Sea region with railways, roads, and ports. By bypassing the Suez Canal, the INSTC significantly reduces both transportation cost and time. Russia approved the construction of Port Lagan in Kalmikiya in 2019 to supplement its Caspian ports in Astrakhan, Makhachkala, and Olya. In 2020, Iran completed its Astara Port on the Caspian Sea to further augment the capacity of the INSTC. The corridor is attracting a variety of other states such as Kazakhstan, Belarus, and Azerbaijan, which aim to increase and diversify their trade.

Financial instruments

Financial instruments are pivotal components to construct regions. The unipolar era was developed with the central role of the US dollar as a trade- and reserve currency; US-led development banks such as the IMF, World Bank, and the Asian Development Bank; and the central role of SWIFT as a payment system.

The Global Financial Crisis of 2008–2009 was interpreted by both Russia and China as an opportunity and necessity to reform global finance. At a speech at the SCO Council of Prime Ministers in 2008, Putin argued: "We now clearly see the defectiveness of the monopoly in world finance and the policy of economic selfishness. To solve the current problem Russia will take part in changing the global financial structure" (RT 2008). In 2011, Putin condemned the fiscal irresponsibility of the US as the administrator of international finance: "The country is living in debt. It is not living within its means, shifting the weight of responsibility on other countries and in a way acting as a parasite" (Smh 2011).

Chinese and Russian financial policies reveal striking similarities and growing cooperation. An intergovernmental Russian-Chinese Commission on Investment Cooperation was established in 2014 at the initiative of the heads of state. The principal task is to facilitate investment projects and reduce trade barriers between China and Russia. China and Russia are cooperating across various institutions such as the BRICS New Development Bank (NDB) and the Asia Infrastructure Investment Bank; creating new rating agencies, establishing cooperation with new payments systems; trading in domestic currencies, diversifying treasury and hoarding gold to de-dollarise. Both Russia and China are also developing digital national currencies to establish greater financial autonomy.

CHINESE PARALLEL FINANCIAL INSTRUMENTS

China's financial instruments finance its technological advancements and infrastructure/transportation projects, and enables the increasing use of the Yuan in international transactions (Huotari and Heep 2015: 153). Chinese financial institutions such as the Silk Road Fund, China Development Bank, and the Export-Import Bank of China provide more finance for foreign energy projects than the World Bank (Hilpert and Wacker 2015: 4). Financing of infrastructure is imperative, especially in regions such as Africa and Latin America, where inadequate infrastructure is the main obstruction to economic growth.

The economic war between China and the US has also incentivised several Chinese technology firms to do a secondary listing in Hong Kong to mitigate the risks of being delisted from the US stock market. Although, the Chinese government is actively promoting Shanghai to replace Hong Kong as the financial centre of China as finance is rewired both globally and domestically (Garcia-Herrero 2020).

China leads the BRICS NDB, which was founded in 2014 as a rival to the Bretton Woods institutions to mobilise financial resources for infrastructure and credit. The Silk Road Fund has also taken a central role in China's growing investments abroad. The launch of the Asian Infrastructure Investment Bank (AIIB) in 2015 represents a direct challenge to the primacy of US-led institutions such as the World Bank and the Asian Development Bank. Irrespective of Washington cautioning its allies not to join the Chinese-led AIIB, all major US allies except Japan joined. China also launched the China International Payment System (CIPS) in 2015 to reduce reliance on the US-controlled SWIFT system.

China's ambition to de-dollarise is intended to support the internationalisation of the yuan. In addition to the gradual increase of its own currency in foreign trade, China is also launching a new payment system known as Digital Currency Electronic Payment (DCEP). The DCEP uses blockchain technology and users do not need to connect with banks, which represents a financial revolution in terms of "banking without banks." The digitalisation of China's national currency is intended to fuel its rise to become the leading international currency.

China's lending of money to pay for infrastructure projects has been criticised as "debt-trap diplomacy." For example, Sri Lanka was unable to repay the loans for the construction of its Hambantota Port, which compelled Colombo to hand over operating rights for its port to China in return for additional finance. In Malaysia, the Prime Minister cancelled $23 billion loans for BRI projects as cautioned against "a new version of colonialism" (Hornby 2018).

China is advancing its geoeconomic power, which by definition entails constructing asymmetrical economic interdependence to extract political power. Beijing's constant references to the win-win logic are accurate as both sides are intended to gain in absolute term. Although, US criticism of its principal geoeconomic adversary is also accurate in terms of China advancing relative gain.

However, the argument of Chinese "debt-trap diplomacy" is politically motivated and flawed. The accusation suggests that Chinese banks lure poor developing countries with low-interest unsustainable loans for infrastructure projects, and when they fail to repay, Beijing seizes the assets to expand its political, geoeconomic, and military power. Warnings of Chinese debt-trap diplomacy is actively pushed by Washington and is too often parroted uncritically by both journalists and academics. Washington is largely motivated by limiting the role of China in the international financial system, and the American efforts to "protect" naïve developing states from poor loans reveal a peculiar paternalism that absolves the recipients of responsibility for risk assessment and economic mismanagement.

Chinese loans have high risks and the recipients must assess whether this is a risk worth taking. Developing states are faced with a dilemma as they need infrastructure to develop, yet should not be overburdened with debt. Investments into infrastructure are imperative for developing countries as rail, roads, ports, electric grids, digital networks, and other physical connectivity is necessary for an economy to be productive and competitive. Although, servicing high-interest loans to fund the infrastructure projects creates an immense burden for the developing states.

Chinese low-interest loans are therefore an attractive solution to resolve the dilemma by acquiring the necessary infrastructure and not being stuck with high-interest loans. However, Chinese banks must also cover their risks. A mortgage for a house has lower interest rates than other loans as the bank has an asset to seize if the loan is not repaid, and infrastructure loans similarly provide China with a tangible asset to seize as reassurance for its low-interest loans.

The accusation of predatory lending as a nefarious geoeconomic strategy benefitting China and not the recipient states is weak and relies on an excessive focus on when the repayment of loans fail. The Belt and Road Initiative has broader geoeconomic logic of organising the international economic system around China, and failing loans are challenging the legitimacy of the new Silk Road. The Chinese banking and financing system is not coordinated to the extent it would need to engage in grand conspiracies to seize foreign assets by design (Jones and Hameiri 2020). Furthermore, the interest of developing states receiving the infrastructure loans have an immense influence over the Belt and Road Initiative as opposed to being pushed solely by China.

RUSSIAN STRATEGIC FINANCIAL AUTONOMY WITHIN GREATER EURASIA

Russia relies on China to augment alternative financial institutions and to de-dollarise, yet a key challenge is to assert itself as an independent pole in the Eurasian financial system as opposed to integrating into a Chinese-led system.

In the late 19th century, the excessive reliance on Western finance became a key challenge for Russia, which became a contributing factor to the instability leading up to the revolution in 1905. The debt crisis and collapse of

the 1990s further taught Russia a valuable lesson to pursue a more conservative financial strategy. Fiscal responsibility and restraint in the 21st century
entailed ending deficits, paying down the debt, diversifying financial lenders,
and making Russia less vulnerable to capital flight. In 2019, Forbes reported
that after five years of the West's anti-Russian sanctions aimed to suffocate
the Russian economy and its financial system, the result was in—the Russian
financial system had become "bulletproof" (Forbes 2019).

Russia aims to develop common investment strategies with China, yet also
diversify. Russia has preferred the Eurasian Development Bank (EDB) of
the Eurasian Economic Union to preserve its strategic autonomy. The EDB
aims to increase trade between member states and strengthening the collective bargaining power vis-à-vis other large power such as the EU and China.
In 2015, Russia and China began harmonising their financial arrangements
by establishing cooperation between the Eurasian Economic Union and the
Belt and Road Initiative under the sponsorship of the Shanghai Cooperation
Organisation.

A dilemma became evident as an SCO development bank with China would
be more powerful, yet it would also undermine Russia's ability to act as an
independent pole of power. Overall, transitioning the SCO from geopolitics
to geoeconomics by endowing the institution with economic competencies
rather than security, entails a transfer of regional power from Russia to China.
Much like a balance of power in the EU depends on French military leadership and German economic leadership, so does the SCO need to balance the
competencies to ensure power does not concentrate in China. Yet, Russia has
been more comfortable developing SCO economic competencies in areas
such as energy, where Russia enjoys a significant voice. The SCO Energy
Club, operational since 2013, has worked towards facilitating cooperation
between energy producers and consumers in Eurasia. The enlargement of the
SCO in 2017, by including India and Pakistan, can mitigate Russian concerns
of Chinese geoeconomic leadership becoming dominant and thus undermining multipolarity (Gatev and Diesen 2016).

Russia has developed the Financial Messaging System of the Bank of
Russia (SPFS) as an alternative system to SWIFT, akin to China's CIPS system. In 2019, several major Russian banks also joined China's CIPS system
to further diversify. A national card payment system has also been launched
as a domestic alternative to Visa and Mastercard, and the Russian cards are
collaborating with the Chinese counterparts such as Unipay for wider usage.
These measures were used to reduce vulnerability to US sanctions and threats
of being suspended from key financial institutions.

De-dollarisation has become an important strategy, and trade with China
in local currencies enables the experimentation of new payments methods
and adopting new practices, which can then be transferred to economic

connectivity with other states. Russia's gold holdings have increased rapidly from 400 tonnes in 2006 to 2,300 tonnes in 2021, and Russia's gold holdings are on the verge of surpassing that of both France and Italy. These efforts have been coordinated by a strategy of reducing the use of the dollar as both the trade- and reserve currency.

These financial instruments are used to connect with key states in the region, Case in point, Russia-Turkey financial cooperation is of growing importance to assert the autonomy of the two Black Sea powers. Agreements were made in 2019 to enhance trade using national currencies, to connect Turkey with Russia's SPFS financial messaging service, and to launch the Russian Mir card in Turkey. In 2019, Iran also connected with Russia's SPFS system and the discussion continue to pursue closer integration between the EAEU and Iran.

COMMON EURASIAN HOME: THE POLITICAL ECONOMY AND CONSERVATISM OF MULTIPOLARITY

Russia's Greater Eurasia can be conceptualised as a Common Eurasian Home. Gorbachev's Common European Home had envisioned a shared European continent with many rooms to accommodate both capitalist and socialist states. This proposal was defeated by the US preference for a Europe Whole and Free, which implied one large room under universal liberal democratic values and thus US leadership. Greater Eurasia can similarly aim to establish a common Eurasian Home with several rooms that can accommodate the distinctive cultures and civilizations, while also rejecting any formats for universalism that legitimises sovereign inequality among the main poles of power.

Competitive geoeconomic regions must facilitate both cooperation and competition. Cooperation is required to eliminate internal barriers for economic connectivity to have clear borders that distinguish from being within or outside the region. Cooperation and integration also enable the participants of a geoeconomic region to assert collective autonomy and influence. Yet, regions should also organise the preservation of competition to maintain competitiveness and vitality.

Western observers commonly believe that the power disparity between China and Russia will eventually fuel distrust to the point that Moscow will seek to break away from the partnership. China's greater economic power is only problematic to the extent Russia develops excessive dependence. This can be avoided with strategic autonomy over strategic industries, critical transportation corridors, and financial instruments. Furthermore, Russia is diversifying its economic connectivity across Eurasia to ensure not all its eggs are in the Chinese basket. Herein lies the difference between the acceptable leadership of Chinese and intolerable Chinese dominance.

The requirement for a common political culture for a regional framework is contested. It has for example been argued that the West's demand for common values rather than compatible values was a calculated initiative to legitimise the exclusion of Russia from European institutions and thus avoid substantial reforms to the regional security architecture (Möller 2003). Instead, the ability to facilitate cultural and civilizational distinctiveness is instrumental to preserve multipolarity within the region.

Conservatism recognizes the need for organic development as each state must position itself between continuity and change. The need to preserve cultural distinctiveness is imperative, which is why universalist ideals and uniformity is largely rejected by conservatives. Russia has returned to its long history as a conservative power after experimenting with the excesses of socialism and liberalism in the 20th century. Putin (2013b):

> I want to stress that Eurasian integration will also be built on the principle of diversity. This is a union where everyone maintains their identity, their distinctive character and their political independence . . . We expect that it will become our common input into maintaining diversity and stable global development.

Irrespective of the official Marxist ideology of the Chinese Communist Party, China has for years been gravitating towards a conservative philosophy that seeks to preserve and reproduce civilizational distinctiveness. China's Foreign Minister, Wang Yi argued:

> The unique features of China's diplomacy originate in the rich and profound Chinese civilisation . . . the idea of peace as of paramount importance and harmony without uniformity, as well as the personal conduct of treating others in a way that you would like to be treated, and helping others succeed in the same spirit as you would want to succeed yourself. These traditional values with a unique oriental touch provide an endless source of invaluable cultural asset for China's diplomacy (Wang 2013: 14).

Any region strives to balance cooperation for collective strength and competition to preserve internal vitality. In geoeconomic regions, the challenge is even greater as a durable geoeconomic region must be naturally reinforced by the balance of dependence. For Russia, it is imperative to maintain strategic autonomy within Greater Eurasia to ensure the construct becomes a multipolar arrangement and not a Greater China. For China, it is also strategic to facilitate a multipolar arrangement as it will make the Chinese-Russian partnership more sustainable, as an excessively asymmetrical partnership between Russia and China will create systemic incentives for the Russians to decouple.

RUSSIAN GEOECONOMICS: A EURASIAN BALANCE OF DEPENDENCE

Russia's foreign policy is undergoing historical change by adjusting to a more modest position in the international system where it no longer controls its periphery. Russia's vast geography has always had a domineering influence on Russian identity and foreign policy. It has been the source of security by absorbing and defeating invading armies from Napoleon to Hitler, although it has also been the source of insecurity due to the vulnerability of long and porous borders. Russia's expansionist impulses throughout its history have largely been influenced by insecurity due to the continuing need to control the periphery of newly acquired territory. Unlike the Europeans, Russia did not have natural geographical borders. The ability and intention to control its periphery is diminished, as Russia is no longer the domineering power in Eurasia. The Russian Empire and the Soviet Union pursued a hegemonic peace by equating power maximisation to security maximisation. The more modest capabilities of the Russian Federation in the 21st century create incentives and constraints, which translates into the role of a balancer without exclusive control over the periphery. With the emergence of a globally multipolar system with the rise of China and other non-Western powers, Russia is positioning itself as a balancer. The new Russian posture informs its region-building and the flexibility of its inter-regional formats in Eurasia.

The EAEU is an important instrument to improve the symmetry in relations with China. The EAEU is also working towards strengthening control over energy trade by developing a single energy market (Perskaya 2020). It is common in the West to compare the EAEU to the Soviet Union. For example, US Secretary of State, Hillary Clinton, accused the Eurasian Economic Union of being a plot to "re-Sovietise the region" and announced that the US is "trying to figure out effective ways to slow down or prevent it" (FT 2012). This is a deeply flawed comparison as the purpose is not to sever the region off from the outside world, rather it is to mobilise collective bargaining power to engage with the wider world from a position of strength. Critics of Russian Eurasian integration tend to contrast independent nation-states with empire, which neglects the potential of regionalism in the modern world (Tsygankov 2003: 114). It would therefore make more sense to compare the EAEU with the EU (Krickovic 2014). During his UN General Assembly speech in 2015, Putin argued:

Contrary to the policy of exclusiveness, Russia proposes harmonizing original economic projects. I refer to the so-called integration of integrations based on universal and transparent rules of international trade. As an example, I would like to cite our plans to interconnect the Eurasian economic union, and China's initiative of the Silk Road economic belt. We still believe that harmonizing the integration processes within the Eurasian Economic Union and the European Union is highly promising (WT 2015).

HARMONISATION OF INTERESTS: BRI MEETS THE EAEU

Russia and China resolved their territorial disputes in 2004, which was a priority for Russia to get out of the way as relative power was shifting rapidly to China's advantage. Solving bilateral disputes was also important to create stability along the 4,200-kilometres-long shared border and instead shift focus towards the challenges from US-led containment. Russia's main threat derives from its western borders with an expansionist NATO and EU, while China's main threat originates from its eastern borders where the US intensifies its island-chain containment to counter the rise of China. There is a high degree of bilateral economic compatibility between China and Russia. China is resource-hungry and seeks to establish reliable transportation corridors through the Eurasian continent. Russia seeks a partner to modernise its economy and can fund economic connectivity in Eurasia.

Russia is pivotal for China's Belt and Road Initiative to gain reliable and competitive access to the European markets (Huasheng 2018). Furthermore, the EAEU establishes one custom zone between Chinese and EU borders. If China and Russia can harmonise their respective formats for Eurasian integration, then the combined strength of these initiatives could construct a new international order (Ziguo 2017). The Secretary-General of the Belt and Road Research Centre at the Chinese Academy of Social Sciences also argued in the language of Mackinder that a Chinese-Russian partnership is essential to integrate Eurasia and "whoever can guide the Eurasian process can lead the construction of a new world order" (Rolland 2019: 17).

In Central Asia, Chinese and Russian interest diverge due to a desire to shift the balance of dependence within a common region. Although, both have additional incentives to cooperate to deny Western powers access to Central Asia. Central Asia is strengthened by economic connectivity with China, which also benefits Russia. Central Asia is a key node in most formats for Eurasian integration, and the region works towards establishing political subjectivity. Kazakhstan stands out in terms of modernising its economy and due to its vast energy resources, which complements its "Bright Path" initiative that mirrors the ambitions of the Chinese Belt and Road Initiative. The Central Asia region occupied a strategic position between the main trading markets during the rule by nomadic powers. The new President of Kazakhstan, Kassym-Jomart Tokaev, argued:

> We believe that the idea of a Greater Eurasia—in the broad sense of that term—opens new horizons for activating economic ties between Asia and Europe and has become a foundation for forming a new system of international relations in the Eurasian space. In my view, the processes taking place on our mega-continent form a new geopolitical reality (Dolgopolov and Fronin 2019).

An early sign of harmonisation of two distinct formats for Eurasian integration became apparent in a summit between Putin and Xi in May 2015. Moscow and Beijing agreed on "cooperation in coordinating the development of the Eurasian Economic Union project and the Silk Road Economic Belt." In June 2016, Putin and Xi reaffirmed their commitment to coordinate their Eurasian initiatives. In June 2017, Moscow and Beijing agreed that cooperation would not take the Western format of subject-object, rather Russia and China would cooperate based on the principles of "sovereign equality and non-interference in internal affairs," and respecting each other's "chosen path of development."

Putin (2018) asserted: The Eurasian Economic Union and the Belt and Road Initiative are efficiently complementing each other. Harmonisation of these projects can lay the foundation for establishing a Greater Eurasian Partnership." Yaroslav Lissovolik (2017), the former chief economist of the Eurasian Development Bank, opined that the Belt and Road Initiative and the EAEU collectively provide the landlocked economies of Central Asia with the connectivity required to be competitive. The agreement to integrate BRI and EAEU under the auspices of the SCO represents the leading format to resolve disputes and harmonise the Russian and Chinese formats for Greater Eurasia. In May 2018, the EAEU and China signed the Trade and Economic Cooperation Agreement.

In 2019, the heads of government of the SCO adopted the Programme of Multilateral Trade and Economic Cooperation of the SCO Member States until 2035. The focus of cooperation included all three geoeconomic levers of power: development of technology, science, education, industry, transportation and logistics, payment systems in national currencies, banking and finance to establish an SCO development bank. The SCO recognises the need to offer Iran membership in the future, while the entry of Afghanistan is premature.

TOWARDS A BALANCE OF DEPENDENCE IN EURASIA

Putin made it clear at the St. Petersburg Economic Forum in 2016 that the Eurasian Economic Union would only be one component of the wider Greater Eurasian Initiative. Putin (2016) argued in favour of a Greater Eurasia that accommodates China's Belt and Road Initiative: "Now we propose considering the prospects for a more extensive Eurasian partnership involving the EAEU and countries with which we already have a close partnership—China, India, Pakistan and Iran." Putin (2016) added: "Let me repeat that we are interested in Europeans joining the project for a major Eurasian partnership."

The Russian Foreign Minister, Sergey Lavrov (2018) specified that the structure of Greater Eurasia was less formal and not intended to endow the founders with a leadership role:

> It is important to understand that the Greater Eurasian Partnership is not something that one should join. It's not a pre-drafted project coordinated by a narrow circle of original participants who tell the others that there are terms and conditions on which we will interact with you . . . The underlying idea is very simple and is based on the fact that the Eurasian Economic Union and the SCO, whose membership partially overlaps that of the EAEU and ASEAN, are already present in that region.

Russia no longer has the upper hand in the east as China's geoeconomic power is far greater. However, by not being the leading power, Russia benefits from the systemic pressures in Eurasia that gravitate naturally towards a balance of dependence. The Chinese economy is the most powerful in the region, yet when a dominant format emerges, the weaker states have an incentive to diversify their ties. Russia benefits, as its role in Eurasia, is that of a geoeconomic balancer. Unlike the US that seeks to contain China with zero-sum balancing, Russia aims to establish a multipolar Eurasian region with a balance of dependence.

China's ability and preparedness to challenge the US-centric economic system makes Beijing an indispensable partner for Russia to attain its goal of diversifying away from excessive reliance on the West. However, the unfavourable asymmetrical interdependence between China and Russia risks demoting Moscow to the status of a junior partner with unacceptable China influence limiting Russian sovereignty. It is therefore imperative that Russia's pivot to Asia does not merely become a pivot to Asia, as Russia must diversify its partnerships in the east to improve the balance of dependence with China (Diesen 2019).

Iran, positioned at the southern edge of Greater Eurasia, is becoming an increasingly important and visible part of the Greater Eurasian partnership. A senior advisor to the Ayatollah argued that stability in Greater Eurasia requires a partnership with Moscow and Beijing (Khabar 2015). China seeks a partnership that naturally extends the China-Pakistan Economic Corridor into Iran, which can include the Iran-Pakistan gas pipeline under construction. In March 2021, China and Iran signed a 25-year "strategic cooperation" agreement that included Iran into the Belt and Road Initiative. Russia also views Iran as an increasingly important partner in the North-South Transportation Corridor. Iran signed a free-trade agreement with the Russian-led EAEU in 2018 and Iran has expressed interest in full membership which would make Iran the only member state that was not a former Soviet Republic. Iran and Russia came closer in the partnership to prevent the Western regime-change efforts in Syria. Moscow and Tehran have aimed to use military cooperation as a foundation for a wider geoeconomic partnership. Both China and Russia have also eyed a possible membership for Iran in the SCO, which would be important to resolve Eurasian issues such as the Afghanistan quandary once NATO eventually withdraws.

The rise of China gives incentives for Central Asian states to align closer with Russia and deepen the integration of the EAEU to create a more tenable symmetry in relations with China. The growing presence of China in Central Asia has fuelled some Sinophobia across the Central Asian region (Kulintsev et al. 2020). The Russian objective is not to take advantage of anti-Chinese sentiments to exclude China from the region; rather it is to create a balance of dependence. This development can also be considered to be in China's interest as the relationship with China becomes tolerable and durable if asymmetries are reduced. China remains the leading geoeconomic power, yet without the contentions fuelled by dominance.

Japan similarly has increased incentives to establish greater economic connectivity with Russia in Northeast Asia to ensure Russia does not become too reliant on China and thus lose its ability to uphold an independent and neutral foreign policy in the region (Diesen 2018). Japan has expressed interest in contributing to modernise the Russian Far East, and also asked to cooperate on the Northern Sea Route through the Russian Arctic. South Korea similarly has incentives for greater economic connectivity with Pacific Russia as alternatives to the partnership with the US and China. Furthermore, South Korea has its own initiative for Eurasian integration that is linked to mitigating tensions on the Korean peninsula with economic cooperation (Kuznetsov 2016: 357–58).

India also has strong incentives to ensure that Russia's pivot to the east does not merely become a pivot to China. The INSTC that connects Mumbai with St. Petersburg via Iran is imperative to ensure the Chinese-led East-West integration of Eurasia is balanced with a North-South integration of Eurasia. India and Russia are also pursuing a maritime partnership with shared ship-building and the establishment of new transportation corridors. India has expressed its interest in partaking in the development of the Arctic route, and a Memorandum of Intent (MoI) was formalised in 2019 for the Vladivostok-Chennai Maritime Corridor (VCMC). A key objective of the VCMC for India is to challenge the centrality of China's BRI (Chaudhury 2018). India has also developed an Arctic policy focused on developing new transportation corridors to access Russian natural resources in the Arctic. Yet, unlike the possibility of joining a US-led anti-Chinese alliance to contain China, the geoeconomic diversification merely skews the balance of dependence in Eurasia.

The Russia-India partnership is troubled by different strategic challenges. Russia and India both benefit from Eurasian integration, yet their different priorities reflect diverse interests as Russia is primarily challenged by the US and India is mainly concerned about China. Subsequently, India has strong incentives to position itself between Greater Eurasia and the Indo-Pacific partnership, while Russia is concerned that the Indo-Pacific partnership is designed to create divisions in Eurasia by mobilising an anti-Chinese alliance. Russia's Foreign Minister, Sergey Lavrov, argued that "India is currently an object of the Western countries' persistent, aggressive and devious policy as they are trying to engage it in anti-China games by promoting Indo-Pacific strategies," while concurrently "attempting to undermine our close partnership and privileged relations with India" (Laskar 2020).

China's pressures on India have created the situation where India relies on the US to the extent Washington can use India as an instrument against China and sow divisions in Eurasia. This is also problematic for Russia as strained relations with India, in combination with deteriorating relations with the EU, threaten Russia's geoeconomic equilibrium in Greater Eurasia (Trenin 2019). Thus, the deepening of Russia-India relations demands that both countries accept the "strategic space they provide each other to deal with the US, China and other great powers" (Unnikrishnan and Kapoor 2021).

Economic connectivity begets more economic connectivity as the system gravitates towards a balance of dependence. When China connects with developing states, economic integration entails significant political influence due to the asymmetries. For example, Pakistan's former commerce minister succinctly phrased it: "China is the only game in town" (Sender and Stacey 2017). Subsequently, Russia and Pakistan have begun forming closer commercial and military relations to ensure Pakistan does not become too dependent on the asymmetrical relationship with China. The same dynamic applies to Iran, which is now looking towards both Beijing and Moscow as its key partners in Eurasia.

The leading position of China creates systemic incentives for other regions in Eurasia to establish greater economic connectivity with Russia to create a more favourable balance of dependence. Russia also seeks to incorporate larger institutions such as the Association of Southeast Asian Nations (ASEAN) and the Asia-Pacific Economic Cooperation (APEC) into the greater Eurasian partnership to diffuse the power on the supercontinent.

The Europeans are similarly under pressure as Russia decouples from Western technological platforms, strategic industries, transportations corridors, and financial instruments. Considering Russia's principal foreign policy objective for decades was to construct a Greater Europe, the alienation of Russia after the Cold War can only be defined as a historical blunder. With Russian economic interests and dependencies shifting to the East, the Europeans are handing over a powerful partner to China. As Chinese geoeconomic power continues to grow in Europe with Russian support, the Europeans will come under greater pressure to end their containment policies against Russia and reach a post-Cold War settlement that reforms the zero-sum structures in Europe.

MILITARY BLOCS VERSUS GEOECONOMIC BALANCE OF DEPENDENCE

The growing military tensions with the US creates a dilemma for the Greater Eurasia Initiative. On one hand, US military posturing in Europe and East Asia are creating systemic incentives for Russia and China to establish a formal military alliance. In recent years, this is seemingly becoming a greater possibility. In October 2020, Putin (2020) alluded to the possibility of a future military alliance with China, as cooperation already entails common military exercises and a "high level of cooperation in the defence industry," which includes "sharing of technologies." Russia is now selling China its most modern weapon systems such as the S-400 missile system and the Su-35 fighter jets. This weaponry will make a vital contribution for China to control the airspace above the disputed South China Sea.

On the other hand, establishing an official Sino-Russian military alliance would undermine the geoeconomics of Greater Eurasia by alienating economic allies. Formal military alliances tend to harden the borders of regions, and the same dynamics undermines the ability to diversify economic connectivity. A Russian-Chinese military alliance would result in Russia alienating countries like Japan and India, while China would alienate European countries and become a larger target of NATO. Russia has already lost some of its foreign policy autonomy in East Asia due to a growing dependence on China (Baev 2018). Similarly, the NATO alliance has resulted in the Europeans alienating Russia that made it imperative to look east instead of economic partnerships.

Usually, when states form alliances they make great announcements. Russia and China have formed an informal alliance as interests are aligned and foreign policies are coordinated, yet are reluctant to define it as an alliance. The official word "alliance" can reduce the gravitational pull towards Greater Eurasia and alienate participants by inferring zero-sum objectives.

CONCLUSION

The strategic partnership between China and Russia creates a format for Greater Eurasia that has previously not existed. The Chinese-Russian partnership is set to create a multipolar region with new strategic industries, transportation corridors, and financial instruments. The asymmetrical geoeconomic power between China and Russia fuels some tensions, although the uneven geoeconomic power also creates systemic incentives to move towards a balance of dependence. More specially, Russia endeavours to establish strategic autonomy and diversify its economic partnership across Greater Eurasia.

Under its Greater Europe Initiative, the Europeans acted on systemic incentives to balance Russia as the largest state on the continent and due to its historical baggage. Russia is discovering that by not being the leading geoeconomic power in Greater Eurasia, it can enjoy a natural inclination by other states to instead accommodate Russia and deepen economic connectivity. India, Iran, Kazakhstan, Japan, South Korea, and other states on the Eurasian supercontinent have strong incentives to establish closer economic ties with Russia to prevent Moscow from aligning too closely with Beijing. These systemic incentives that push Greater Eurasia towards a balance of dependence are also being felt to a greater degree in Europe. By abandoning Greater Europe in favour of Greater Eurasia, Russia will paradoxically have the greater bargaining power to restructure its relations with the Europeans.

6

China as a European Power

Until recently, it was common in Europe to consider China to be an economic competitor primarily in the developing world. China is now rapidly establishing itself as a European power with meticulous use of its geoeconomic levers of power. Chinese strategic industries are now taking a growing market share in Europe, Chinese transportation infrastructure has penetrated Europe, and Chinese financial institutions have asserted a formidable presence.

Observers were perplexed by China's geographical acrobatics by categorising itself as a "near-Arctic-state," and the concept of China as a European power also appears to defy geography. Yet, this is what Greater Eurasia represents—the restructuring of regions as Europe and Asia are integrated into one large region. Much like the trans-Atlantic region made the US the leading power in Europe, so is China emerging as a key geoeconomic power on the old continent. In 2020, China became the EU's largest trading partner of goods—a leading position that is set to continue to grow. What initially seemed to be unrelated Chinese economic initiatives now demonstrate a cohesive grand geoeconomic strategy. Subsequently, political loyalties in Europe are challenged as well.

This chapter first assesses China's regional approach to favourable economic connectivity with Europe. China engages the EU as an autonomous regional entity within the Greater Eurasian region. Albeit, China has also developed the sub-regional format of 17+1 or bilateral engagement with individual member states for when the EU resists economic connectivity on terms that are acceptable to Beijing.

Second, China's three-pillared geoeconomic power in Europe is harmonised and complements each other. Strategic industries in Europe are targeted for mergers and acquisitions, while China's ambitious high-tech innovations are aimed to create economic dependencies in European economies. Bimodal transportation corridors by land and sea are developed with southern, eastern, and northern bridgeheads. Financial instruments are important to fund strategic industries and infrastructure projects, and a collective approach to

China is undermined by the tendency of EU member states to compete among themselves to attract Chinese capital.

Last, Chinese geoeconomic power in Europe is explored by assessing the extent to which economic power can be converted into political influence. Beijing has relied on geoeconomics as a covert influence that creates a gravitational pull, although Beijing is also becoming more comfortable with the use of economic sanctions. It is concluded that the Europeans are presented with a dilemma as enhancing their economic competitiveness requires aligning their economies closer to China.

REGIONAL FORMATS FOR ECONOMIC CONNECTIVITY

Geoeconomic regions are vulnerable to efforts by external powers seeking to sow divisions. Geoeconomic regions must provide some benefits to external actors to justify the preparedness to cooperate with a bloc that attempts to benefit from collective bargaining power. China must have incentives to engage with the collective bargaining power of 27 EU member states instead of negotiating with each member bilaterally in a more advantageous format. China will support the EU to the extent the EU engages in a formal partnership with China that provides sufficient market access. China will thus support the EU if the EU cooperates within China's Greater Eurasia region, similar to how the US supports the EU to the extent the EU remains committed to the trans-Atlantic region.

China is reaching out to the EU as an entity, its sub-regions, and individual member states. The alternative formats for engagement are intended to present Brussels with a dilemma concerning the EU's role in Greater Eurasia. If the EU takes an anti-Chinese approach by blocking China's access to Europe, then Beijing can pursue alternative formats that are less favourable to the EU. China, much like the US and Russia, will only have an incentive to support the internal cohesion of the EU to the extent the EU is prepared to harmonise its interests and policies with China. Beijing considers "regional groupings as useful in facilitating integration into an increasingly dynamic regional economy" (Freeman 2018: 85).

The message to Brussels is therefore that the EU can preserve its collective strategic autonomy as an independent pole of power within Greater Eurasia, or it can be picked apart with formats for economic connectivity that undermines its internal political cohesion. The Chinese approach to the EU thus resembles its approach to the EAEU. Russia was similarly presented with the dilemma concerning the growing geoeconomic presence of China in Central Asia—Russia could either establish closer economic connectivity between the EAEU and China's Belt and Road Initiative under the auspices of the multilateral SCO, or China would approach Central Asian states on a bilateral basis and thus have greater ability to dictate the terms. Russia prefers a format for economic connectivity between the EAEU and China as it improves the symmetry of relations, and in return, China establishes a more benign form for geoeconomic leadership which is not opposed by Russia.

A formal EU-China partnership is supported by both carrots and sticks. A carrot entails assigning a privileged role for Germany as a de-facto geo-economic leader of the EU and a node in the Greater Eurasian region. Yet, sticks are also available with alternative entry points to dissuade any efforts to contain Chinese geoeconomic incursion into Europe. The EU subsequently identifies China as both an essential partner and a "strategic rival." There is nothing contradictory about this definition and the purpose of a collaborative arrangement is to manage both cooperation and competition.

THE 17+1 FORMAT

The main alternative sub-region to establish China as a European power is the 17+1 format. The collaborative framework between Central and Eastern European countries and China was initially known as the 16+1 for-mat, which included Albania, Bosnia and Herzegovina, Bulgaria, Croatia, Czech Republic, Estonia, Hungary, Latvia, Lithuania, Montenegro, North Macedonia, Poland, Romania, Serbia, Slovenia, and Slovakia. The 16+1 for-mat was proposed in 2012, the year before the launch of the Belt and Road Initiative. The 16+1 format became 17+1 when Greece joined in 2019.

Following the collapse of communism, the shared Marxist past had become a burden rather than an asset for China in Central and Eastern Europe. Beijing has subsequently looked towards new ways to restore its influence in Central and Eastern Europe (Tubilewicz 1999). China's economic miracle has become a source of soft power that several former communist states aspire to replicate, which can be seen as an alternative model for EU members who disprove the thesis that economic prowess demands liberal democracy. The Global Financial Crisis of 2008–2009 demonstrated the feeble state of many Western economies, appearing as sandcastles built on a weak foundation of debt and spending. Furthermore, several Central and Eastern European states aim for a more central role as opposed to playing second fiddle to the Western European states in the EU.

Central and Eastern Europe is a region with the historically justified fear of being crushed between the East and West. The founding Prime Minister of Singapore, Lee Kuan Yew, on several occasions argued: "When elephants fight, the grass suffers, but when they make love, the grass suffers also."

This modified African proverb frames the historical challenge of Central and Eastern Europe and the challenge of being positioned between two giants, Germany and Russia. For this reason, the presence of the US in Europe after the Cold War has been a source of relief, especially for countries like Poland that remains extremely hostile to Russia and is apprehensive about excessive reliance on a more assertive Germany. For the same reason, China has an appeal for Central and Eastern European countries. The 17+1 format is structured to elevate the role of Central and Eastern European countries, which can be instrumental for a more cohesive and tenable EU within Greater Eurasia. Alternatively, the format can be used to sow divisions and fragment an EU that is hostile to China.

The loyalty of Central and Eastern European countries towards the EU has been receding incrementally. The prospect of EU membership was initially the main source of motivation to accept political reforms and implement unilateral adjustments. Yet, once on the inside, the loyalty to the EU becomes more dependent on the material benefits of membership. Liberalism as the common denominator of shared European identity has become a burden to many of the more conservative states in Central and Eastern Europe. The excesses of liberalism and centralisation of power in Brussels has especially fuelled resistance in Poland and Hungary where a common European identity entails reproducing the traditional Christian values and culture of the nation-state.

China enjoys greater asymmetrical interdependence within the smaller 17+1 format, which are also more willing to integrate economically. The format can be a stepping-stone towards a wider EU-China arrangement and thus not undermine EU solidarity. It is noteworthy that Belarus, Moldova, Georgia, and Ukraine have not been invited to cooperate within the 17+1 format, which would influence Russia to a greater extent. Instead, the countries involved as more firmly positioned within the Western European sphere of influence and a bridgehead into the heart of the EU.

THE US COUNTERS CHINESE GEOECONOMICS IN EUROPE

The US National Security Strategy of 2017 cautioned that "China is gaining a strategic foothold in Europe by expanding its unfair trade practices and investing in key industries, sensitive technologies, and infrastructure" (NSS 2017: 47).

The US enjoys great influence in Central and Eastern Europe due to security dependence, which makes the states cooperating in China's 17+1 especially vulnerable to US pressure. By citing security challenges, the US has been more successful to establish a clear link between security dependence and geoeconomic loyalty. Across Central and Eastern Europe, governments are cancelling tenders and contracts with Chinese companies (Michaels and Pop 2021). Romania and Lithuania have spearheaded the exclusion of China, although Slovenia, the Czech Republic, and Croatia have also cancelled some contracts for Chinese-built and Chinese-financed infrastructure.

US pressure on Romania is yielding results. Romania's state-owned nuclear company, Nuclearelectrica, yielded to pressure and cancelled a contract with China to construct new units at its Cernavoda nuclear plant. Romania also agreed to almost exclude China completely from contributing to developing its 5G networks, irrespective of the adverse impact on Romania's economic development. While Romania has attempted to avoid the anti-Chinese rhetoric, the US has been boasting about the decision to block China's market access. The White House press release in 2019 states: "Romania is committed to working with the United States to combat the cybersecurity threats posed by Chinese vendors in 5G networks" (Melenciuc 2020). The US military presence in Romania as an expanding frontline against Russia, evident by the US missile defence base on Romanian soil and the US effort towards increasing NATO's presence in the Black Sea. Hence, the US has been able to convert security dependence into geoeconomic loyalty in Romania and other states.

The US negotiated and pushed through the economic normalisation agreement between Serbia and Kosovo in 2020, which also enabled the US to use its role as a security provider to advance a geoeconomic agenda. Washington added provisions within the normalisation agreement that aimed to enhance the US position vis-à-vis China in all three geoeconomic levers of power. Technology was addressed as the agreement stipulated: "Both parties will prohibit the use of 5G equipment supplied by untrusted vendors in their communications network. Where such an agreement is already present, both parties commit to removal and other mediation efforts in a timely fashion" (Vuksanovic 2020). Furthermore, the agreement committed both Kosovo and Serbia to "work with the U.S. International Development Finance Corporation and EXIM on memorandums of understanding to operationalize" various infrastructure projects and their financing.

STRATEGIC INDUSTRIES

China seeks to assert greater control over strategic industries in Europe, which by definition creates asymmetrical interdependence due to the difficulty of diversifying. China initially climbed global value chains by using its huge trade surpluses for acquisitions. Having caught up with the West in key technologies, the next phase of climbing global value chains entails establishing technological leadership as the foundation of market leadership.

The technological leadership of China also has severe implications for the development of international technical standardisation. Standardisation is important for interoperability as an absolute gain, although defining the technical specifications also influences which technologies will dominate the markets in the future (Seaman 2020). The growing influence of the Chinese government in setting new standards will contribute to make standards a subject of power competition. While Europe has traditionally held a strong influence over technical standards, this benefit is now contested (Rühlig 2021).

China's acquisition of strategic assets in the EU can make China the leading industrial superpower on the European continent and the world (Rabe and Gippner 2017). Technology transfer has been China's principal motivation for mass acquisitions, and Chinese staff tends to eventually replace their European counterparts (Le Corre and Sepulchre 2016: 54). In 2010, China took over Volvo, the Swedish car company. In 2012, the German construction machinery giant Lutzmeister was sold to its Chinese rival, Sany. In 2015, China National Chemical Corporation acquired the Italian tire manufacturer Pirelli. In 2016, China National Chemical Corporation acquired the Swiss giant Syngeta for $43 billion. In 2018, a Chinese investment group became the largest shareholder in the German car manufacturer Daimler AG. The Chinese consumer electronics giant Midea bought the German robot manufacturer Kuka, and in 2019, China's Alibaba purchased the German big data company Data Artisans. The acquisition of Kuka and Data Artisan is especially significant as Germany's industrial policy *Industry 4.0* is in direct competition with the *China 2025* industrial policy.

Access to the vast Chinese market was conditioned on foreign companies establishing joint ventures with local Chinese firms. Incrementally, the transfer of technology and know-how elevated the capabilities of Chinese companies. As China transitions from catching-up to establishing technological leadership, the commercial strategy is changed. Currently, European companies that want to remain economically competitive in the Fourth Industrial Revolution must connect with Chinese technologies and open their home markets. Case in point, the German car manufacturer Audi has engaged in a partnership with Huawei to launch self-driving cars. The partnership made Audi the first foreign car manufacturer to participate in the testing on public roads in the huge city of Wuxi in 2017 with LTE-Vehicle (LTE-V) technology, which connects telecom operators with automobile manufacturers. Roads in Wuxi have been custom-made for self-driving cars as the roads communicate with the cars. A limitation of self-driving cars is the limited data and information that individual cars can extract from their immediate environment. In Wuxi, the roads, street signs, traffic lights, bus stops, and other adjacent infrastructure has been equipped with censors and cameras that share the information with the cars—and the cars also "talk" to each other. Technological independence from Chinese technologies subsequently entails self-harm for European companies that want to remain competitive.

There are concerted efforts in the West to limit the access of Chinese digital platforms to prevent Chinese strategic industries from obtaining a leading position within Europe. The US has pushed back against Huawei's rollout of its 5G infrastructure in Europe. In an effort to create a "Concert of Democracies" of the current era, the UK has pushed towards creating a 5G club of democracies to limit China's technological footprint in the West and restore Britain's political-economic role in Europe following Brexit.

China announced possible measures against efforts to limit its market access. China cautioned retaliation against that Nokia and Ericsson, two leading European telecom giants, if the EU or its member states ban Huawei from contributing to the development of 5G networks. Sweden banned Huawei and ZTE from partaking in the 5G network and China responded that the discrimination against Chinese companies would have "serious consequences" by limiting the access of Swedish businesses in China. The CEO of Ericsson, a Swedish company, cautioned the Swedish government about the consequences of excluding Chinese tech companies. China is under great pressure to make an example of Sweden as other European states are also seeking to limit the inclusion of China in the European 5G infrastructure. With large Swedish companies that have made significant investments in China, such as IKEA and H&M, China will have plenty of targets.

Sweden's actions against China have been emboldened by the EU, which in January 2020 released a set of tools to limit the EU's dependence on Chinese telecom giants as a strategic industry with security implications (European Commission 2020a). The EU initiative fell short of Washington's push towards a total EU ban of Huawei and ZTE, as Brussels wanted to be able to claim that Chinese tech companies are not discriminated against. The EU also insisted that unfair economic practices had to be addressed trade been adamant that further negotiations with China are necessary with China. More specifically, Chinese industrial subsidies in areas such as high-tech (European Council 2020b).

China has more leverage among European states that have not yet joined the EU. Case in point, Serbia has become a central node in China's Digital Silk Road. China and Serbia signed the Agreement on Economic and Technical Cooperation in the Field of Infrastructure in 2009, which contributed to make Beijing the "fourth pillar of Serbian foreign policy, along with Brussels, Washington and Moscow" (Republic of Serbia 2009). In 2019, the Safe City project was rolled out across Serbia in which Chinese high-tech industries such as Huawei and HIKVision established a surveillance system based on facial recognition technology. After China and Serbia established a visa-free regime in 2018, Serbia experienced a large influx of Chinese tourists. Joint Chinese-Serbian police patrols in Serbian cities with large amounts of Chinese tourists became common, and also in regions with economic interests such as the Chinese ownership of steel mills or Chinese funded high-ways. Serbia became the first European state to buy Chinese drones and the Sinopharm Covid-vaccine.

TRANSPORTATION CORRIDORS: BRIDGEHEADS FROM THE SOUTH, WEST, AND NORTH

The EU can reap many economic benefits from the new transportation corridors, yet the restructuring of corridors is organised to make China the leading geoeconomic power in Eurasia with growing influence in Europe (Yu, Tettamanti, and Rizzi 2020). Simply put, the new transportation corridors are integrating Europe into Greater Eurasia.

The Port of Piraeus in Greece has become the main physical bridgehead into Europe from the south of the continent. Proving the enduring relevance of geography, Mackinder (1919: 116) argued more than a century ago: "the possession of Greece by a great Heartland power would probably carry with it the control of the World-Island; the Macedonian history would be re-enacted." After the global financial crisis of 2008–2009, China became a leading investor in Greece.

The investments included the Chinese shipping company, China Ocean Shipping Company (COSCO), acquisition of the strategic Port of Piraeus in 2016, and the subsequent management and operation rights until 2052. The acquisition was followed by renovations to expand the capacity and efficiency of the port. In 2016, the Greek Prime Minister, Alexis Tsipras, announced his country would "serve as China's gateway into Europe" (Le Corre 2018). As its bridgehead into Europe, China expands into the adjacent regions. A network of roads, railroads, bridges, tunnels, airports, and logistic centres is also constructed to connect Greece with the Western Balkans and thus further enhance the competitiveness of the Port of Piraeus. Along with the new transportation network, China is developing or taking over strategic industries such as coal plants, cooper mines, and steel plants.

From the Western Balkans, the Chinese infrastructure project heads farther north. China's upgrade of the railway network from Budapest to Belgrade reduces travel time from 8 hours to 3.5 hours, and an extension is added to connect with the Macedonian capital. An air link also appears to be in the making as China Everbright Limited acquired full control over the operations of Albania's only international airport. China is also constructing part of the S14 expressway in Poland (Paszak 2020).

From the eastern borders of Europe, the trans-Eurasian land-bridge connects through China and Kazakhstan before going south towards Turkey or north towards Russia before entering Europe. The corridors are subsidised, although as the trade volume by rail continues to increase sharply, the subsidies are withdrawn. The land corridor has been growing rapidly as it becomes efficient with new infrastructure, harmonisation of standards, and reduction of administrative barriers. This land corridor can then also connect with the maritime Silk Road through the Mediterranean. While Central and Eastern Europe have been physically connected to the world through Western Europe, the Chinese infrastructure projects are rewiring this connectivity towards the east.

From the north, the Russian-Chinese Arctic corridor is still in its early stages, yet with great potential due to lower costs and shorter travel time. A very likely European connection node is the Russian port of Murmansk, which can connect with Finland by rail and transit southwards. A feasibility study on an Arctic Railway corridor between Finland and Norway was completed in 2019, which could link Finland with a modernised deep-sea harbour in Kirkenes. Norway is less likely to play a central role, partly due to the lack of a domestic utility of the infrastructure costs in the low-populated northern region that would also disrupt the communities of Sami people (MTC 2019). In contrast, Finland has a greater potential to become a central node in an Arctic transportation network that would also contribute to greater domestic connectivity.

China is constructing the Helsinki-Tallinn tunnel under the Baltic Sea, which is expected to be linked directly to the Arctic corridor. In the Baltic, states such as Latvia have pledged to cooperate with China in logistics, infrastructure, and trade (PRC 2017). Xi Jinping personally lobbied for the Rovaniemi-Kirkenes railway line and the Helsinki-Tallinn tunnel to gain further access to Central and Eastern Europe. Furthermore, China is working with Russia and Northern European states to lay a shorter data cable connection along the seabed of the Northern Sea Route as a part of the Digital Silk Road (Spohr and Hamilton 2020: 25).

The leading economies in Western Europe, the centre of power in the EU, has been more critical of China's BRI. In 2017, the leaders of Germany, France, UK, and the president of the European Commission declined to attend the Belt and Road Forum in Beijing. In 2018, French President Macron and British Prime Minister May also declined to sign a Maritime Silk Road memorandum of understanding (MoU) with the Chinese government. Recognising that control over maritime corridors is a central component of a hegemon,

Macron argued that "these roads cannot be those of a new hegemony, which would transform those that they cross into vassals" (Rose 2018).

With the power centre of the EU pushing against the BRI, China has instead shifted focus to intensify bilateral initiatives with EU member states. Brussels realised the limitations of regional solidarity when Italy broke ranks with the EU in March 2019 by unilaterally signing on the BRI, and thus becoming the first major Western economy to join the Chinese initiative, in defiance of both the EU and the US.

FINANCIAL INSTRUMENTS

Europe has become a critical region for China to expand its financial power. Access to the huge Chinese market is often conditioned on economic and political decisions, including the choice of Chinese capital. With trillions of dollars accrued in foreign reserves, China has become the world's leading creditor. The financial power is easily converted into political influence as almost all of China's lending is done by the Chinese government, the Chinese central bank, and Chinese state-owned or state-affiliated companies (Horn, Reinhart, and Trebesch 2019).

China's Foreign Direct Investments support the two other geoeconomic pillars of power—strategic industries and transportation corridors. Chinese investments are focused on mergers and acquisitions within innovative technologies and strategic industries (Hanemann, Huotari, and Kratz 2019). Chinese lending enables its trading partners to run higher deficit spending, which contributes to further de-industrialisation in Europe as its people can temporarily live beyond their means and import goods that would otherwise have to be produced locally. Enabling deficit-economies in Europe that borrow and spend rather than produce and save is causing a systemic decline as these states eventually lose their productive power and obtain unsustainable and unmanageable debts. Investments are also instrumental to finance infrastructure for the Belt and Road Initiative that ensures all roads lead to Beijing. Kaplan (2018) labels China's finance as "patient capital" due to the long-term horizon and high tolerance towards risks, which enhances Chinese geoeconomic power and develops export markets for its goods.

European states have flouted EU legislation to pursue Chinese capital. The Hungarian government seemingly broke the market competition laws of the EU and its rules on tenders by financing the Chinese-constructed Belgrade-Budapest railway with Chinese capital. The terms of the loan were not disclosed and the Hungarian government also decided to pay for the infrastructure itself rather than taking advantage of the EU's programs.

A similarly peculiar case can be found in the Czech Republic. While the former Czech president Vaclav Havel was deeply suspicious of communists and China, the current Czech President Milos Zeman has embraced China and Chinese capital in the effort to make the Czech Republic a central node in China's regional Eurasian network. In 2017, President Zeman hired Ye Jianming as his advisor, who is the founder and former Chairman of CEFC China Energy Company Limited (Kowalski 2017).

FINANCIAL INSTITUTIONS

In 2015, Germany, the UK, France, and Italy as the largest economies of the EU became founding members of the Chinese-led AIIB. The event represented a tectonic shift of financial power from the US to China as the AIIB is a direct competitor to the US-led World Bank and the US/Japanese-led Asia Development Bank. The launch of the AIIB also displayed the waning influence of the US in Europe as Washington had urged the Europeans to not join the Chinese initiative. Washington was especially surprised by London's decision to break ranks as Britain strives to be the main partner of the US in Europe. Yet, the major economies of Europe realised that their economic power, and thus also value to the US, depends on their ability to adapt to new realities. The wealthier states in Europe were more inclined to join the AIIB (Chen 2017), which suggests an interest to develop strategic autonomy from the US. Even Washington recognised the folly of self-inflicted damage caused by ignoring the shifting international distribution of power. The former US Secretary of State, Madeleine Albright, acknowledged that by attempting to isolate China, the US had isolated itself as "all of a sudden everybody was in" except for the US (Ting 2015).

EUROPEANISING THE YUAN

China aspires to internationalise a yuan and Europe is a key region towards this end. China has developed a sophisticated trading infrastructure and financial institutions in Europe. Clearing banks for trade in the yuan and trade of Chinese securities have been set up across Europe's financial centres. The UK has been the main focus in Europe to internationalise the yuan, and Brexit has thus represented a temporary set-back for China aspirations to become a financial superpower (Kärnfelt 2020).

The internationalisation of the yuan presents the EU with a dilemma. The growing commercial use of the yuan by European companies presents great economic opportunities by creating more favourable terms for exports to China. Furthermore, the commercial earnings of the yuan can easily be invested into Chinese financial assets. However, it also represents a geostrategic risk as global financial power is rewired towards Beijing. The growing use of the yuan will also give China greater ability to finance its grand geoeconomic initiatives, such as the acquisition of high-tech companies and funding of infrastructure projects. The growing use of the yuan also enables China to reduce its reliance on the US dollar for its economic activities around the world, which is imperative to sink the domineering role of the US in the global economy.

The EU's ability to establish a common approach towards the internationalisation of the Yuan has been problematic as EU member states compete with each other to attract Chinese clearing banks and financial infrastructure. Britain's departure from the EU will further undermine the ability of the EU to manage and limit the internationalisation of the yuan.

THE EU RESPONDS

The EU, supported by the US, has cited spying concerns and national security as the principal reason for limiting China's financial footprint in Europe. Geoeconomic rivalry commonly entails erecting barriers for competing powers to restrict market access. This includes tariff and non-tariff barriers such as policies for bureaucratic, environmental, health and safety, industrial, and national security (Jones 1986; Cwik 2011). Sometimes these policies are justified by their claimed intention, while other times they are merely geoeconomic instruments of power. The restrictions on Chinese digital systems support both national security and the geoeconomic interest of enhancing the EU's strategic autonomy.

In his 2017 State of the Union address, the Commission President Jean-Claude Juncker embraced economic nationalist rhetoric as he called for improved measures to protect the EU's strategic industries:

> we are not naïve free traders. Europe must always defend its strategic interests. This is why today we are proposing a new EU framework for investment screening. If a foreign, state-owned, company wants to purchase a European harbour, part of our energy infrastructure or a defence technology firm, this should only happen in transparency, with scrutiny and debate (European Commission 2017).

In 2018, Sigmar Gabriel, the German Minister for Foreign Affairs and Vice-Chancellor of Germany, accused China and Russia of "constantly trying to test and undermine the unity of the European Union," and introduced ideological arguments to geoeconomic competition as he criticised China's

Belt and Road Initiative as an effort to create "a comprehensive system alternative to the Western one, which, unlike our model, is not based on freedom, democracy and individual human rights" (Miller 2018b).

In March 2019, the EU officially identified China as a "strategic competitor" in the "pursuit of technological leadership, and a systemic rival promoting alternative models of governance" (European Commission 2019: 1).

Yet, on 30 December 2020, the EU and China agreed in principle on the EU-China Comprehensive Agreement on Investment (CAI). The deal can be defined as the most significant investment deal of the century and the most ambitious agreement that China has signed. Germany had held the rotating presidency of the EU and was determined to push through the deal before the end of the German presidency.

After seven years of negotiations, it is noteworthy that the agreement was reached merely weeks before the inauguration of the Biden administration. Biden had promised to revive relations with Europe and to mobilise a common front against China. The timing of the agreement appears to signal clearly that the EU intends to chart an independent path on China to assert the EU's strategic autonomy. Equally, the Chinese had a greater interest to push through the CAI before Biden took office and attempts to organise the Europeans in an anti-Chinese campaign.

However, following the US lead, the EU imposed sanctions on China in March 2021 over human rights concerns in Xinjiang. China's retaliatory sanctions were thus cited as a possible reason for cancelling the CAI.

THE CARROT AND STICK: CONVERTING ECONOMIC DEPENDENCE TO POLITICAL INFLUENCE

Geoeconomics entails converting economic power into political capital, either through carrots or sticks. The main carrot offered by China is to become central nodes in its region-building initiative that entails developing local industries, establishing transportation hubs, and attracting foreign capital. The stick is also an important tool against European states that either resists Chinese geoeconomic incursion or express political hostility.

Political influence is imperative as Beijing asserts its control over Xinjian, Tibet, Hong Kong, Taiwan, and rectifies domestic divisions as a colonial legacy from the Century of Humiliation. While Beijing recognises these domestic initiatives can tarnish its international reputation and disrupt its grand geoeconomic project, it must also take into account vulnerabilities as the US and Europe can weaponise ethnic minorities and Taiwan to weaken China. Case in point, the US only ended its CIA operation in Tibet following the Nixon-Kissinger deal in the 1970s. As China rises, it is therefore imperative for Beijing that the Europeans are deterred from following the efforts by Washington to gradually abandon the One-China Policy, interfere in Hong Kong, and decry human rights abuses in Tibet and "genocide" in Xinjiang. While China has severe human rights abuses, Beijing is adamant to prevent this from becoming an instrument in great power rivalry akin to what the Europeans do against Russia.

Norway was an early recipient of the Chinese stick. Liu Xiaobo, a Chinese dissident, received the Nobel Peace prize in October 2010, in which China responded by freezing economic and political relations with Norway. The economic sanctions were profound in salmon exports and other exports. After the sanctions, Norway voting on human rights resolutions has become more cautious, which indicates that the sanctions were effective in terms of changing Norway's "bad behaviour" (Kolstad 2020).

The 17+1 grouping has been conducive to soften EU policies towards China. While not publicly opposing the EU's effort for a common approach towards China - Greece, Hungary, Portugal, and Croatia have been advocating for an "open door" policy regarding Chinese investments. China has demonstrated its ability to wield influence in the 17+1 format to undermine the EU's ability to reach a common position on issues ranging from the South China Sea dispute to preventing common EU statements criticising China's human rights record. China has in the past been able to divide the EU when its collective bargaining power is seen as detrimental to China.

Similar trends are also found among non-EU member states such as Turkey. Turkey used to be a fervent critic of China's treatment of its Uyghur minority population in Xinjiang, which are a Muslim and Turkic ethnic group with cultural affiliation to Central Asia. In 2009, Erdogan opined that the "The incidents in China are, simply put, a genocide" (Alemdaroglu and Tepe 2020). By 2016, Turkey arrested and extradited a leading Uyghur political activist. Since 2019, Turkey stepped up its efforts and has arrested hundreds of Uyghurs and began processing their deportation. In the unipolar era, the US monopolised on technologies, transportation corridors, finance, and security, which demanded certain loyalties to Washington to thrive. In the multipolar era, Turkey is working towards diversifying its strategic partnerships to avoid excessive reliance on more power states. China is becoming an indispensable partner to ensure a more independent Turkish foreign policy.

THE AUSTRALIAN CAUTIONARY TALE

The case of Australia provides valuable lessons for how the geoeconomic rivalry between the US and China will have consequences for the Europeans. China usually employs targeted economic coercion with limited consequences, such as targeting Norwegian salmon, French aircrafts, South Korean K-pop, or Japan's access to rare earth metals. In contrast, China's economic coercion against Australia targeted a wide range of industries that threatens its entire economy.

Australia is to some extent a unique case, yet it is indicative of Beijing's ability and preparedness to use devastating economic coercion against states that align with US efforts to contain and confront China. Australia relies on the US for security and safeguarding the transportation corridors that connect it to the world, yet its main trading partner is China. For many years, Australia was adamant it did not need to choose between the US and China. This was part of Australia's wider effort to reconcile its European history with its Asian geography.

The ability to remain neutral became untenable once the US stepped up its efforts to contain China. The "pivot to Asia" under the Obama administration entailed agreements with Australia to station US marines on its soil and improve cooperation on ballistic missile defence systems. On the behest of American requests, Australia also targeted key pillars of China's geoeconomic power. Australia excluded Huawei and ZTE from the rollout of its 5G networks, and the federal government passed legislation allowing the federal government to cancel the Belt and Road agreement between the state of Victoria and China and limiting Chinese investments. The political posturing of Canberra also aligned with the US in terms of criticising China's actions in the South China Sea, human rights violations in Xinjian and Hong Kong, and supporting Washington's call for investigating the origins of Covid-19. China listed these grievances and rapidly intensified the economic coercion against Australia. In no uncertain terms, Beijing informed Canberra that it was the responsibility of Australia to fix the problems it had caused (PRC 2020). By making a public spectacle of the China-Australia dispute through Twitter, Beijing ensured the wider world was informed that joining US initiatives against China would come with a price.

CONCLUSION

China's economic rise consisted of three stages. First, it was a valuable contribution to the Western-led system by providing low-cost manufactured goods and capital as the proceeds from its export-based economy was reinvested back into the West. Second, China became a competitor in international markets such as Africa. Third, China has already caught up and in many areas surpassed the West—and China is asserting its geoeconomic leadership in Europe.

European states face a dilemma in terms of hitching their wagon to the Chinese economic miracle. Economic connectivity with China is necessary to remain economically relevant in the new world. China offers win-win geoeconomic solutions to the Europeans, yet the relative gain is in China's favour. China's geoeconomic presence in Europe creates economic incentives for the EU to position itself between the trans-Atlantic partnership and Greater Eurasia, while efforts to align too closely with either the US or China will result in punitive actions by the other.

European states react differently to China based on their geoeconomic power and preferences for regional frameworks. For example, Germany is more concerned about high-tech rivalry with Chinese strategic industries, while the UK is more apprehensive about China asserting itself in transportation corridors. China's preparedness to recognise Germany as the central geoeconomic node in Europe will make Berlin more favourable to Chinese geoeconomic region-building, while the British commitments to the trans-Atlantic partnership will translate into greater willingness to confront China. Among the weaker states in Europe, especially in Central and Eastern Europe, the privileged position in a Chinese Greater Eurasian region makes them more inclined to welcome China's geoeconomic incursion into Europe. Although, their US security dependence limits economic connectivity with China.

China's geoeconomic region-building in Europe creates systemic incentives for the EU to integrate into Greater Eurasia. If the EU attempts to balance China's efforts to establish itself as a European power, then China will have incentives to sow divisions within the bloc. If the EU uncritically accepts China full access to the European market, then China will develop intolerable asymmetrical interdependence. The EU thus has systemic incentives to accept a Greater Eurasian geoeconomic architecture to the extent the EU can maintain strategic autonomy as an independent pole of power within Greater Eurasia. China does not seek to destroy the EU, merely reformat it to fit within greater Eurasia. Beijing is therefore not inherently pro-or anti-EU, rather it depends on the compatibility between Europe and Greater Eurasia.

7

Eurasian Russia Skewing the Balance of Dependence in Europe

Russia's Greater Eurasia skews the balance of dependence in Europe. Russia does not have the same geoeconomic capabilities as China, although the purpose of creating a Greater Eurasian region remains the same - Eurasian Russia will become less dependent on Europe and Europe will become more reliant on Russia. There is neither the geoeconomic capability nor intention of Russia to strive towards a hegemonic position in Europe; rather Russian efforts are devoted to scaling back the collective hegemony of the West and establishing symmetry in relations. Russia's Greater Eurasia is not inherently pro-or anti-European, rather the objective is for Europe to matter less in Russian foreign policy by making it one of many sub-regions in Greater Eurasia.

Under Yeltsin, Russia attempted to integrate *into* Europe with the implicit acceptance of unilateral concessions. After the liberal approach collapsed due to NATO expansion, Putin sought to integrate Russia *with* Europe as equal partners. After the Ukraine crisis eliminated Moscow last illusions about the gradual integration of Greater Europe, Russia set new regional ambitions with Greater Eurasia. The third and contemporary integration approach entails integrating Europe with Greater Eurasia.

This chapter first explores why the format for Russia-EU cooperation fundamentally changes as Russia has transitioned from Greater Europe to Greater Eurasia. The EU's concentric circles format is incompatible with the multipolar format of Greater Eurasia, and Moscow will no longer be able to work extensively with the EU as an entity until a new format emerges.

Second, Russia's geoeconomic levers of power in Greater Eurasia contribute to shift the symmetry of dependence in its favour. The shifting balance of dependence derives primarily from Russian strategic industries, transportation corridors, and financial instruments becoming less reliant on the EU, while Russia's economic footprint in Europe has not yet markedly increased.

Last, it is assessed the extent to which the EU and Russia can convert their economic power into political influence. Greater Eurasia enables Russia to develop its own path to economic modernisation and to reproduce its distinctive culture—thus achieving the conservative goal of positioning society between continuity and change. Russia's conservative vision for Europe repudiates the EU's liberal hegemony, and the support among European conservatives can result in Europe adapting to Russian values. It is concluded that the changing symmetry of economic dependence in favour of Russia is altering Russia's role in Europe.

REGIONAL FORMATS: FROM GREATER EUROPE TO GREATER EURASIA

Ever since the European continent was divided following the Second World War, the Europeans and Russians have aimed to develop a format for cooperation that mitigates conflict based on power and regime type. The Conference on Security and Cooperation in Europe (CSCE), also referred to as the Helsinki Accords of 1975, represents the foundational document for cooperation in Europe. The document encompasses both components to mitigate conflicts: first a common European framework by developing mechanisms for reducing political and military tensions between the two blocs, and second the commitment to making human rights an integral part of discussions over international security.

The Helsinki Accords inspired Gorbachev's Common European Home concept that sought to reform and open up the Soviet system and integrate the capitalist and communist states under one common European roof. When the Cold War was declared over in 1989 and the Berlin Wall came down, the Helsinki Accords were to be further developed. The Charter of Paris for a New Europe in 1990 was established on the foundations of the Helsinki Accords and sought to deepen its two components—a common Europe and human rights. The Charter of Paris called for "ending of the division of Europe" and affirmed that "security is indivisible and the security of every participating State is inseparably linked to that of all the others."

In 1994, the Organisation for Security and Cooperation in Europe (OSCE) was founded as the successor of the CSCE / Helsinki Accords, which would continue to work towards ending the Cold War legacy of dividing lines on the continent. However, the OSCE was soon thereafter undermined as the new Europe would be constructed by NATO and the EU, which aim to include all states in Europe except Russia. Washington deemed the OSCE as a potential challenge to its hegemonic rule as it prevented the US to obstruct the rise of competing states (Sarotte 2011).

The EU, seeking collective hegemony in partnership with the US, also sought to absorb the responsibilities of the OSCE, such as reforming law enforcement bodies and border control, and fighting corruption, organised crime, drug trafficking, and terrorism (Entin and Zagorsky 2008: 27). Thus, the Secretary-General of the OSCE, Marc Perrin de Brichambaut (2009), accused the EU of "undermining the OSCE" with its unilateral approach to pan-European security. The EU also supported the closure of the OSCE missions in Estonia and Latvia and absorbing the responsibilities despite not recognising Russian-speakers as citizens and the subsequent denial of basic rights.

At the 1999 OSCE Istanbul Summit, Russia had committed itself to withdraw its peacekeepers from both the Georgian and Moldovan break-away regions. Although, as the role of the OSCE as a collective format for security was seen to be systematically diminished and replaced with an expansionist NATO, Russia began to walk back its previous commitments. In 2003 the Dutch Chairman of the OSCE, Jaap de Hoop Scheffer, proposed that the Russian peacekeeping forces in Moldova should be replaced with an OSCE Peace Consolidation Force, which would then "outsource" the peacekeeping to the EU (Löwenhardt 2004: 107). Symbolic of the shift from a common Europe to bloc policies, the following year Jaap de Hoop Scheffer became the Secretary-General of NATO.

THE EU'S WIDER EUROPE VERSUS RUSSIA'S GREATER EUROPE

The Helsinki Accords were subsequently largely in tatters as the OSCE, the successor of the CSCE, had been deprived of a leading role in Europe. In its place, the EU developed its Wider Europe concept that envisioned the pan-European space governed under Brussels' leadership. As the EU's policies in Wider Europe perpetuated Russian weakness and sustained Russia as a political object, the EU-Russian partnership reached an impasse. In contrast, Russia pushed for the development of a Greater Europe, which was reflected in its proposal for a new European security architecture in 2008 and an EU-Russia Union from Lisbon to Vladivostok in 2010 (Diesen and Wood 2012).

Wider Europe decoupled the two initial components of the Helsinki Accords—a common Europe and commitment to human rights. By merely moving the dividing lines in Europe towards Russian borders, the shared commitment to human rights and democracy became an instrument of Western extraterritorial governance over the East.

Geoeconomic theory suggests that Russia's Greater Europe Initiative had little prospect for success as the West never had strong incentives to include Russia. Including Russia in European institutions would drastically shift the internal balance of dependence within a pan-European infrastructure as Russia has the largest population and territory in Europe, and great geoeconomic potential. Furthermore, the failure to include Russia did not have any significant costs for the West as Russia had not diversified its economic connectivity and did not have anywhere else to turn. The worst deal presented to Russia would nonetheless be the best option for Russia.

Relations with Russia could be managed under asymmetrical interdependence, facilitated by the EU27+1 format. The EU could further skew the balance of dependence in its favour by expanding its membership and also pursue partnerships with the shared neighbourhood to further augment collective strength against Russia. The neighbourhood between the EU and Russia was subsequently defined by zero-sum logic as every state that aligned itself with the EU would create further asymmetries between Brussels and Moscow, thus enabling the EU to dictate the terms of cooperation in its concentric circles' format. Furthermore, the EU was reluctant to support any regional integration initiatives in the post-Soviet space that includes Russia.

The European Neighbourhood Policy, launched in 2004, is a bilateral format between the EU and individual neighbouring states. This initiative was rejected by Moscow as the bilateral format aimed to maximise the EU's asymmetrical interdependence with individual neighbours and it failed to accommodate Russia's relations with its neighbours. Due to the calculated power disparity, the EU bilateral initiatives are merely camouflaged unilateralism (Tassinari 2005; Vahl 2005; Browning and Joenniemi 2008).

Brussels and Moscow agreed on the Common Spaces Agreement of 2005 to align their approaches to their shared neighbourhood as the European Neighbourhood Policy was unacceptable to Russia. The "common space of external security" agreed that regional cooperation and integration must be promoted "in a mutually beneficial manner, through close result-oriented EU-Russia collaboration and dialogue, thereby contributing effectively to creating a greater Europe without dividing lines and based on common values" (Common Spaces Agreement 2005). Although, the EU had few incentives to abide by its commitments as Russia did not have any other partners.

The EU's Eastern Partnership of 2009 betrayed the Common Spaces Agreement by rejecting regional integration in a "mutually beneficial manner" (Chizhov 2012). The Eastern Partnership established a multilateral format that included all of EU's Eastern neighbours, except Russia. The regional format was structured to deprive Russia of its main strategic industry, energy, by pursuing "energy security" in the format of aligning the pan-European space under EU rules. The Eastern Partnership support INOGATE, an international energy cooperation program that includes all the former republics of the Soviet Union, except Russia (European Commission 2008a). The Eastern Partnership also aims to restructure transportation corridors under EU control with the Transport Corridor Europe-Caucasus-Asia (TRACECA) that penetrates the Eurasian space while bypassing Russia.

GREATER EURASIA AND THE CANCELLATION OF THE HELSINKI LEGACY

Greater Eurasia signifies the end of the Helsinki Accords. By abandoning Greater Europe, Russia cancels both the aspirations for a shared European continent and the notion that its domestic affairs, which includes human rights and democracy, should be an integral part of discussions on international security. When Moscow signed the agreement in 1975, it had not expected that discussions of human rights would be used as an instrument to organise subject-object relations instead of facilitating a common continent. Furthermore, Washington's efforts to reduce economic connectivity between the EU and Russia incentivises the weaponisation of human rights. As the Navalny incident demonstrated, a human rights issue on Russian soil was used as an effort to cancel major energy project and sever relations. Russia is unlikely to consider further gas pipelines to Europe.

Greater Eurasia inevitably reorganises the relationship between Russia and Europe in terms of power and values. Russia's Eurasian orientation aims to reduce its own reliance on Europe, and increase the reliance of Europe on Russia. A multipolar Greater Eurasia reopens the fundamental question of whether the EU is the sole option for organising Europe's affairs. In the past, Russia used its relations with China, Iran, and other states in the East to elevate its market value, although these relations were often treated as bargaining chips to negotiate a more favourable position for Russia in Europe. Under Russia's Greater Eurasian Initiative, these relations are imperative to avoid excessive reliance on the West.

Greater Eurasia presents an alternative mode for organising the European space and Russia subsequently sees two alternatives—the EU can integrate *with* Greater Eurasia or *into* Greater Eurasia. Brussels' willingness to establish an equal and non-EU centric partnership, for example in the EU-EAEU format implies integration with Greater Eurasia. Alternatively, Brussels' insistence on an EU-centric format for cooperation with Russia, such as "Wider Europe," is a non-starter and Russia will pursue strategies of integrating the EU *into* Greater Eurasia by undermining the EU's strategic autonomy.

The EU-centric concept of concentric circles to transform the European continent is rejected by Russia as it is incompatible with Greater Eurasia.

The concentric circles' approach signifies a flexible approach to integration whereas the inner circles move towards federalist initiatives while the approach to the outer circles of non-members entails exporting EU rules for external governance (Lavenex 2011). Moscow's rejection of the concentric circles' concept denotes that the EU and Russia have incompatible formats for cooperation, which will obstruct mutually beneficial and pragmatic cooperation. Thus, Brussels will discover that the EU has little if any value to Moscow as a partner.

For Russia, it would then be preferable with no diplomatic ties with EU institutions compared to cooperation in EU-centric formats that feed Brussels false expectations—such as the prerogative of the EU to interfere in the domestic affairs of Russia. This old format is obsolete and dangerous by provoking conflicts. Russia thus benefits from conceptually decoupling from the EU's Wider Europe and thus engage with the EU from the same external position as China and India.

Russia's Greater Eurasian Initiative will also impact EU policies towards the shared neighbourhood between the EU and Russia. Brussels' zero-sum victories in the shared neighbourhood do not strengthen the EU vis-à-vis Russia, rather it compels Russia to shift its economic connectivity towards China and other powers in the East. Case in point, during Russia's Greater Europe Initiative, the EU imposing a zero-sum integration on Ukraine would strengthen asymmetries of the EU and Ukraine vis-à-vis Russia. Although, under Russia's Greater Eurasia Initiative, the coup in Ukraine and ensuing anti-Russian sanctions push Russia into the arms of China.

By reducing its excessive reliance on the EU, Russia can also alter the content of cooperation. For example, the domestic affairs of Russia are no longer a subject of international affairs. The sovereign inequality embedded in the subject-object framework of relations is rejected by Moscow. Russia therefore has no interest in a "re-set" of relations with the EU to the extent it entails a return to the framework of a teacher and a student. In February 2021, the EU foreign policy chief, Josep Borrell, went to Moscow to improve relations. Brussels stretched out a hand to Moscow in the form of a long list of criticism of issues in Russia's domestic affairs and guidance on how Russia could rectify them. Moscow was condemned for the jailing of Navalny and demanded his unconditional and immediate release. Moscow was appalled by the lecturing and interference into its domestic affairs, while Brussels was humiliated by Moscow's rebuke. Russia's effort to decouple liberal democratic values from power relations was predictably interpreted by the EU as Russia rejecting liberal democratic norms. In response to the EU's "humiliation," it immediately began discussing further sanctions.

Hence, communications between the EU and Russia were evidently in limbo as Brussels had not acknowledged that Greater Europe has been replaced with Greater Eurasia. Russia's excessive reliance on an asymmetrical partnership with the EU has come to an end, and Russia has no reason to let Brussels dictate the content and framework of the partnership. Foreign Minister, Sergey Lavrov, had previously cautioned that communication with the EU was counter-productive:

> Those people who are responsible for foreign policy in the West do not understand the need for mutually respectful communication. So we should probably stop communicating with them for a while. Moreover, Ursula von der Leyen declares that geopolitical partnership is not working with the current Russian government. So be it, if that's the way they want it (Lavrov 2020).

In the Greater Eurasian space, where the EU matters less, Russia can afford to take a break from engaging with Brussels. Russia sees little if any purpose in engaging directly with the EU. As Lavrov informed Borrel, Russia considers the EU to be an "unreliable partner" (Tass 2021).

Inter-regionalism creates incentives for mutual recognition and legitimacy (Hettne and Söderbaum 2000: 469). The EU's reluctance to engage with the Russian-led EAEU incentivises Russia to embrace similar wedge tactics. Inter-regionalism based on sovereign equality could mitigate tensions between the EU and Russia as an agreement that Russia does not disrupt European institutions if the EU similarly does not oppose and undermine Russian-led institutions (Gvosdev 2008). The EU has been supportive of regions around the world, except for its eastern borders due to the zero-sum rivalry with Russia. Whilst the EU has rejected diplomatic ties with the EAEU, the EAEU has become engaged in the Western Balkans. In October 2019, the EAEU and Serbia signed a free-trade agreement. Although, the agreements have been instrumental by Serbia to gain leverage vis-à-vis the EU that is experiencing enlargement fatigue.

Russia aims to give the EAEU a role in Europe. The EU has interests to support the EAEU to mitigate the zero-sum game in the European neighbourhood. While the EAEU represents a challenge to the EU, it is also an opportunity to make Russia a stakeholder with an interest to uphold the European order. Even the US would in theory have some interest in supporting the EAEU to limit China's influence in Central Asia and ensure a balance of dependence in Greater Eurasia as its historical objective. Although, US objectives of global hegemony prevents support for EAEU.

RUSSIA ACCOMMODATING CHINESE POWER

Russia's Greater Eurasia Initiative enhances the challenge from China for the EU. Russia benefits from strengthened Chinese influence to the extent it displaces zero-sum formats of the West. While China attempts to harmonise its interests and accommodate Russia's strategic interest, the West tends to organise relations in zero-sum terms to "liberate" states from Russian influence. For the US, there is not a single relationship Russia has with a foreign power that is not deemed harmful to global primacy and that must be limited.

China's growing influence in Central Asia is thus beneficial to Russia to the extent it enables the Eurasian duo to contain Western objectives against Russia. Chinese geoeconomics is important to balance the EU in areas such as the Western Balkans, which the EU considers its backyard for exclusive influence. Although, Chinese influence in the EU is also beneficial to the extent it directs economic interests to the East and dilutes internal cohesion that is used to mobilise resources against Russia.

By replacing the EU's market share in Russia and becoming the main partner for modernising Russian digital infrastructure, China's relative vis-à-vis the EU increases further. The technological cooperation with Russia and the establishment of joint research centres enable China to improve the competitiveness of its strategic industries. China's prospect of becoming a future leader in space exploration is greatly aided by Russia, which aims to scale back its partnership with the West and instead cooperate with China.

If the partnership expands into cyber cooperation, it could have many applications ranging from joint cyber espionage for commercial purposes to collective counter-intelligence. In the military sphere, the Russia-China strategic partnership strengthens China's military capabilities that will influence Europe. Joint military exercises have brought Chinese troops on Russian soil in the Vostok military exercises in the Russian Far East. In September 2021, China may also join Russia's Zapad military exercise that prepares for and simulates war in the West against NATO. Russia has previously accommodated the Chinese blue-water navy in the Mediterranean and the Baltic Sea, which could be expanded to the Arctic in the future. A tit for tat is making Europe a chessboard for military conflicts between the great powers as Russia invites the China military to Europe in response to the Europeans accommodating the US military. Beijing asserts that if European navies enter the South China Sea, then the Chinese navy will establish a presence in the Mediterranean. Russia is making it possible by accommodating a Chinese military presence in joint exercises and what appears to be an alliance in all but name.

EURASIAN RUSSIA'S THREE-PILLARED GEOECONOMIC POWER IN EUROPE

Russia's Greater Eurasian Initiative alters the symmetry of dependence. The main impact on the asymmetry of relations derives from Russia's ability to reduce its reliance on the EU, while to a lesser extent Russia will likely make the EU more dependent on Russia.

The collapse of the Soviet Union made Russia excessively reliant on the West as regional transportation networks and industrial connectivity within Eurasia were severed (Rastogi and Arvis 2007: 6). The extensive influence of the EU over Russia during the past decades has been the result of the EU's economic footprint in Russia, while Russia's economic footprint in the EU has largely been restricted to energy exports. In 1995, 40 percent of Russia's import originated from the EU and by 2002 the asymmetries had grown even further to 53 percent (Garcia-Herrero and Xu 2019: 6). Chinese trade with Russia has since grown rapidly and the EU is subsequently losing market share rapidly to China, an unmistakable trend even before the Ukraine crisis of 2014.

Strategic industries

Many European corporations have viewed the growing Russian market as an immense opportunity for exports, which is especially of importance when there is little growth at home. The interest in Russia as an export market differs between EU member states as Germany exports heavy machinery and motor vehicles, while the Italians export agricultural products.

The interregnum period between Greater Europe and Greater Eurasia has been defined by mutual sanctions due to the Ukraine crisis and different expectations about the partnership. Sanctions have hurt the Russian economy and prevented many important investments, although it has also enabled Russia to push through important reforms that were neglected when market forces prevailed. The mutual sanctions between the West and Russia gave Russian companies some breathing space to reverse market liberalisation and provide government support for the development of strategic industries (Connolly 2016: 770). More specifically, Russia has taken advantage of the sanctions to develop autonomy within strategic industries and diversify foreign partners to avoid excessive reliance on foreign strategic industries.

Since the 1990s, Russia de-industrialised as energy exports were used to pay for imports of manufactured goods. Yet, under sanctions, Russia has been using proceeds from energy exports to subsidise infant industries to develop them into mature industries capable of competing in international markets.

Government interventions into the development of national industries have taken the form of tariffs supported by sanctions and subsidies supported by foreign acquisitions. The Russian authorities have also supported the acquisition of foreign-based assets that create a demand for Russian-supplied components (Yevtushenkov 2015). Putin was explicit that import substitution was not intended to isolate Russian companies and thus make them uncompetitive, rather it was temporary initiatives to mature infant industries to become competitive in international markets:

> The import replacement programme's aim is not to close our market and isolate ourselves from the global economy. We need to learn how to produce quality, competitive goods that will be in demand not just here in Russia, but on the global markets too (Russian Federation 2015).

The import substitution program intensified in 2014, out of necessity, to reduce reliance on Western imports. Russia has over 1,100 import substitution projects with various degrees of development and success (Novikov, Lastochkina, and Solodova 2019). Import substitution has been especially successful in the machine-tool industry, electronic industry, aviation shipbuilding industry, pharmaceutical industry, agricultural engineering, oil and gas engineering, and medical industry (Novikov, Lastochkina, and Solodova 2019: 3).

The initial import substitution focused on critical products such as engines for military helicopters from Ukraine, as the conflict severed supply chains. Although, Russia has also been able to reduce its reliance on German machinery. What Russia could not develop itself has been outsourced to China, which has replaced German supplies. Many of the exports from China are indeed products that China reengineered from Germany.

A key success story has been Russia's counter-sanctions against European agriculture as part of a strategy to develop Russia as an agricultural superpower. The vast export market in Asia is encouraging the development of more farmland, and improvement of technologies and transportation infrastructure to enjoy economies of scale not previously possible. Furthermore, While global warming is causing desertification, flood and, drought in other parts of the world, the warming climate is contributing to transform the Eastern half of Russian territory (Lustgarten 2020). Agricultural development spurs advancements in biotechnology and other high-tech industries (Barbanov and Bordachev 2012: 60). While reliance on agriculture in the 19th century slowed down industrialisation, the development of smart agriculture can make the digitalisation of the industry a stepping-stone into the Fourth Industrial Revolution. Agriculture is also an important industry to develop Russian regions that have been underdeveloped, and thus improve the distribution of wealth and social cohesion. The sanctioning of European agriculture also has the bonus of making sanctions unpopular and sow divisions due to the lobbying power of the EU's agricultural industry.

RUSSIAN EXPORTS

Russian strategic industries pursuing exports in Europe include high-tech products and natural resources. A leading high-tech industry of Russia is the weapon industry, which is enjoying rapid modernisation with automation and other modern technologies. Yet, the US aims to limit Russian exports with threats of sanctions against Russian customers under the Countering America's Adversaries Through Sanctions Act (CAATSA). Smaller states are more vulnerable to US economic coercion as they cannot withstand the pressure and they cannot establish themselves as an independent pole of power. For example, after US threats of sanctions, Serbia had to walk back its statement in 2019 about a future interest in buying the Russian S-400 surface-to-air missile systems.

However, larger states have both the incentive and capability to withstand US threats of economic coercion. Turkey and India have demonstrated preparedness to break rank with their Western allies. The emergence of a multipolar Greater Eurasian region incentivises larger states such as Turkey and India to diversify economic ties to pursue an autonomous foreign policy. Turkey and India, seeking an independent role between East and West, decided to buy the Russian S-400 irrespective of threats of US sanctions. Washington can, however, end up isolating itself with economic coercion as Turkey and India will be compelled to align their economies closer towards Greater Eurasia.

Russia endeavours to grow its high-tech footprint in the world in less controversial industries. As Russia's digital ecosystem matures, there are plans to make inroads into Europe. Case in point, Yandex, the Google of Russia, endeavours to make a global use of self-driving cars for taxi services and food delivery. Yandex announced in 2020 its intention to launch its robot-taxis in the European market (FT 2020).

Although, Russia's main and dominant strategic industry in Europe remains energy. Russia exports both oil and gas to Europe, although the latter creates greater dependence due to the difficulty of transportation and the natural competitiveness of proximity as it enables the use of pipelines instead of the more expensive infrastructure that Liquified Natural Gas (LNG) demands.

The US and the EU have consistently sought to undercut Russia's energy as a strategic industry to further skew the balance of dependence. The nationalisation of energy resources led to the vast resources ending up in the hands of a few oligarchs, who were courted by Western powers. By the end of the 1990s, it appeared that much of Russia's energy resources would fall under Western control until Russia began nationalising energy resources. The most important event being the arrest of Mikhail Khodorkovsky in 2003 and the subsequent nationalisation of his oil empire as he was preparing to sell a major share to ExxonMobil and Chevron-Texaco (Tsygankov 2009: 146).

The EU and US then moved the energy war towards controlling transit states and diversifying energy suppliers. Western support in the Georgian "Rose Revolution" that installed an anti-Russian government was linked to the establishment of an energy corridor to the Caspian Sea and Central Asia. These proposed pipelines, between Georgia and Azerbaijan, follow nearly the same path as the Batumi-Baku rail corridor that Halford Mackinder, the British Commissioner to South Russia, advocated that Britain should seize during the Russian revolution to undermine the economic power of Russia. Following the Western support for the Ukrainian "Orange Revolution" in 2004 to install an anti-Russian government, the West appeared to have struck a geoeconomic prize as 80 percent of Russian gas to Europe transitted through pipelines in Ukraine.

Russia's energy policies initially reflected a somewhat naïve understanding of economic statecraft. Russia had offered gas discounts to its neighbours such as Ukraine, believing that this would automatically translate into improved political relations. Yet, the excessive reliance on the European market, and the excessive dependence on transit through Ukraine, meant that Russia lost significant influence over its strategic industry.

Following the Western-supported "Orange Revolution" of 2004 in Ukraine sent a clear signal to Moscow that it was merely subsidising an anti-Russian government. Moscow's energy policies and economic statecraft had to be revised to make tangible demands in return for energy subsidies (Makarkin 2010). Although, the Yushchenko administration in Ukraine could take advantage of Russia's disproportionate reliance on Ukraine for transit by siphoning gas from pipelines transiting to Europe. Ukraine's energy blackmail by demanding discounts to prevent it from siphoning gas was to some extent tacitly supported by the EU as an effort to elevate Ukraine's strength vis-à-vis Russia. The West lambasted Russia for using the "energy weapon" by cutting off gas to Ukraine in response to Ukraine siphoning gas off the pipelines. Once Yanukovich won the presidential election in 2010, Russia offered energy discounts in return for tangible rewards such as extending the lease of the naval base in Sevastopol, Crimea. However, by 2014, the West yet again supported the toppling of the Russian-friendly government in Ukraine and replace it with the anti-Russian opposition.

The great energy diversification game between the West and Russia was largely limited to diversifying energy suppliers and transit states. The

EU sought to control the transit states while limiting Russian alternatives through the Black Sea and the Baltic Sea. The EU exports its energy legislation to neighbouring states to control the transit. In a threat to Moldova, the EU Commissioner for Energy warned that "whoever leaves the Energy Community indirectly leaves the partnership with the EU. It becomes the next Belarus" (Keating 2012). Germany, seeking a reliable supply of affordable energy resources and to become a central node in the EU's energy network, constructed Nord Stream 1 pipeline through the Baltic Sea to connect Germany directly with Russia. Bulgaria, a weaker state within the EU, was pressured to abandon construction of the South Stream pipeline through the Black Sea, which Russia replaced with the Turk Stream to Turkey. The more recent Nord Stream 2 pipelines, positioned along a similar underwater route as Nordstream 1, have resisted fierce pressures of cancellation—largely due to the Greater Eurasian Initiative.

The Greater Eurasia Initiative enables Russia to also diversify energy consumers, as opposed to the former rivalry of diversifying suppliers and transit. Interdependence between Europe and Russia has previously been somewhat symmetrical as Europe relies on Russia for supplies, and Russia depends on the EU for demand. The integration of Greater Eurasia skews the symmetry of interdependence between Europe and Russia, in the favour of the latter.

Russia establishes itself as a "swing supplier" with new infrastructure that enables the supply of energy from the same sources to either Europe or Asia (Paik 2018: 133). Russia became a swing supplier of oil in December 2009 with the inauguration of the Eastern Siberian-Pacific Ocean (ESPO) pipeline. After the West supported the coup in Ukraine in February 2014, Russia rushed to sign the $400 billion Power of Siberia gas pipeline with China in May 2014. Putin argued in September 2016 that Gazprom was becoming a swing supplier: "If any problems arise in Europe, we will easily re-direct flows to the East" (Paik 2018: 135).

Oil and gas exports to China are growing rapidly, an opportune partnership between the world's largest energy exporter and importer, and without any transit states. This partnership reduces the ability of the West to apply pressures and conditions for Russian gas, or seek to assert influence over transit states. The West has been pushing for Russia to maintain Ukraine as a gas corridor to give economic gains for Ukraine and strengthen the balance of dependence of Ukraine vis-à-vis Russia. Yet, in the era of Greater Eurasia, Russia can respond to unreliable transit states in Europe by shifting its exports to Asia as Russia relies significantly less on Germany as an export market.

Germany has recognised the limits on pressuring Russia over energy supplies. Greater Eurasia has altered the equations as blocking Nord Stream 2 through the Baltic Sea will not result in the preservation of the pipeline infrastructure through Ukraine. Instead, Russia is rapidly expanding its gas and oil deliveries to the East and thus preparing itself for the EU's self-isolation. The continued obstacles and threats of cancelling Nord Stream 2 have increased the perception in Moscow that the EU has become an unreliable partner, and Russia is unlikely to engage in new pipeline projects in Europe. Merkel recognised that Nord Stream 2 had to be built to prevent pushing Russia further towards China, and due to the diplomatic purpose of maintaining a bridge to Russia (FT 2021).

However, the Europeans have pursued a strategy whereas Nord Stream 2 is conditioned on also preserving the Ukraine corridor (Ischinger 2021). Although, this appears to be a political theatre for the internal European audience to defend the construction of Nord Stream 2. Russia will continue to bring Ukrainian gas transit down to a bare minimum to avoid future pressures, and to reduce the geoeconomic importance of Ukraine as a motivation for Western expansionism.

Transportation corridors

The limited access to European maritime corridors has been an enduring challenge for Russia since the 13th century. The curse and attraction to Eurasia have historically been a reaction to Western efforts to deny Russia access to maritime transportation corridors. In Greater Eurasia, Russia can revive its initiatives from the 19th century to reduce reliance on Western-controlled transportation corridors by developing strategic autonomy over Eurasian transportation corridors.

Russian land-corridors into Europe are connected with East-West land-corridors in cooperation with China's Belt and Road Initiative, and North-South bimodal corridors are established with Iran and India. Yet, Russia's Eurasian transportation routes also gain a strong maritime component. The Northern Sea Route through the Arctic is a leading example of Russia asserting itself in maritime corridors for transit between Europe and Asia, and access to energy resources in the Arctic. In February 2018, Russia passed a law that reserves cabotage in the Russian Arctic to Russian-flagged vessels. The law covers all kind of maritime activity within Russia's exclusive economic zone and continental shelf, which also includes the transportation of energy resources (Moe 2020). The development of the Arctic has focused on energy extraction, which contributes to developing infrastructure that can be also used for transit. Northern European countries such as Finland can be included in the Northern corridor to enhance efficiency and to recruit regional stakeholders. Although, Russia also develops autonomous infrastructure.

Russia aims to strengthen connectivity along its European coastlines by reducing reliance on hostile and unreliable neighbours such as the Baltic States. Geography has historically endowed the Baltic States, especially

Latvian ports, with a favourable position to connect Russia with the Baltic Sea. Yet, with growing traffic from Russia's East-West corridor, it is not conducive to rely on the Baltic States they have positioned themselves as bulwarks against Russia. Russia's construction and modernisation of ports and terminals on Russian territory in the Baltic Sea and the Black Sea have contributed to a drastic decline in the use of ports in the Baltic States (Klyuev 2018).

The reunification with Crimea also strengthens Russia's presence in the Black Sea, although commercial use of Crimean ports has been reduced by Western sanctions. The Crimean port has thus focused on military missions to Syria and Libya, and Crimean ports have also been offered to Iran to skirt US sanctions and piracy.

Russian influence over the Black Sea and the Sea of Azov will have an immense value by connecting the seas with the Eurasian space. At the EAEU summit in May 2018, the president of Kazakhstan proposed the construction of a Eurasia Canal—a shipping corridor along with rivers from the Caspian Sea to the Black Sea (Ma 2018). The corridor could commercially benefit the entire Caspian region and China (Bekturganov and Bolaev 2017). The corridor could be incorporated into the International North-South Corridor as the project gains steam. In contrast, allowing Crimea to fall into the hands of the US and NATO would have marginalised Russia in the Black Sea and the Sea of Azov, undermining Russia's ability to connect the Eurasian heartland with the maritime periphery.

Financial instruments

In the 1990s, Russian foreign policy largely consisted of meeting the conditions of the West to obtain much-needed aid and investments. These days are long gone. Russia has survived two financial crises, of 2008 and 2014, and has been able to work around the sanction regime against its financial sector by developing alternatives. Russia's financial strength derives from fiscal discipline by spending the years of high energy prices to pay down its debts and build up foreign reserves (Miller 2018a). Furthermore, conservative financial policies have limited Russia's vulnerability to market fluctuations.

The financial role the EU previously held in Russia has shifted towards China since the Ukrainian crisis of 2014 as the anti-Russian sanctions left a large market share available to Chinese lenders. The EU's anti-Russian sanctions will remain for the foreseeable future, and the Russian financial industry is experimenting, learning, and adapting to the new financial markets in the East. The EU maintains a larger share of finance in Russia, although China is catching up rapidly (Garcia-Herrero and Xu 2019: 9). In terms of FDI in

Europe, Russia tends to focus its efforts on the Western Balkans, with a particular focus on Serbia and Montenegro.

Russia also began increasing the yuan in its foreign exchange reserves, which assists China in internationalising its currency. While Russia and China are spearheading the use of local currencies, Russia's de-dollarisation initiative is benefitting the EU as the Euro gains a larger share of Russian treasuries. Anti-Russian sanctions initially reduced the value of the Russian ruble, although the depreciation has contributed favourably to the import substitution program and competitiveness of industries required to diversify away from exports of natural resources (World Bank 2016).

Russia's purchase of Volksbank of Austria operations enabled Russia's Sberbank to become the largest bank operating in Eastern Europe (Kramer 2012). Sberbank continued buying Turkey's Denizbank and by 2020 Sberbank remained the second largest European bank by market capitalization.

Sberbank is also contributing to merge Russia's financial power with strategic industries. Sberbank has become a national leader in artificial intelligence and has developed e-commerce platforms, blockchain, cloud technology, virtual reality, mapping service, public transportation payments system, the Internet of Things, and robotics (Sberbank 2018). By 2019, Sberbank added self-driving cars and automated systems for agricultural machinery and trains to its digital economy projects. Subsequently, the Russian financial industry is converging with the tech-industry to develop a sophisticated autonomous domestic digital ecosystem. The transformation of Russian finance and industry to develop autonomous capabilities from Europe is aided by the partnership with China. In 2020, Sberbank announced a strategic partnership with China's Huawei to further develop Russia's digital economy (Marrow 2020).

POLITICAL INFLUENCE

The EU is gradually coming to terms with its diminished influence over Russia and the costs of continued economic coercion. Germany and France both recognise the need to restore functional relations with Moscow to avoid pushing Russia further towards China. Yet, the question remains how relations can be improved. France appears to recognise the need to resolve the underlying problems in Europe—the absence of a mutually acceptable post-Cold War solution that recognises a role for Russia in Europe. In contrast, Germany is more committed to the status-quo and seeks to treat the symptoms or consequences of the zero-sum relations with Russia.

Emmanuel Macron recognised that the enduring divisions on the European continent undermined the capacity for strategic autonomy as EU-Russian relations are hostage to US-Russian relations. Macron (2019) argued for rethinking relations with Russia as "We cannot rebuild Europe without rebuilding a connection with Russia." Macron advocated for Russia's return to the Council of Europe and he supported Trump's efforts to invite Putin to the next G7 meeting, although the latter was unsuccessful. Furthermore, Marcon has argued that "pushing Russia away from Europe is a deep strategic error because we are pushing Russia either to isolation which increases the tensions, or to ally with other great powers like China" (Élysée 2019).

The German Foreign Minister; Heiko Maas (2021) cautioned against continuing on the same path of sanctions as it is "driving Russia and China into each other's arms, and thereby also be creating the largest economic and military alliance in the world. I do not think this should be the West's strategy when critically engaging with Russia."

However, the EU is nonetheless divided as several states in Central and Eastern Europe, mainly Poland and the Baltic States, are content with maintaining severed relations with Russia. This represents continuity as Central and Eastern European states have over the years sabotaged EU-Russian relations (Sakwa 2017). Germany's position remains uncertain as the former status-quo disappears. Germany and Russia have enjoyed a special partnership for decades that contributed to soften Western policies against Moscow. However, the foundation for the partnership has eroded.

Willy Brandt's Ostpolitik began in 1969 to restore the political subjectivity of Germany. As a medium-sized power in the Western bloc, the Germans benefitted from engaging the Soviet Union independently to obtain access to the Eastern bloc. After the Cold War, Germany has prioritised establishing its leadership in Central and Eastern Europe above establishing amicable relations with Russia. Thus, Ostpolitik has been abandoned as an effort to transform European politics by softening bloc politics and instead become an instrument of bloc politics. The German Foreign Minister, Heiko Maas (2020), wrote:

> Unlike Brandt, we no longer have to go via Moscow to talk to our eastern neighbors nowadays. Many partners in Eastern and Central Europe now view Russia very critically—and German foreign policy must take our neighbors' concerns seriously. In addition to offers of dialogue, clear German positions vis-à-vis Moscow are therefore important for maintaining trust in Eastern Europe.

AN AMICABLE DIVORCE: WITHOUT
RUSSIAN RESPECT AND RESENTMENT

Russia's foreign and domestic policies have for centuries been measured in comparison with the West. Russian politics have been defined and divided by central questions such as attempting to get closer to Europe or further away, to advance pro-Western or anti-Western policies. Since Peter the Great's Cultural Revolution, modernisation has been conceived as Europeanising Russia, while preserving Russian traditions and culture meant falling behind on modernisation. The Russian Empires pivot to Asia in former centuries was advanced under the banner of imperialism as Russia and Britain fought for dominance over the supercontinent. The Soviet Union similarly saw itself in the mirror of the West. After the Cold War, Russia's foreign policy was defined by Western-centrism.

The obsession with the West is now drawing to an end due to the changing international distribution of power. The West is no longer the centre of economic and technological development, which disrupts the traditional view of the West. Russia should not define itself as pro-or anti-West, rather the West does not matter anymore to the same extent.

The declining interest in the West can improve relations. A deep-seated resentment in Russia towards the West has grown as a result of continued exclusion from the continent. Resentment derives from a place of respect for the other part, and Kortunov (2019) therefore argues that "resentment is the sincerest form of respect." As Russia's interest and respect for the West continue to dwindle, Moscow's foreign policy will be less influenced by resentment. For the Europeans, the end of Russia's Western-centric domestic and foreign policies will present both opportunities and challenges.

RUSSIA AS AN INTERNATIONAL
CONSERVATIVE POWER

Russia does not enjoy the economic capabilities and reputation of China, yet the ability to diversify away from excessive reliance on Western economies culminates in soft power. Russia relies less and less on the EU and without any aspirations for Greater Europe it has no reason to accept intrusive interference into its domestic affairs under the auspices of promoting democracy and human rights.

The EU developed on the premise that commitment to political liberalism was imperative for economic development. European countries exhausted by the excesses of liberalism over the past decades often view Russian conservatism favourably. As the liberal international order recast the former capitalist-communist divide into an ideological liberal-authoritarian divide, Russia has sought to alter the discussion to a liberal-conservative discourse with a natural and traditional middle ground. Russia's conservative agenda in Europe seemingly aims to establish a more favourable and tenable foundation for relations between equals as opposed to attempting to subvert the West (Sakwa 2020). Case in point, Putin preferred the social conservative François Fillon rather than Marine Le Pen in the 2017 French presidential election (Sakwa 2020).

Russia returned to its conservative roots under Putin—an ideological inclination that has defined most of Russian history (Robinson 2019). Conservatism is devoted to managing change as the new must be built on the foundations of the old, which is the anti-thesis to revolutionary change when the past is uprooted to give way to the new (Diesen 2021b). After the revolutionary decades under communism, Russia had strong domestic needs to revive traditional social institutions such as the Orthodox Church, the nation, culture, and traditions. As Solzhenitsyn (1978: 26) had cautioned, both communism and liberalism were on unsustainable paths by neglecting spiritual life following the industrial revolution: "In the East, [Our spiritual life] is destroyed by the dealings and machinations of the ruling party. In the West, commercial interests tend to suffocate it. This is the real crisis." Russian conservatives are also deeply critical of liberals as they share the communists' neglect of the traditional and spiritual, as evident by the belief in universal values for "transcending classes" and "transcending the nation" (Lukin 2000: 194). Moscow considers the ills of "Communist Man" that degraded Russia to currently manifest itself in "Western Man," seeking to be liberated from his own past and constraining social structure, which will also produce cultural, spiritual, and political decay. Putin (2013a) scorned the undesirable path of the West:

> We see that many Euro-Atlantic states have taken the way where they deny or reject their own roots, including their Christian roots which form the basis of Western civilization. In these countries, the moral basis and any traditional identity are being denied—national, religious, cultural, and even gender identities are being denied or relativised.

In an interview at the G20 meeting in June 2019, President Putin expressed his belief that the ideology of structuring society solely around liberal ideals had failed:

> The liberal idea has become obsolete. It has come into conflict with the interests of the overwhelming majority of the population . . . Deep inside, there must be

some fundamental human rules and moral values. In this sense, traditional values are more stable and more important for millions of people than this liberal idea, which, in my opinion, is really ceasing to exist (FT 2019a).

Russian Eurasianism paradoxically enhances its ideological appeal in Europe. By embracing its Eurasian traditions and developing a geoeconomic strategy for Greater Eurasia, Russia can balance the preservation of traditional values with economic modernisation. Russia's conservative message, criticising the excesses of liberalism, has been well received among traditional conservatives and populists in Europe. The sentiment on the new political right in Europe was expressed by Salvini, the former Deputy Prime Minister of Italy, who wore a t-shirt of Putin in the European Parliament and later proclaimed: "I feel at home in Russia in a way that I don't in other European countries" (Squires 2018).

The efforts to establish common ground on conservative ideals would entail Europe adapting to Russia by abandoning liberal internationalism in favour of political and social conservatism. The implications of this development can hardly be overstated as it "would be 1989 in reverse," with the West rather than Russia, which has to "go through a traumatic conversion to foreign ideas" (Maçães 2019).

CONCLUSION

When we are confronted with the consequences of our own choices, the last thing we want is to be reminded of what we asked for. Yet, the efforts to exclude Russia from Europe after the Cold War have resulted in Russia looking towards the East for strategic partnerships.

A principal assumption of geoeconomic regions is that economic dependence is followed by political loyalties. Russia's marginal position at the periphery of Europe demanded profound asymmetrical interdependence and was based on the assumption that Russia's weakness in the 1990s would perpetuate. The economic revival of Russia from the early 2000s changed the balance of dependence and conflicts have since focused on Russia attempting to use the improved symmetry to negotiate its accommodation in Greater Europe, while the EU has sought to restore the former asymmetries.

The Greater Eurasia Initiative is a reaction to the asymmetrical relations between the collective West vis-à-vis Russia. The key objective of Eurasian Russia in Europe is thus to skew the balance of dependence by becoming less reliant on Europe, and ideally making Europe more dependent on Russia. However, the objective of Greater Eurasia is to end Russia's Western-centricism rather than merely altering relations with Europe.

Russia's Greater Eurasian orientation signifies the abandonment of the Greater Europe Initiative and thus challenging the Helsinki Accords it was founded upon. Europe and Russia are thus without a format for cooperation for the foreseeable future, which limits the scope for diplomatic solutions at a time the world undergoes a dramatic transformation.

Should Russia's Greater Eurasia be an inter-regional initiative with the EU for mutual legitimacy or common gain, or a project where each side seeks to delegitimise and fragment the other region? The EU's accusations of Russian efforts to divide the EU while concurrently refusing to even establish diplomatic relations with the EAEU are indicative of the current disorder and incompatible expectations. A Russian-European partnership would restore stability in Europe positioned between the trans-Atlantic region and Greater Eurasia. As Russia inhabits a central middle position at a time when global power is organised around a US-Chinese rivalry, the Europeans have a lot to lose from failing to reach a mutually acceptable political settlement with Russia that was never achieved after the Cold War.

8

The Three Levels of Trans-Atlantic Fragmentation

The influence of the Greater Eurasian region on Europe depends on the extent to which the existing regions of the West are robust and enjoy internal cohesion. The rise of Greater Eurasia occurs as the trans-Atlantic region fragments on three levels: First, North America and Europe are decoupling; second, Europe is fragmenting between North and South as well as between West and East; third, individual states are polarising as liberalism decouples from the nation-state.

International institutions and geoeconomic regions are a reflection of power, and the EU emerged under hegemony and a liberal international system. European unity was first established after the Second World War under the bipolar international distribution of power to balance the Soviet bloc, and then the Europeans adapted to the unipolar era by seeking equal partnership with the US for collective hegemony in the pan-European space and the wider world. The dual trans-Atlantic and European region enter uncharted waters as interests diverge under a multipolar distribution.

The rise of China incentivises the US to shift its focus away from Europe and towards the Indo-Pacific region, while at the same time demanding greater geoeconomic loyalties for its security guarantees to the extent any resemblance of EU strategic autonomy falters. The EU's relations with China are defined less by zero-sum considerations due to mere geography, and the EU will therefore prioritise an autonomous foreign policy. However, the EU itself has been organised as a collective hegemony in partnership with the US, which has been a key source of its ability to deliver tangible goods to its member states. The efforts to continuously widen and deepen the integration of Europe has left the region fragile. The EU being the only game in town enables Brussels to ignore dissent within the EU today its federalist push towards a homogenised supranational union. These problems were already simmering towards the surface and will further intensify as member states have alternatives in a multipolar world.

This chapter first explores the decoupling of the trans-Atlantic region. A benign hegemon provides collective goods for states within its region in return for political loyalty towards the hegemonic system. In the multipolar era, the US has fewer resources to buy political influence, and its political allies have more to lose from selling their political allegiance. Second, the EU's existing problems are intensifying as the cost-benefit calculations of loyalty towards the union are changed. The EU demands excessive and often unnecessary compliance by member states as a cost to sovereignty, while its ability to deliver material benefits declines. Last, after decades under a neoliberal economic system and excessive political liberalism, the member states themselves are polarising as liberalism and conservatism become less compatible in Western societies. It is subsequently concluded that unity in the West has been weakened remarkably, which creates incentives for militarising disputes with external rivals to boost internal cohesion.

FRAGMENTATION OF THE TRANS-ATLANTIC REGION

The French President, Emmanuel Macron, recognised the need for Europe to adapt to the multipolar world, and acknowledged that "we are undoubtedly experiencing the end of Western hegemony over the world" (Élysée 2019). Macron opined that in a world increasingly divided between the US and China, Europe cannot simply become a political object by positioning itself under the leadership of one side. Macron cautioned against an untenable European vassalage status under the US and even pointed to differences in values and humanism. The EU would also need to reassert its strategic autonomy through geoeconomic regionalism, as Macron called for reducing dependence on foreign technologies and the US dollar (Élysée 2019). While France has always had internal Gaullist impulses, the tone set by the French president also responds to systemic pressures.

The rise of China has become a key source in the divisions between the US and the EU. For the US, China is seen as a direct competitor that must be challenged, while the EU does not have the same zero-sum calculations with a more distant economic partner. The US demands more geoeconomic loyalty from the EU, yet is less capable of offering material support as its relative power declines and its focus shifts towards Asia. Thus, the US will pursue a strategy aimed to uphold its hegemonic position, while the EU will see an increased need to establish sovereign autonomy. As expressed by French President, Macron, the EU must pursue an independent foreign policy to "prevent the Chinese-American duopoly," as "we are not the United States of America." Macron continued: "It is therefore not tenable that our international policy should be dependent on it [the United States] or be trailing behind it. And what I am saying is even truer for China" (FR 2020).

The US 2018 Annual Report to Congress identified that China uses economic statecraft to sow divisions between the US and its allies (US Congress 2018: 304). While this is undoubtedly true, the mere shift towards a multipolar distribution of power contributes to decouple Europe and the US.

The US and Europe have since the Second World War developed a shared geoeconomic region. Whilst the balance of power of the trans-Atlantic region was profoundly asymmetrical following the Second World War, it has incrementally gravitated towards equilibrium as the Europeans developed collective bargaining power by deepening and widening European integration. The US-European balancing act between cooperation and competition has tilted mostly in favour of the former due to common interests. During the bipolar distribution of power during the Cold War there was a shared interest to balance the Soviet Union and in the ensuing unipolar era, the West has established a common purpose of collective hegemony to advance the so-called liberal international order.

The US-led international system created a dilemma between the external and internal distribution of power. The need to strengthen the Western alliance contributed to a favourable external balance of power vis-à-vis its Soviet and Chinese adversaries, albeit the security umbrella and delivery of collective goods as a benign hegemon entailed a wealth transfer within the US-led alliance system.

President Truman and Eisenhower considered trade concessions to allies as preferable to aid, which culminated in several asymmetrical trade agreements that were designed to develop strong allies. The transfer of productive capabilities from the US to its allies were justified by the external challenges. As Eisenhower argued to congressional leaders: "all problems of local industry pale into insignificance in relation to the world crisis" (Eckes 2015: 64). Eisenhower had previously also cautioned against the economic burden of an enduring security presence in Europe, as opposed to making the security guarantees a temporary subsidy to develop Western European military capabilities to restore a natural balance of power in Europe. Eisenhower argued in 1951: "If in ten years, all American troops stationed in Europe for national defence purposes have not been returned to the United States, then this whole project will have failed" (Carpenter 1992: 12).

For the US, which developed its geoeconomic strength under the economic nationalism of the American System, free-trade agreements that undercut US industrial strength was controversial. The hegemonic responsibilities in the trans-Atlantic region began to tear away at the US by the mid-1960s. Already by the 1950s, the unilateral tariff reduction by the US for its capitalist allies were imperative to achieve foreign policy objectives, albeit preserving US strength demanded further import restrictions (Eckes 1995). A report by the US Senate Finance Committee argued:

> Throughout most of the postwar era, U.S. trade policy has been the orphan of U.S. foreign policy. Too often the Executive has granted trade concessions to accomplish political objectives. Rather than conducting U.S. international economic relations on sound economic and commercial principles, the executive has set trade and monetary policy in a foreign aid context (Senate Reports 1974).

US leadership in the trans-Atlantic region became unsustainable as generous trade agreements transferred productive power to allies and eroded US trade surplus. Without a trade surplus, the US was also less able to finance foreign aid and military expenditures as two other vital means for sustaining US leadership in the world. The loss of productive power also eroded financial power. The growing US trade deficit incentivised the Western European allies to convert a weakened dollar into gold. Security dependence on the US had temporarily been translated into geoeconomic loyalty as the Western Europeans recognised that exchanging dollars for gold would undermine the trans-Atlantic alliance. Although, economic interests eventually dictate policy and the US supply of gold began to shrink. Thus, the IMF introduced the Special Drawing Rights (SDRs) in 1969 as an alternative reserve currency to bolster the financial system. In August 1971, Nixon closed the gold window as the fixed conversion rate between the US dollar and gold was suspended. The US ending a key obligation of the Bretton Woods system made the principal trade-and reserve currency in the trans-Atlantic region a fiat currency.

The US responded to the diminished trust in the US dollar by transitioning from the gold-dollar to the petrodollar. In 1973, US secretary of State Henry Kissinger negotiated a deal with Saudi Arabia to exclusively sell oil in US dollars, and in return, the US committed its military to provide security for the Saudis. In 1975, the Gulf States joined the petrodollar system and the US dollar subsequently became the sole currency for energy trade, which sustained its central role for all international trade and thus also the role as a reserve currency. The petrodollar recycling-system further militarised US geoeconomics, making the US more reliant on overt coercion as opposed to the more covert influence of economic dependence. At the end of the Second World War, the US had primarily been a geoeconomic power, but in the confrontation with a communist Soviet adversary largely decoupled from economic statecraft, the US became increasingly reliant on military power (Blackwill and Harris 2016: 167).

To ensure the collective strength and internal cohesion of the trans-Atlantic region, the US provided its support to Western European integration from the establishment of the Coal and Steel Community, the European Economic Community, and the European Union. Yet, the Western European sub-region of the trans-Atlantic region gradually developed its own geoeconomic capabilities. Western European states pursued aggressive industrial policies to develop strategic industries. Case in point, heavy investments were made in the form of subsidies to develop competencies in the airline industry. Airbus Industrie penetrated the US market with subsidies, at one point leasing out twenty-three of its A300 airliners to US Eastern Air Lines for $1 per year: "Just as in the past when young men were put in uniform to be marched off in pursuit of schemes of territorial conquest, today taxpayers are persuaded to subsidize schemes of industrial conquest" (Luttwak 2010: 34). While the European taxpayers subsidised cheap airfares for American consumers as a short term investment, industrial capacity was transferred to Europe as a long term industrial gain. European airlines rose to become world-leaders and Germany used the same industrial policies to develop cars, communications, superconductor, and other strategic industries (Luttwak 2010: 34). In 2011, Germany first began discussing its *Industry 4.0* industrial policy to digitalise industrial production and thus get a head-start on the Fourth Industrial Revolution.

TRANS-ATLANTIC DISUNITY IN GREATER EURASIA

As the unipolar era has drawn to an end and a multipolar international order asserts itself, the foundation for the convergence of interests and policies in the trans-Atlantic community erodes. The *quid pro quo* of economic benefits in return for political influence loses its foundation, which has been at the geoeconomic foundation of the relationship between the benign hegemon delivering collective goods.

Meanwhile, the multipolar distribution of power incentivises the Europeans to assert strategic autonomy as opposed to retreating under US patronage as it did during the Cold War. Europe, which gains less from the trans-Atlantic partnership, must develop an independent foreign policy towards China and the East to bolster its strategic autonomy and not be demoted to a US vassal. Brexit also represents a blow to the trans-Atlantic partnership as Britain had a central role in ensuring that Europe did not drift away from the trans-Atlantic region. For Brussels, multipolarity implies that the US will become more adversarial in its geoeconomic policies, and the same applies to post-Brexit Britain.

The rapid shift of power from the West to the East has precipitated the US to shift its focus to Asia, thus the US has less to gain from the transfer of economic power to Europe by paying for its security and accepting the economic rivalry. This was expressed by Obama's "pivot to Asia" in 2010 that aimed to balance the rise of China (CRS 2012), which intensified under the Trump administration by launching a trade war against China.

Although, the Obama and Trump strategies towards containing China differed in terms of the dilemma between prioritising the external or internal balance of dependence. Obama prioritised leading a strong alliance to counter its adversaries, at the cost of transferring economic power to its allies. Trump was more concerned about the unsustainability of the shifting balance of dependence within the US-led alliances, as the US was seen to crumble by transferring economic power from the American centre to the periphery in Europe and East Asia.

Obama aimed to mobilise the Indo-Pacific region under US leadership to subvert the geoeconomic power of China, which was complemented by the military balancing of China with augmented forward deployments and enhancing the military competencies of its East Asian allies. Obama initiated the development of the Trans-Pacific Partnership (TPP) to unite the region under US geoeconomic leadership and thus limit the role of China. Yet, while Obama shifted focus towards East Asia, he also sought to maintain US power in Europe with the proposed Transatlantic Trade and Investment Partnership (TTIP), which would unite the trans-Atlantic region against Russia. US Secretary of State, Hillary Clinton, even referred to TTIP as an "economic NATO" (Oreskes 2016).

In contrast, Trump was concerned that the transfer of economic strength from the US to its allies was a losing strategy as the reduced relative economic power and domestic disruptions in the US limited the ability to confront China. Trump withdrew the US from NAFTA, while effectively cancelling both the TPP and TTIP.

Without common interests naturally aligning policies, the US becomes more dependent on economic coercion against the Europeans. To recalibrate the relationship between the US and its allies, Trump hit the Europeans with countermeasure tariffs on various products to punish the Europeans for subsidising Airbus in the rivalry with Boeing (Donnan, Ryan, and Stearns 2020). The Trump administration also demonstrated hostility towards the EU as an economic rival, by openly supporting Brexit and advocating further disintegration.

Trump aimed to develop a return on investment by seeking pragmatic and transactional relationships where the US would convert security dependence into tangible geoeconomic loyalty. The policy change resembled Russia's decision to remove energy subsidies for neighbouring states in 2009 and instead demand tangible benefits in return for subsidies, as political loyalties did not naturally emerge. A *quid pro quo* was demanded during the NATO Summit in July 2018, as Trump told the NATO Secretary-General in no uncertain terms that the US expected the continent to buy American LNG rather than Russian gas in return for financing European security: "We're supposed to protect you from Russia, but Germany is making pipeline deals with Russia. You tell me if that's appropriate. Explain that" (Keating 2018). Similarly, the US threatens European states that include Huawei in the development of 5G infrastructure with reduced intelligence sharing and economic sanctions.

The Biden administration does not have a clear answer to the dilemma of the US, as a shrinking power. Biden seeks to restore the US leadership among allies that distrust US capabilities and intentions. The US has scaled back sanctions against Nord Stream 2 and in March 2021, the US and EU agreed to suspend tariffs in the Airbus-Boeing dispute. While relations with the Europeans stabilise, it can be interpreted as a temporary concession by the US as the relationship between the benign hegemon and allies have not been reformed. The Europeans will still seek to develop strategic autonomy, while the US will see its relative economic power continue to decline.

Furthermore, the world has moved on. While the US and EU began negotiating TTIP in 2013, a European Council decision in April 2019 stated it was effectively cancelled this initiative was officially cancelled as "negotiating directives for the TTIP are obsolete and no longer relevant" (European Council 2019b: 2). Instead, the EU and China agreed on the EU-China Comprehensive Agreement on Investment (CAI) in January 2021. The future of TPP is similarly obstructed as the Asia-Pacific region moved on. In November 2020, China signed the Regional Comprehensive Economic Partnership (RCEP) trade deal with 14 other Asia-Pacific economies, which was a Chinese-led rival to the US-led TPP. Hence, the EU's engagement in the pan-European space and East Asia will demand an autonomous position from the US.

There are indications that while the Biden administration is more capable of mobilising the Europeans than his predecessor, he is less prepared to take on China directly in an economic war. The US is a corporate state, defined by the excessive influence of corporations over the state, which enables China to influence Washington through Wall Street. As a prominent and influential professor in China boasted—with the return of Biden, China could rely on a network of "our old friends who are at the top of America's core inner circle of power and influence" (Jacobs 2020). While the US-China decoupling is beneficial for Europe to the extent they can catch additional market share, it is nonetheless beneficial for reduced tensions to reduce US pressure of displaying geoeconomic loyalties.

The Biden administration has suggested that the US will not demand that the Europeans pick a side and can freely engage with China. However, this seems disingenuous as the US actively uses sanctions against Russia and

China, and then Washington denounced the ensuing counter-sanctions as economic coercion that must be confronted collectively by the West:

> we must not separate economic coercion from other forms of pressure. When one of us is coerced, we should respond as allies and work together to reduce our vulnerability by ensuring our economies are more integrated with each other than they are with our principal competitors (Blinken 2021).

EUROPE DISTANCES ITSELF FROM THE US

The EU itself is deeply divided on the decoupling from the US. Some argue that EU-US unity to preserve the internal cohesion of the trans-Atlantic region, which is imperative to meet the challenges from the rise of new poles of power with different values and uncertain foreign policy ambitions. Others recognise that as unipolarity erodes, the Europeans cannot simply retreat under US patronage and thus forfeit decades of European region-building. This is especially important in a multipolar world as EU interests diverge from the US.

From a geoeconomic perspective, the EU's strategic autonomy is a condition for preserving the partnership with the US; a balance of dependence is a vital condition for a tolerable and enduring trans-Atlantic region. While extremely asymmetrical ties with the US would demote the Europeans to American vassals, it would also incentivise Eurasian powers to engage in fierce wedge tactics in Europe.

The unilateral US withdrawal from the Iran nuclear agreement (JCPOA) demonstrated the vassalage status of the EU as Washington imposed sanctions on European countries that would still honour their obligations under the international agreement. The former Swedish Prime Minister, Carl Bildt (2018), even referred to the US decision as a "massive attack" on Europe. While much of the loss of trust was caused by the brazenness of Trump, it is also necessary to recognise that Trump was a symptom of changing international distribution of power as US policies will not change significantly under other administrations.

The Europeans have sought to decouple security from geoeconomics. Irrespective of threats of US sanctions, several European states have joined China's Belt and Road Initiative, Germany engages in a tech-partnership with China and approves the Nord Stream 2 pipeline, Turkey buys the Russian S-400 missile system, and most of Europe has joined the Asian Infrastructure Investment Bank (AIIB). Almost four-fifths of Germans prefer not taking sides in the US-China economic conflict (Keqin 2021), which is an indication that political loyalties are weakening as economic interests diverge.

THE GROWING DIVISIONS IN EUROPE

Geoeconomic regionalism explains the initial strong foundation for European integration, and the more recent fragmentation of Europe between the North and South, and the East and West. The strength of the US derived from the Single Market and the Schengen Treaty. The EU's decline derives from an overextension caused by two flawed policies—the Euro and excessive enlargements (Münchau 2015). Both initiatives further strengthen the geo-economic power of the EU as the common currency represents a "deepening" of integration, while successive enlargement signifies the "widening" of European integration. However, both initiatives upset the internal balance of dependence within the EU.

THE COMMON CURRENCY

The Euro was largely a federalist initiative aimed to transition the EU from a balance of dependence between nation-states, to the United States of Europe. A political union is required to develop a financial union, and a fiscal union is necessary for a monetary union. Without the consensus for a political union, the EU began at the other end with a monetary union that created structural flaws that could only be solved with a fiscal union, and a fiscal union would demand political integration (Feldstein 2012). The Euro was thus designed as a "half-built house" (Bergsten 2012), a flawed economic project creating a chain reaction towards political union (Padoa-Schioppa 2004; Spolaore 2013).

The Euro has instigated geoeconomic rivalries between EU members, which has concentrated power in Germany. First, the federalist impulse had not achieved political consent, which fuelled resentment in countries such as Britain that aspires for functionalist integration—when the function of integration informs the form of Europe as opposed to a federalist approach when the centralised form of Europe informs its functions (Mitrany 1965). The eventual departure of Britain from the EU further disrupted the balance of dependence within the bloc as power concentrated in Germany.

Second, a common currency for vastly different economies has caused a tremendous transfer of productive power and wealth. The Euro becomes a deeply devalued currency for Germany, which contributes significantly to a positive trade gap as German exports are more competitive and local industries have greater protection from imports. The Euro is thus commonly presented as the equivalent of German currency manipulation akin to that of China (Mattich 2011; Baru 2012; Krugman 2013). The weak currency has been supplemented by economic statecraft as Germany "coordinates constant discussions between labour, government, and industry to arrive at agreements on wages, investment, productivity gains, and prices that will assure continued competitiveness to producers based in Germany" (Prestowitz 2012). While Germany pursues a neo-mercantilist export-based economy based on production and saving, the Mediterranean EU members have been demoted to an economic model of borrowing and spending. The Euro prevents weakened economies from devaluing their national currencies to price their way back into the market. The first chief economist of the European Central Bank, Otmar Issing, labelled the Euro a "house of cards" that would unavoidably collapse (Evans-Pritchard 2016).

The Euro's logic of a chain reaction replaces the carrot with a stick as the driving force for integration. The current state of the EU and the Euro is not sustainable, and the Union must either integrate further towards fiscal union and political union or proceed with an orderly disintegration process and return to national currencies. Amid an economic crisis caused by the EU and the Euro, it is proving difficult to sell the message that "more Europe" is the solution. Similarly, the ability of Germany to present itself as the solution to systemic problems as an economic locomotive to pull the EU out of an economic crisis is paradoxical, as member states recognise that Germany is also a key problem (Veebel 2015: 225).

As the EU stumbles from crisis to crisis and excitement about the European project dwindles, Germany becomes increasingly reliant on using its asymmetrical power to extract political concession and use economic sticks to punish member states that deviate from the project (Stockhammer 2014; Brattberg and De Lima 2015; Stiglitz 2016). Preserving unity through pressure worked in Greece, although it will prove more difficult with larger Mediterranean states that linger towards economic crisis, most importantly Italy. By relying excessively on coercion, the EU replicates the weakness of the Napoleonic Continental System.

Germany's image is subsequently worsened in Eastern and Southern Europe, with unflattering historical references of German dominance becoming increasingly common. During the first months of the Covid-19 outbreak in 2020, in which Italy did not receive assistance from the EU, 59 percent of Italians stated that the EU no longer makes sense. Furthermore, the majority of Italians characterised China as a friend, while almost half of the Italians labelled Germany an enemy (Follain and Migliaccio 2020).

ENLARGEMENTS

Successive rounds of enlargements contribute also contributed to skew the balance of dependence within the EU as the German economy has benefitted the most. More importantly, enlargements have made the geoeconomic bloc less homogenous, which causes socio-economic disruption to the extent the EU cannot act as a unitary actor. The weaker economies in Central and Eastern Europe has resulted in economic transfers going from West to East, while labour is transferred from the East to the West. The predictable consequence has been Western European states criticising wealth transfer and demographic changes causing a surge in nationalism, while Eastern Europe experiences a disastrous demographic decline and loss of skilled labour.

Meanwhile, internal cohesion further erodes as the ability of Western European states to manage the Central and Eastern European states declines. The US and the EU believed that Eastern European nationalism could be mitigated with inclusion into the trans-Atlantic region. Initially, this assumption was correct as membership in the trans-Atlantic region laid the foundation for a broad political consensus for a smoother transition to capitalism and democracy. Eastern European desired to join NATO and the EU that shielded them from Moscow influence and enabled them to seek historical vengeance on Russia. Yet, once membership was attained, there was less incentive to accept lecturing from Washington and Brussels. Poland and Hungary are especially standing out in terms of challenging the authority of Brussels. Poland began diversifying its economy following the global financial crisis to reduce reliance on Germany as Berlin became increasingly assertive.

Concerned about the excessive liberalism of the EU, Poland and Hungary have spearheaded an alternative concept of "Europe" that reproduces the traditions and cultural distinctiveness of Europe as a limitation on liberal universalism. Furthermore, playing second-fiddle to Western European states within the EU incentivised Eastern European states to diversify ties. The Prime Minister of Hungary, Victor Orban, displayed the changing sentiment as he argued liberal democracies "will not be able to sustain their world-competitiveness in the following years . . . today, the stars of international analyses are Singapore, China, India, Turkey, Russia." An identity shift is also evident as Orban indicates the embrace of turanism, a unique strand of Hungarian nationalism that identifies Hungary as a successor of the Huns. As Orban announced: "Hungarians see themselves as the late descendants of Attila the Hun" (MTI 2018).

OPPOSITION: ADAPTING OR KICKING
THE CAN DOWN THE ROAD?

The problem of different interests of EU member states is exacerbated under a multipolar international distribution of power. Dissent could previously be ignored in the unipolar era, while in the multipolar era the member states can look to alternative centres of power.

Socio-economic and political differences can be accommodated in a multi-track Europe to maximise the benefits of membership and minimise the costs. The advocates of "more Europe" present a false dichotomy that suggests accommodating differences within the bloc will weaken the geoeconomic bloc. Advocates of a homogenous supranational union can fuel internal divisions and resentment that can be exploited by external actors, while the aspiration for homogeneity reduces the internal vigour of the region. The geoeconomic region consists of states with various socio-economic and political systems and differing cultures.

The EU's federalist approach has tended to treat political opposition as a problem to be overcome. The ideological struggle towards overcoming its own nation-state past, resistance towards further integration has been viewed as remnants of a bygone era. Referendums that did not get the desired result were either run again or ignored, a problem the EU sought to avoid by merely ending the use of referendums. By ignoring rather than resolving differences within the EU, problems begin to fester.

The attitude towards dissent was exemplified by a speech by Václav Klaus, the president of the Czech Republic in the European Parliament. Klaus expressed his commitment to the European Union and that his country considered no alternatives. However, Klaus (2009) opined that "the methods on forms of European integration do, on the contrary, have quite a number of possible and legitimate variants" and he denounced the efforts to monopolise on the concept of European integration and the attempts by some to be "the owner of the keys" to European integration. In response to President Klaus's request for more debate around the format for European integration, half of the MEPs in the European Parliament marched out in protest.

The geoeconomic glue that holds the EU together is weakening as evident by the UK vision of a future "global Britain" by severing its institutional connections with an EU in relative decline. From Greece, Italy to Hungary, maintaining loyalty towards Washington and Brussels against Beijing and Moscow is becoming an economic burden. Even Germany's growing economic interests in the east are influencing its political considerations. Divergent interests gradually tear away at the trans-Atlantic relationship and the internal cohesion within the EU.

Without the geoeconomic foundations for internal cohesion, the EU will become increasingly reliant on coercion against its own members to ensure the ability of the EU to act as a sovereign entity of power. Mitrany's (1965) thesis of federalist versus functionalist formats for integration concluded that European integration should be functionalist by only being pursued in areas where it augments sovereignty of the member states by strengthening the economic, security and political power of the member states. Mitrany (1965) cautioned against the federalist approach that made the centralisation of power the principal objective as this would dictate the form of European integration. Without the functionalist foundation, the federalist approach would become too reliant on coercion by not delivering tangible benefits to its neighbour.

Hence, Mitrany (1965: 130–1) cautioned federalist European integration would "introduce the factor of fixity in the index of power" and resemble the federal system of the Soviet Union rather than the United States. The fallacy of unity and harmony through one-track supranationalism was also a key flaw in the Soviet system. However, a more appropriate comparison may have been the Napoleonic Continental System that became excessively reliant on coercion to uphold loyalties.

Considering the nation-state as a competing centre of power represents a dangerous mindset, as the effort to marginalise the nation-state then imposes unnecessary costs to sovereignty, which ultimately weakens the EU. There appears to be growing awareness in Brussels that federalist ideologies conflict with geoeconomic realities, which is counter-productive, as the deliberate effort to minimise national sovereignty unnecessarily increases the cost of EU membership and thus reduces political loyalties. The President of the European Council, Donald Tusk (2016), recognised that the view of the elite of Europe does not enjoy popular support among the peoples of Europe:

> It is us who today are responsible for confronting reality with all kinds of utopias. A utopia of Europe without nation-states, a utopia of Europe without conflicting interests and ambitions, a utopia of Europe imposing its own values on the external world. A utopia of a Euro-Asian unity. Obsessed with the idea of instant and total integration, we failed to notice that ordinary people, the citizens of Europe do not share our Euro-enthusiasm. Disillusioned with the great visions of the future, they demand that we cope with the present reality better than we have been doing until now.

A strong functionalist case can be made for integrating the economic power of the EU under multipolarity to enhance collective autonomy and influence, which is weakened by obsessions about federalist integration. The shared economic interests thus substitute the need for centralised control.

POLARISATION OF THE NATION-STATE

Domestic socio-economic stability is an important element of geoeconomic analysis as the ability of the state to act as a unitary actor depends on domestic cohesion. The failure to organise society undermines the ability to mobilise resources to pursue strategic interests in the international system.

Managing industrial society has been difficult since the industrial revolution created the conditions for a market economy. Polanyi (1944) famously noted that the market economy created a schism in human nature and society as the market economy is disembedded from society. Both the political Left and the political Right respond to flaws in the market economy and recognise the social responsibility of the state to intervene in the market to restrain the excesses of economic liberalism. The political Left recognises that the balance between capital and labour is unstable in a capitalist society as power gravitates towards the former, which is why redistribution is required to ensure the vast majority of the population remain a self-interested stakeholder in the economic system. On the political Left there are thus initiatives such as workers Unions to organise the collective strength of labour to balance the symmetry with capital. On the political Right, there has traditionally been an effort to restrain the excesses of the free-market to mitigate the impact of creative destruction and unfettered market forces on the ability to reproduce traditional communities and values. Thus, on the political Right there has traditionally been an effort to prevent economic determinism to ensure that social institutions such as the family, Church, community, and culture do not get washed away due to their lack of economic utility. Polanyi (1944: 239) opined that the failure to manage industrial capitalism had given birth to two extreme political ideologies—communism on the political Left and fascism on the political Right.

After the Second World War, the unity of the capitalist bloc was established based on compatible values—accepting various forms of capitalism. The capitalism of the West from 1945 to the 1980s can be defined as "embedded liberalism" as it balanced market efficiency with the social responsibilities of the political Left and Right (Ruggie 1982). The state was therefore endowed with a central role to mitigate creative destruction from new technologies and unrestrained market forces (Luttwak 1993).

However, political legitimacy after the Second World War became excessively reliant on continuous economic growth, which created great pressure during economic downturns. The economic stagnation and corrections of the 1970s created strong pressures for boosting the economy by enhancing market efficiency at the expense of the social responsibilities of the political Left and Right. Reaganism and Thatcherism revolutionised and corrupted the concept of conservatism and the political economy of the Right as the free-market became the leading principle. Reagan (1984) recognised the imperative of preserving traditional values, communities, and the central role of the Church to prevent from getting "mired in the material," as it would culminate in the "coarsening of the society" and eventually a "nation gone under." Although, by accepting society to be moulded by unfettered market forces, any references to family values and traditional communities would merely become a superficial culture war as opposed to anything meaningful. The hollowing out of the political Right was aptly summarised in the manifesto of Ted Kaczynski (1995: 7):

> They whine about the decay of traditional values, yet they enthusiastically support technological progress and economic growth. Apparently it never occurs to them that you can't make rapid, drastic changes in the technology and the economy of a society without causing rapid changes in all other aspects of society as well, and that such rapid changes inevitably break down traditional values.

The political Left followed the path of the political Right by embracing unfettered market forces, and thus foregoing its ideological commitments to redistributing wealth. The concept of economic justice was largely abandoned by the Clinton administration, which began to destine itself from unions and redistribution (Rorty 1998). The repeal of the Glass-Steagall Act by the Clinton administration eliminated the separation between investment banking and commercial banking, which deregulated the finance industry and set the conditions in place for the financial crisis of 2008 that devastated the middle class.

A neoliberal consensus established itself as both the political Right and Left abandoned their social responsibility in favour of economic competitiveness in the international system. Europe, largely reinventing itself in the image of America, followed the path towards the neoliberalism consensus. After the Cold War, the common identity of the trans-Atlantic region and Europe became even more reliant on a shared liberal identity. The former morality of state ownership and state intervention was discredit and became immoral under the liberal West. While the state had previously been assigned the role of a guarantor of public interest, the state has since become a symbol of corruption, inefficiency, and technological inertia (Luttwak 1993). Neoliberalism was introduced at a dangerous time as the digital economy created a demand for a flexible labour market and fewer regulations and worker protection. The intensification of globalisation was creating intolerable social costs, while the removal of trade barriers between vastly different economies was placing downward pressures on salaries at a time when the overall world economy was growing (Rodrik 1997).

The radical international division of labour further disembedded the economy as the US was treated as an economy instead of a society. The technology elite and financial elite in cosmopolitan regions thrived, while the manufacturing class was gutted. The free-market logic has assumed that outsourcing jobs would enable the US to direct its capital and labour to more productive areas. However, the workers belonging to the traditional economy were directed towards low-skilled and low-paid jobs that did not provide the same status and meaning. The socio-economic polarisation of the country began to tear away at the middle class and undermine the resilience and unity of society (Luttwak 2010). The uneven distribution of economic power within the US fuelled radical alternatives as social mobility diminished and a growing part of the population no longer stakeholders in the status quo. Macron cautioned that political and economic liberalism had reduced poverty and integrated the global economy, yet it had also brought society to a "break point" (FR 2020).

The global financial crisis of 2008 became a breaking point for societies across the West as the solution was the greatest wealth transfer from the middle class to the super-rich. Instead of allowing the market to eliminate bad debts with bankruptcies of banks and states, there was a toxic combination of bail-outs and austerity. Fiscal stimulus has continued since the global financial crisis as a clear indication of the immeasurable challenge to resolve the financial system. Low rates are causes of malinvestments in the economy, yet increased rates make it difficult to service private and public debt. Subsequently, the problem is continuously delayed and worsened to the point it becomes uncontrollable.

THE NATIONALISM-GLOBALISM DIVIDE

The growing gap between the thriving elites and struggling populations across the West resulted in the rise of populist politics. Populism is expressed by rhetorically distancing the elites from the people. Populism is thus inherently anti-establishment as a response to the polarisation of society between the cosmopolitan elite and the "people" left behind from the forces of globalisation. The "people" is commonly defined by the political Left as working class, and by the political Right as those adhering to traditional values. Populists on the political Right proclaimed to take the mantle of classical conservatives, seeking to intervene in the economy to protect traditional values, culture, and faith. Populists on the Left declared they were fighting for traditional redistribution. Meanwhile, populists on both the Right and Left are confronted by the existing political class as systems tend to reproduce and defend themselves.

Populists can develop respectability and claim the moral high-ground by representing the cause of democracy. Globalisation is largely incompatible with national sovereignty and thus the foundation of democracy, which is why globalist elites are despised as a threat to the democratic nation-state (Rodrik 2011).

Mudde (2016: 30) suggests that "the populist surge is an illiberal democratic response to decades of undemocratic liberal policies" deriving from the liberal consensus disembedded from society. Once the people who did not benefit from globalisation began to question the growing economic inequality, erosion of national culture, and mass immigration, they were merely denounced as backward fools lured by xenophobic tribalism. In *Dead Souls*, Huntington argued the average citizens seek national unity through traditional values, identity, culture, and manufacturing jobs. In contrast,

> for many elites, these concerns are secondary to participating in the global economy, supporting international trade and migration, strengthening international institutions, promoting American values abroad, and encouraging minority identities and cultures at home. The central distinction between the public and elites is not isolationism versus internationalism, but nationalism versus cosmopolitanism (Huntington 2004: 5).

Populism can be considered a mechanism to restore the traditional role of the political Right and Left. Albeit, to reproduce the existing systems there is a tendency to treat populism as a problem or abnormality to be overcome rather than a symptom of systemic problems. Resonant of Plato's thesis in *The Republic*, democracy crumbles when people seek to liberate themselves from constraining external structures, and in the ensuing chaos seek out a strongman to restore order. Rorty (1998: 89) projected that the excesses of economic liberalism would give rise to radical alternatives:

> Members of labor unions, and unorganized and unskilled workers, will sooner or later realize that their government is not even trying to prevent wages from sinking or to prevent jobs from being exported. Around the same time, they will realize that suburban white-collar workers—themselves desperately afraid of being downsized—are not going to let themselves be taxed to provide social benefits for anyone else. At that point, something will crack. The nonsuburban electorate will decide that the system has failed and start looking around for a strongman to vote for—someone willing to assure them that, once he is elected, the smug bureaucrats, tricky lawyers, overpaid bond salesmen, and postmodernist professors will no longer be calling the shots. . . Once the strongman takes office, no one can predict what will happen.

Resolving the polarisation of Western societies requires constraining the excesses of political and economic liberalism, which is problematic as liberalism has grown to occupy such a dominant place in Western identity. The EU largely embodies the excesses of liberalism in the post-Cold War identity of the West. When the proposed European Constitution was debated in the early 2000s, it was noted that the text made no mention of Europe's Christian heritage. Leading conservatives in the US have similarly asked if the foundation for a common country with liberals is possible. Case in point, Rush Limbaugh opined:

> I actually think that we're trending toward secession. I see more and more people asking what in the world do we have in common with the people who live in, say, New York? . . . there cannot be a peaceful coexistence of two completely different theories of life, theories of government, theories of how we manage our affairs (MMS 2020).

Liberalism and the nation-state grew up until liberalism decoupled from the nation-state more recently. The European nation-state is a deeply conservative construct based on ethno-cultural demos, which became the sturdiest vessel to elevate human freedom. The effort to liberalise the individual from collective social institutions has culminated in multiculturalism and radical secularism to the extent it becomes problematic to reproduce the distinctive culture of Western societies. Prosperity is commonly followed by stagnation as prosperous societies tend to embrace liberal values of tolerance and openness, which undermines the conservative values of in-group loyalty by reproducing the traditional, family values, and community (Haidt 2012).

Liberalism has a dangerously optimistic view about the prospect of transcending the primordial instincts in human nature. The liberal belief suggests that ignoring and denouncing traditionalism and instinctive tribalism creates conformity around liberal ideals. Instead, the self-indulgent approach to structuring society fails to address imperishable instincts in human nature, and the political elites subsequently lay the foundation for radical alternatives.

In the book review of *Mein Kampf,* George Orwell argued that Hitler "grasped the falsity of the hedonistic attitude to life" that assumed "human beings desire nothing beyond ease, security and avoidance of pain." Orwell cautioned that hedonism cannot be the sole alternative to fascism: "The Socialist who finds his children playing with soldiers is usually upset, but he is never able to think of a substitute for the tin soldiers; tin pacifists somehow won't do" (Orwell 1940). The structuring and values of society have to recognise rather than ignore that the people also "want struggle and self-sacrifice, not to mention drums, flags and loyalty-parades" (Orwell 1940). In the struggle against Hitler, Orwell (1940) warned that "Fascism and Nazism are psychologically far sounder than any hedonistic conception of life." Fascism has been misinterpreted as "merely a version of Conservatism" (Orwell 1940), while in reality, it was a nefarious ideology emerging in the vacuum left behind by the decline of conservatism.

The dividing lines in both Europe and Asia were not removed but moved after the Cold War. Subsequently, the capitalism-communist divide of the Cold War was recast as a liberal-authoritarian divide to revive the ideological scaffolding of the West against Russia and China. The excessive reliance on a shared liberal identity resulted in liberalism decoupling from the nation-state. Multiculturalism and radical secularism became indicators of collective social institutions weakening in favour of a common identity based on values. With the decline of classical conservatism, a political vacuum opened for right-wing populists. The right-wing populists reject the liberal-authoritarian ideological divide of the world and instead consider the main dividing line to be national-patriotism versus cosmopolitan-globalism. Through this prism, countries such as Russia are viewed as a possible ally instead of an adversary.

CONCLUSION

The emergence of multipolarity is altering the foundations for the trans-Atlantic region. The systemic incentives for harmonising policies are coming to an end and both the US and Brussels/Berlin rely increasingly on economic sticks to punish deviations. The reliance on economic coercion to maintain a geoeconomic region can function as a dam to delay the day of reckoning, although as the pressure builds up, it will only make collapse more sudden and uncontrolled once the dam is breached.

The weakened internal cohesion of the trans-Atlantic region, the EU, and states place the entire region at a crossroads. The states of the trans-Atlantic region can be more susceptible to embracing compromise and inter-regional solutions with the Greater Eurasian region, or the West can bolster solidarity by converting the geoeconomic rivalries with the East into a military and ideological zero-sum competition.

9

Developing Strategic Autonomy for European Sovereignty

The multipolar distribution of power creates systemic pressures for the EU to pursue "strategic autonomy" to assert "European sovereignty." The reduced concentration of economic power in the international system removes the conditions for a liberal economic system. Preserving internal cohesion and remaining competitive in the international system demands that the EU abides by geoeconomic realities. Strategic autonomy to enhance European sovereignty is a geoeconomic strategy, and it demands that the EU revises its post-national and post-sovereign liberal ideology.

Strategic sovereignty of a geoeconomic bloc entails enhancing the ability of the bloc to act as a unitary actor, and avoid unfavourable asymmetrical interdependence on more powerful actors. The sovereignty of a geoeconomic bloc entails the same as sovereignty for rising nation-states in the 19th century—autonomous control over strategic industries, transportation corridors, and financial instruments. However, the concept of "European sovereignty" is nonetheless more complex than the economic nationalism of the 19th century that linked industrialisation of nation-building, as the EU is not a sovereign entity.

What in Europe is the sovereign? By reintroducing the concept of sovereignty in Europe there is a need to recognise a rivalry for sovereignty between the nation-state and the EU, which cannot be resolved by a winner-takes-all approach. An important implication of the European sovereignty concept is therefore the recognition that geoeconomic cooperation and competition must be managed between EU member states. The ability of the EU to mobilise its resources and political support of member states to act strategically in the international system requires a reconceptualisation of the EU as a vehicle for aligning common interests, as opposed to a vehicle for transcending national interests.

Furthermore, by embracing the concept of European sovereignty, the EU must redefine its relationship with its neighbours and the wider world. The pursuit of strategic autonomy and European sovereignty is an acknowledgement that the EU is an entity of power that competes with other sovereignty entities. Thus, the principle of sovereign equality must replace former ideas of normative power and other post-sovereign authority in international affairs.

This chapter first explores the EU's embrace of strategic autonomy and European sovereignty, which represents an ideological transformation. The effort to transform the EU as an actor is incentivised by the emergence of a multipolar world as evident by the Gaullist undertones of the endeavour to establish European sovereignty. Second, the EU needs to reinvent the strategic industries, transportation corridors, or financial instruments required to preserve strategic autonomy. Aspirations for a Digital Single Market correctly identifies that path ahead, yet the ability to deliver this result is undermined by internal divisions and outdated thinking about the international system. Last, a sovereign Europe with strategic autonomy will have a greater ability to adapt to the multipolar distribution of power and improve relations with other poles of power.

TOWARDS STRATEGIC AUTONOMY
AND EUROPEAN SOVEREIGNTY

Strategic autonomy is emerging as the new catchphrase of the EU, yet the term remains ill-defined. Angela Merkel proclaimed that the time "when we could rely completely on others" had come to an end and "we Europeans must take our destiny into our own hands" (Joffe 2017).

The European Council President, Charles Michel, proclaimed in September 2020 that "The strategic independence of Europe is our new common project for this century . . . European strategic autonomy is goal number one for our generation" (European Council 2020c). Ursula von der Leyen, the President of the European Commission, aimed to develop a "geopolitical commission" using the EU's economic and financial power in concert with its diplomatic power to assert itself as a "pillar of the multilateral system" (European Commission 2020b).

The EU has begun to adopt geoeconomic lingo by recognising the imperative of skewing the balance of dependence to maximise autonomy and influence. Michel defined the concept of strategic autonomy: "It means more resilience, more influence. And less dependence" (European Council 2020c). French President, Emmanuel Macron, defined strategic autonomy as "meaning our sovereignty, our ability to reduce our dependence vis a vis the rest of the world, strengthen our production companies" (Figaro 2020).

Yet, "European sovereignty" is a paradoxical term. On one hand, it is an acknowledgement that the process of globalisation does not entail transcending the nation-state by embracing neoliberal and cosmopolitan free-market capitalism. On the other hand, the EU as a region is largely founded on the ideology of globalism, and Brussels remains committed to a federalist project of transcending the nation-state through liberal ideals. There has been a long competition to monopolise on the concept of Europe, and the federalist concept of "pro-European" tended to be anti- or post-sovereignist.

The highest sovereign remains the nation-state and geoeconomic initiatives of the EU must account for the balance of dependence within the bloc. By recognising the EU is a geoeconomic bloc where states aim to maximise their sovereignty, a pragmatic approach must be developed to address the integration dilemma: Member states seeking to maximise their sovereignty will accept the "cost" of transferring of sovereign powers to Brussels to the extent it is outweighed by the "benefit" to sovereignty as the EU uses collective bargaining power to negotiate a favourable geoeconomic position in the world. If the costs to sovereignty are higher than the benefits to sovereignty, the political loyalty of member states will rescind.

The emergence of a multipolar international order can strengthen the internal cohesion of the EU as new poles of power create systemic incentives for European solidarity. The ability of individual nations to uphold their sovereignty in an era of competing poles of power enhances the benefits of the EU, which can further enhance the appeal of the EU if Brussels also reduces the costs to national sovereignty. A former advisor to President Macron wrote: "The choice is not between national and European sovereignty . . . It is between European sovereignty and none at all" (Pisani-Ferry 2019). In the lack of a better phrase, the new EU strategy implies "Europe first."

ADAPTING TO MULTIPOLARITY

The concept of European sovereignty is an effort to adapt to a multipolar international distribution of power, as evident by the Gaullist connotations. It should therefore not be a surprise that the current calls for European sovereignty are led by President Macron. De Gaulle was a Eurosceptic who championed the nation-state as the highest sovereign, although he dreamed of a powerful and unified Europe that could exist independently between the Soviet Union and the US.

France aimed to reform NATO to assert European autonomy from the US and the UK in 1959 and 1960, although these efforts failed. Thus, France sought to use the European Economic Community (EEC) as an instrument for autonomy from NATO. In 1961, the Fouchet Plan sought to create a politically united Europe. A French-German partnership was envisioned to be at the heart of a united Europe. However, other members feared the grouping would become excessively dominated by France, akin to the Napoleonic Continental System. Thus the Fouchet plans eventually failed.

De Gaulle was committed to the nation-state, although French sovereignty and European sovereignty were not mutually exclusive as France was expected to be the leader of a united Europe. In 1962, De Gaulle asked:

> What is Europe about? It must serve to avoid being dominated by either the Americans or the Russians. With six of us, we should be able to do as well as each of the two super majors. And if France manages to be the first of the Six, which is within our reach, she will be able to wield this Archimedes' lever. She will be able to lead the others. Europe is the way for France to become again what it ceased to be at Waterloo: first in the world (Schuman Foundation 2021).

In 1966, de Gaulle withdrew France from the NATO military command structure to limit the intrusive power of the US and pursue multipolarity. In 2009, France eventually rejoined NATO's military command as the sole centre of military power, which implicitly recognised that France was isolating itself.

De Gaulle endeavoured to transform the bipolar order to a multipolar order by pursuing European sovereignty, independent from the Americans and the Russians. This was eventually rejected in favour of gradually enhancing European autonomy within the US-led bloc. The current challenge is different from the days of de Gaulle as a multipolar system has already asserted itself and the conditions for European autonomy within a US-led trans-Atlantic region diminishes. In a multipolar world, European sovereignty becomes a necessity to avoid becoming a chessboard of independent poles of power.

The EU gravitates towards the more Westphalian understanding of international relations shared by the major powers in Greater Eurasia. This implies a redefinition of globalisation as a state-centric phenomenon as opposed to being a process to transcend the relevance of the state. This also represents a return to a Gaullist European tradition as De Gaulle cautioned in 1962 that Europe must be based on the state: "The nation is a human and a sentimental element . . . there cannot be any Europe other than that of the states, apart from in myths, fiction, and parades" (Carden 2020).

THE EUROPEAN SWING POWER

The EU's ability to preserve its strategic autonomy in a multipolar world requires maintaining a mutually beneficial partnership with the US, while fomenting independent policies towards Russia and China. The EU is in a similar position as India and Turkey, and must therefore pursue similar policies of positioning itself between the trans-Atlantic partnership and Greater Eurasia.

Buzan defined a "swing power" strategy by being "engaged in several regions but not permanently wedded to any of them" (Buzan 2005: 193). Once the EU commits solely to the trans-Atlantic partnership, the US will have the confidence and ability to exert greater geoeconomic power and political influence over the EU. Concurrently, by being solely devoted to the trans-Atlantic region, the EU has little value in Greater Eurasia and thus incentivises adversaries of the US to engage in wedge tactics in Europe. Similarly, the EU cannot commit itself solely to the Greater Eurasian region as it by design limits the power of the US, which would therefore incentivise Washington to employ similar wedge tactics to reward and punish individual EU member states. Diversification and an autonomous foreign policy are thus imperative to preserve the EU's strategic autonomy.

The swing power strategy can mitigate competing interests within the EU, which recognises that individual member states have strategic interests with different poles of power in the world. Linking the EU solely to one pole of power entails strengthening some EU member states above others, which further divides the bloc.

De Gaulle was never able to establish a sound France-German political axis, and the eventual accession of the UK to the EU limited the ability for European sovereignty. The UK's participation was to a great extent motivated by preventing the EU from drifting away from the trans-Atlantic partnership. The departure of Britain weakens the overall power of the bloc and creates a new competitor on the western periphery, although it also represents an opportunity to advance European sovereignty. Britain's EU membership has also been used to uphold its historical role of ensuring dividing lines between Germany and Russia. Britain has been one of the most ardent critics of Russia and has pushed for ultimatums without compromise. A compromise is more possible over Ukraine, and Brexit also presents the opportunity to establish cooperation between the EU and the EAEU.

THE GEOECONOMIC LEVERS OF POWER
OF A SOVEREIGN EUROPE

The EU foreign policy chief, Josep Borrell, wrote in December 2019 that the geostrategic rivalry between countries such as the US, China, and Russia presented the EU with "the option of becoming a player, a true geostrategic actor, or being mostly the playground" (Barigazzi 2019). In other words, the

EU risks being demoted from a political subject to a political object in the world of global multipolarity.

In June 2019, the European Council had similarly agreed on a five-year strategic plan: "A new strategic agenda 2019–2024." The strategic agenda includes "developing a strong and vibrant economic base" and "promoting European interests and values on the global stage" (European Council 2019a). More specifically, strategic industries were to be revamped with a focus on the digital revolution and artificial intelligence, and financial instruments by deepening the Economic and Monetary Union and strengthening the international role of the Euro. In April 2020, the European Council also concluded "it is of utmost importance to increase the strategic autonomy of the Union and produce essential goods in Europe."

Strategic industries

The EU's Single Market for goods was a critical tool to develop a geoeconomic region. Although, technologies and the economy have since been transformed and the EU has lost sight of its geoeconomic foundations.

The world is entering the Fourth Industrial Revolution and technological sovereignty is imperative for political sovereignty. Digital technologies are integrating with the physical world and thus transforming production with automated production, transportation with self-driving cars, the financial industry with new payment systems and digital currencies, the medical industry, every-day items with the internet of things (IoT), and restructuring other industries with smart agriculture, smart cities, and automated weapon systems.

A Single Digital Market is essential to integrate the European economies for collective autonomy and influence. Unlike its American, Chinese, and Russian counterparts with various degrees of sophisticated domestic digital ecosystems to buttress technological sovereignty—there is no European equivalent of Google, Amazon, Facebook, Microsoft, and Apple that is given a domestic primacy. This is imperative as an economic power is increasingly concentrated around digital platforms. The EU risks technological colonisation as foreign powers develop core-periphery relations by dominating and saturating European markets. Digital sovereignty in the 21st century is as vital to nation-building and region-building as a manufacturing base was in the 19th century.

The current US-China rivalry over 5G in Europe represents a dilemma of having their data mined by and being spied on by either the Americans or the Chinese. Similarly, the US Cloud Act (Clarifying Lawful Overseas Use of Data) of 2018 announced the right of US companies to extract data from foreign corporations stored on US cloud services providers. The Cloud Act undercuts European privacy laws and endows the US with a competitive advantage by harvesting more data to develop superior AI software.

There is subsequently a growing awareness in the EU that technological sovereignty is crucial. EU leaders announced an agreement in April 2020 aimed towards strategic autonomy: "It is of utmost importance to increase the strategic autonomy of the Union and produce essential goods in Europe" (European Council 2020a). The European Commission (2020b) recognised that "Technologies such as artificial intelligence, 5G networks and quantum computers have the potential to revolutionise our way of life." The European Commission's ambition for the EU to become a global leader in digital innovation, although this would require a complete reversal of the current relative decline of European patents in leading technologies.

In Gaullist tradition, the French are pushing forward to assert strategic autonomy. Case in point, the digital service tax introduced by France in July 2019 to tax American tech-giants such as Google, Facebook, Amazon, and Apple can set a precedent for Europe to follow. Furthermore, Germany and France entered into discussion with the European Commission regarding "measures to strengthen the development of future technologies in Europe and reduce our dependence," which includes technological sovereignty by developing digital technologies such as data storage, cloud infrastructure, 5G, and artificial intelligence (Élysée 2020). Albeit, a dilemma becomes evident as these are primarily initiatives from German and French cooperation, which will create further asymmetries within the EU. Furthermore, strong industrial policies and restructuring supply chains can cause severe disruptions to the rules of the Single Market.

Technological sovereignty counteracts US efforts of asserting its geoeconomic dominance and influence over Europe. Case in point, the EU seeks to develop greater production capabilities of semiconductors for commercial and technological gain, as well as political autonomy. The EU became vulnerable to US unilateralism as evident by the US Export Control Reform Act (ECRA), which pressured the Europeans to limit technology exports to China and re-exporting of American technologies to third countries. China has responded to the US sanctions regime by passing the "Rules on Counteracting Unjustified Extraterritorial Application of Foreign Legislation and Other Measures" in January 2021. The new rules release firms from compliance obligations and enable Chinese corporations to sue foreign companies in Chinese counts that comply with US extraterritorial laws. In the absence of technological sovereignty, the EU is pushed towards picking a side and facing the subsequent economic consequences.

The EU endeavours to extend its existing geoeconomic model as a regulatory power into the digital sphere. Brussels has, much like China, benefitted from its large market. While China sets conditions for market entry, the EU wields geoeconomics power as a regulatory power. The European Council President proclaimed:

> We have unique and undeniable strengths. Our market of 450 million people. And with it, comes our regulatory power. The famous "Brussels effect" – that enables us to set the highest standards for our citizens, while projecting these standards across the world. This is especially true in the digital domain (European Council 2021).

The EU is framing its values in a language consistent with geoeconomics as opposed to a liberal free-market economic system. In the new language, technological sovereignty does not represent a repudiation of liberalism, rather technological sovereignty is presented as enabling the EU to defend and promote its liberal and green values: "A European approach to the digital transformation deepens our democratic foundations, respects fundamental rights and contributes to a sustainable, climate-neutral and resource-efficient economy" (European Commission 2020b). The Covid-19 pandemic also contributed to restoring the legitimacy of the states' responsibility to intervene in the economy to enhance technological self-reliance. The absence of masks and medical equipment demonstrated the need for domestic production for vital industries. As digital technologies penetrate all sectors of society, the conclusion is subsequently that "everything" is a critical industry.

Transportation corridors

The development of new Eurasian transportation corridors is rapidly reorganising trade between Europe and Asia. The growing efficiency of the East-West and North-South Eurasian land-bridges have the commonality of shifting control of transportation corridors from the US to Eurasian powers. While the US will attempt to push for "freedom of navigation" in the Russian Arctic and the South China Sea, the administrative control of Washington over transportation corridors diminishes.

European economies must partially gravitate towards Eurasian transportation corridors to remain competitive, which will benefit some European states more than others. The main challenge to European strategic autonomy and sovereignty is to ensure open access to new transportation corridors. Eurasian powers have greatly incentivised to ensure trust in new transportation corridors, and abusing that trust for short-term gain would undermine long-term benefits. Yet, the West's concept of a rules-based system has existed under hegemonic control. Eurasian transportation corridors decouple EU and US interests, and a rules-based system shifts towards sovereign equality with Eurasian powers.

Federica Mogherini, the EU High Representative for Foreign Affairs and Security Policy, sought to elevate the EU as a political object in Eurasian transportation corridors. Recognising that Europe and Asia account for more than 60 percent of global GDP, improving transportation corridors presents an absolute gain. The EU attempts to obtain greater influence over the political and regulatory environment that impacts its trade. Eurasian powers, primarily China, enjoy greater influence over regulatory frameworks in Central and Eastern Europe. Mogherini opined: "Connectivity cannot be confined to regional pockets, cannot exclude legitimate actors and put environmental considerations last: we need common standards, we need common rules" (EEAS 2018).

In a new strategy on China, the EU demanded that cooperation with the Belt and Road Initiative would depend on the initiative committing to being "an open platform which adheres to market rules and international norms in order to deliver benefits for all and to encourage responsible economic behaviour in third countries." Furthermore, the EU expressly demanded that its standards and regulation should remain outside EU borders:

> Cooperation in this field should be based on full respect for relevant policies, and applicable regulations and standards, including with regard to public procurement, and guarantee a level playing field for economic operators from both sides. This should also apply to those countries outside the EU which have pledged to apply EU standards (European Commission 2016).

The EU seeks to shift the balance of dependence with the US by reducing its own reliance on the US, and increasing US dependence on the EU. In the security sphere, this can be expressed in the form of partaking in military campaigns to assert control over transportation corridors in the Indo-Pacific. Europe is no longer the centre of gravity of US geostrategic focus, which creates certain systemic pressures for the Europeans to be pulled into Asia irrespective of interests deviating from the US (Fiott 2018). These systemic incentives account for increased European military support for military posturing along maritime corridors in the Indo-Pacific region. In late 2017, Macron aimed to reassure Australia that France was aware of the situation in the Indo-Pacific and Australia would not need to stand alone (Ang 2021). After the French announcement of its "pivot" to the Indo-Pacific, the Germans and Dutch followed and began drafting the EU Indo-Pacific strategy. The UK, a non-EU member, also committed itself to the US efforts to develop Western leadership in the Indo-Pacific region. Yet, the Europeans are embracing a strategic ambiguity similar to that of NATO expansionism from the 1990s, which was argued to not be directed against Russia. The French

Indo-Pacific ambassador argued that "Our Indo-Pacific strategy is not at all directed against China" (Ang 2021).

Financial instruments

The EU is also asserting strategic autonomy over its financial instruments to assert European sovereignty and avoid being compelled to choose between the trans-Atlantic region and Greater Eurasia. Two key initiatives for strategic autonomy in the financial sector is the EU foreign direct investment screening mechanism and the Instrument in Support of Trade Exchanges (INSTEX).

The protection of strategic industries is imperative to develop strategic autonomy. In October 2020, the EU's Foreign Direct Investment regulation became fully applicable. The mechanisms on screening Foreign Direct Investment is intended to protect critical technologies and infrastructure, sensitive information and pluralism of the media. The screening mechanism does not have the same force as the US counterpart, the Committee on Foreign Investments in the United States (CFIUS). However, as a geoeconomic region, the EU does not have the same sovereign powers like the US.

The financial dominance of the US has been a key instrument for extraterritorial jurisdiction. The SWIFT system is particularly invasive that enables the US to pass unilateral sanctions that must be adhered to by the rest of the world, which is why both China and Russia have established alternatives. In January 2019, the EU launched INSTEX to facilitate non-USD and non-SWIFT transactions with Iran and possibly other states, which is designed to bypass US unilateral sanctions.

The SWIFT system claims to be politically neutral, yet both Iran and North Korea were cut off from the SWIFT network to undermine their banking systems. The US fined the French banking group BNP Paribas almost $9 billion in 2014 for violating US embargoes against Iran, Cuba, and Sudan. The US similarly accused Alstom, the French energy and transportation conglomerate, of bribery in a third country—Indonesia. The US Department of Justice ended the investigation into Alstom in 2014 when it was agreed that General Electric, its main US rival, would procure the French national champion. However, it was the sanctions against Iran that spurred the EU's development of INSTEX. As the US Treasury Secretary, Steven Mnuchin, informed its European partners at the G7 meeting in 2019: "If you want to participate in the dollar system you abide by US sanctions."

Militarising the EU

Adopting military capabilities is a key instrument of establishing sovereignty. Strategic autonomy cannot be discussed independently from militarising the

EU, as US security guarantees remain the principal source of Washington's influence on the continent—an influence that is diligently converted into US geoeconomic power.

Max Weber famously stated that sovereignty or statehood is defined by the monopoly of the legitimate use of violence within a territory. The EU has subsequently sought to increase autonomous competencies for decades, which has mostly been limited by the primacy of NATO.

Yet, reduced reliance on the US military after the Cold War has provided the EU with greater room for manoeuvre. Six months following the collapse of the Soviet Union, the members of the Western European Union agreed to develop autonomous military capabilities in an agreement that has become known as the Petersberg tasks.

A militarised EU strengthens European sovereignty due to three reasons. First, nation-states rely increasingly on Brussels for security, which is a key competency for pooling sovereignty. Second, by endowing the EU with greater military competencies, the growing imbalance in the German-French partnership can be improved as France asserts leadership in the security sphere in partnership with Germany's geoeconomic leadership. Third, the EU can gain greater independence from the US. However, militarising the EU could sow further divisions in the bloc as Poland and other East European countries view US security guarantees as indispensable.

What is the functional value of an EU army? Critics often comment that Europe does not successfully carry out military interventions without the US, and it is doubtful the EU could defeat Syria, Libya, or prevent Russia's annexation/reunification with Crimea (Youngs 2021). However, the aggressive and often illegal military interventions were part of NATO's "out of area or out of business" rationale as a new reason for existing. NATO's outward focus was incentivised by the absence of an international balance of power in the unipolar era. International law that imposes mutual restraints emerges when there is a balance of power and a desire to maintain the status quo—as it creates a condition where states are willing to accept limitations on foreign policy in return for reciprocity and thus predictability.

Multipolarity incentivises a change in international law that refocuses on mutual constraints and sovereign equality. An EU army would not be comparable to NATO, although the case for an EU army would need to shift towards a national defensive. If not, a militarised EU would become even more vulnerable to wedge tactics. Russia is the only potential adversary to justify and direct these military capabilities, thus threatening to further militarise the dividing lines in Europe.

Converting economic power into political power— reconceptualising globalisation

Geoeconomics entails converting asymmetrical economic power into political power. The EU's geoeconomic influence in a multipolar era must be adapted to two main changes in the process of globalisation—first, globalisation will be state-centric as opposed to transcending the state; second, globalisation will to a lesser extent be a Western-led initiative. The absolute gain of economic connectivity must thus be balanced with the relative gain. More and more European companies are experiencing that enhanced economic efficiency in the new world requires accepting higher dependence on China and Russia, which is a greater challenge than the previous gravitational pull towards the US.

The EU must recognise that its former hegemonic role in the pan-European space and its collective global leadership with the US has come to an end. Political influence must reflect the actual power, otherwise, the pursuit of unrealistic goals will undermine achievable goals. The EU's conversion of economic power into political power occurred under the format of liberal hegemony—as asymmetrical economic dependence enabled the EU to establish sovereign inequality in subject-object partnerships. As the geoeconomic foundations that enabled liberal hegemony have passed, the EU must redefine partnerships.

The Holy Roman Empire came to an end when it was no longer holy, not Roman, and not an empire. The liberal international order is similarly no longer liberal as political realism comes first, it is not international are a large part of the world repudiates it, and it is hardly orderly by being unable to create a format for cooperation. Ambitions to restore the "liberal international order" is commonly presented as an issue of values, which neglects the changing distribution of power. In a multipolar order, the EU cannot maintain its commitment to liberal economics and liberal politics to preserve internal cohesion and influence the international system. The EU can remain committed to liberal values internally and externally, yet recognise that values cannot be decoupled from power as evident by the student-teacher format of relations with Russia.

This will prove to be an immense challenge for the EU as the understanding of its past and present will no longer apply in the future. The EU will need to re-examine its own place in the world both ideologically and conceptually. The fall of the Berlin Wall did not entail the victory of liberal democracy and free-market capitalism, rather these ideals were the result of a temporary concentration of economic power. Since the end of the Cold War, the conviction and guiding principle of the EU has been the assumption that under the collective leadership of the West, the world would incrementally integrate under free-market capitalism, liberal democracy, and technology. In a multipolar world, preserving the EU's strategic autonomy will require the embrace of fair-trade, liberal democracy that is more accommodating to conservative principles, and focus on interoperability of a regionally fragmented digital space.

Those insisting that there was no alternative to emulate the West's liberal democracy and capitalism can no longer ignore the rise of China, as soon to be the largest economy in the world. Ascribing liberalism as the silver bullet for the enduring stability and power of the West is ahistorical and neglects the centuries of brutal rivalry to control strategic industries, transportation corridors, and financial instruments.

Over the past three decades, the ability of the EU to align values and interests has gradually diminished—and self-preservation demands that power is prioritised. Humanitarian interventionism has resulted in a partnership with criminal and militant groups in Kosovo, Libya, Syria, and Yemen. Democracy promotion has legitimised the toppling of a democratically elected government in Ukraine, followed by a deafening silence as post-coup government has launched an "anti-terrorist operation" against its own people in Donbas. Similarly, Kiev's marginalisation of political opposition and independent media has been celebrated as being part of a democratic revolution by decoupling from Russia. Efforts to maintain a "socialising" role will continue to be fiercely rebuked by Moscow, and the failed liberal agenda will undermine the prospect of developing a partnership for mutual interests.

The triumphalism of the 1990s must be tempered and the renewed division of the post-Cold War world into liberals versus authoritarians must be walked back. The world view that, for example, contrasting an authoritarian Russia with a democratic India results in the self-imposed delusion that fails to appreciate the democratic processes in Russia and the role of Hindu nationalism in India. As the relative power of the EU declines, there is greater opposition from the East to accept the West to use moral authority as a currency for power.

The EU's impulse of using sanctions to correct the "behaviour" of partners becomes an exercise of self-harm towards the EU's own geoeconomic position. First, it neglects that the socialising role and moral authority is contested and will be counterproductive as it heightens suspicions about liberal ideals and domestic liberal political groups as a Trojan horse for Western influence. Second, the consistent sanctions make the EU an unreliable partner, which compels states like Russia to reduce reliance and exposure to the EU. It also makes the EU an unreliable power that makes it necessary for Russia and China to engage individual EU member states.

International law and the rules-based system must also adapt to multipolarity. From a neoclassical realist perspective, the severely skewed balance of power following the collapse of the Soviet Union resulted in the introduction of concepts of sovereign inequality that enables the unchecked power to diminish the sovereignty of rival states. During the unipolar era, the West introduced humanitarian interventionism, democracy promotion, preventive attacks, the global war on terror, and other concepts with the common denominator of sovereign inequality.

As articulated by Tony Blair's (1999) speech: "we are witnessing the beginnings of a new doctrine of international community . . . we are all internationalists now, whether we like it or not." However, it was was implied the violating sovereignty was the prerogative of the post-sovereign West. Furthermore, once the international distribution of power would return towards equilibrium, the world would return to international law based on mutual constraints on the use of force as opposed to enabling the use of force. The modern rules-based system of legality is decoupled from legitimacy as liberal democratic norms challenge the uniform application of rules. The invasion and dismemberment of Serbia was a violation of international law, which was justified by decoupling "legality" from "legitimacy."

THE EXTERNAL BALANCE OF DEPENDENCE
FOR A SOVEREIGN EUROPE

The EU's engagement with the wider world has largely been influenced by the idea that the EU is a post-sovereignist project, and the EU has sought to shape the world in its image. The purpose of the European project was to transcend the sovereign nation-state and the sovereign concept altogether (Kundnani 2020). As the EU pursues "strategic autonomy" to augment "European sovereignty," it demands a reconceptualisation of relations with adversarial poles of power.

The EU has largely defined itself by concepts such as "Normative Power Europe" (Manners 2002), which suggests that the EU is not comparable to other entities of power as its main source of power was to radiate liberal democratic norms. The sentiments and ambitions of the EU at the turn of the century were encapsulated by Kristeva (2000) who also argued in 2000, the EU was not only a European project but a "global civilising effort." The mere debate about the EU being a normative power demoted analytical focus and made the EU less aware of the power it competes for and accumulates to promote its values (Diez 2005: 626). The supposedly benign intentions of the EU created a double narrative of the EU as both a "force for good" and a power aspiring for hegemony as asymmetrical relations were imperative to establish its leadership position (Haukkala 2010: 162). Even the scholar who coined the concept, Manners (2006: 168), acknowledged that Normative

Power Europe was a concept developed in the 1990s to argue what "the EU *should* be (doing) in World politics."

The EU's self-perception as a vehicle for globalisation under liberal values rather than an entity of power competing against other actors have impacted its actions and reduced the ability to compromise. Case in point, Russia and the EU have been unable to establish a mutually acceptable format for cooperation due to the conceptual decoupling of Russia from Europe. The EU's supposed post-sovereign status has contributed to a binary division of Europe whereas the postmodern EU is contrasted with modern Russia. Sub-binary categories have thus developed: "post-sovereignty compared to sovereignty; normative foreign policy compared to realpolitik; free trade compared to autarky; soft power compared to hard power; and decentralisation compared to centralisation" (Klinke 2012: 934). The EU Commissioner for Enlargement confirmed that the differences between the EU and Russia made it difficult to establish a mutually acceptable format for cooperation:

> Russia is also trying to build a modern nation-state which relies on hard power. By contrast, the EU is a postmodern entity which wields a vast soft power of attractiveness, but which lacks strong sanctioning mechanisms. No wonder it is often hard to find common language (European Commission 2008b).

As Europe pursues strategic autonomy and "returns" to sovereignty and great power politics, an opportunity emerges for restoring conceptual comparisons. The return to "European sovereignty" can be considered a gradual process. During most of the Cold War, the European Community viewed itself as the "other" in terms of preventing another German-French rivalry. Recognising the destructive history of Europe, the European Community sought to develop security *with* its fellow members instead of security *against* non-members (Wallander and Keohane 1999). The purpose of the European Community was to advance peace by constraining the use of force.

However, after the Cold War, the EU began changing its underpinning function as it would collectively seek security and *against* non-members. The former French President and a key architect of the rejected European Constitution, Valery Giscard d'Estaing, opined: "over the decades, the basis of the EU's existence has changed. We've moved from seeking peace to seeking greatness" (Rettman 2013). Tony Blair similarly expressed his support for the new rationale of the EU:

> The rationale for Europe in the 21st century is stronger than it has ever been. It is essentially about power, not about peace anymore. We won't fight each other if we don't have Europe, but we will be weaker, less powerful, with less influence (Scheuermann 2013).

While the post-Cold War challenge was to replicate the German-French security community with Russia based on constraints, the EU became a project of sovereign inequality protecting the bloc *against* the influence of Russia. The EU developed an awkward posture vis-à-vis Russia as the EU claimed to be a "force for good" as a benign post-sovereign identity based on its relations with other member states, while acting as a sovereign entity of power competing for interests against Russia. The post-sovereign narrative was central in harmonising the double narrative of being a "force for good" and simultaneously asserting leadership with asymmetrical relations (Haukkala 2010: 162).

Relations with Russia must be recalibrated as the EU defines itself as a sovereign great power, as opposed to a post-sovereign normative power. The opportunity for conceptual comparison between the EU and Russia is the ability to manage relations. If there is a relationship between two sovereigns, then a discussion can be opened about formats recognising sovereign equality, as a requirement by Moscow for cordial relations. Furthermore, by recognising the competing geoeconomic interests of two sovereigns, a framework can be established to facilitate common rules for both cooperation and competition in the shared neighbourhood.

The EU's gravitational pull and soft power reduce as its partners have alternatives. Much like NATO aimed to monopolise the role as a security provider, the EU similarly was the main economic actor in the pan-European space. By no longer being the only game in town, the negotiation power shifts away from Brussels. From Turkey to Serbia, there is an effort to position themselves within the Greater Eurasian framework to benefit from the multipolar structure. Instead of accepting unilateral concessions for the prospect of possible future membership in the EU, countries like Serbia and Turkey recognise they can gain more from an independent foreign policy.

THE EU CHOICE: UNIPOLARITY OR
INTER-REGIONALISM IN GREATER EURASIA

The EU faces a similar dilemma as the US in terms of resisting or accommodating multipolarity. By accommodating a multipolar framework the EU can shape the emerging formats and create incentives for the mutual legitimisation of regions. Alternatively, by opposing the emergence of multipolarity the EU can to some extent extend the collective leadership of the West, although the multipolar system will then develop without the participation of the EU and very likely in opposition to the EU.

The EU has an obvious dilemma in terms of regional formats. Geoeconomics regions such as the EU require external powers to cooperate. The EU frequently complains, for good reason, that Russia and China employ wedge tactics and cooperate with individual member states instead of dealing with the EU as an entity. This approach by Moscow and Beijing makes perfect sense as states will always act in their own interest by pursuing formats that skew the symmetry of interdependence to maximise both autonomy and influence. Brussels should ask itself why Russia and China would engage directly with a geoeconomic bloc that enables 27 member states to leverage from collective bargaining power, which by design creates an interdependent economic partnership with favourable symmetry for the Europeans.

Geoeconomic blocs must be able to create some value for external powers as an incentive for cooperation. Washington has supported the EU as a competitor because the bloc supports the unipolar ambitions of the US. Washington has accepted a more even balance of dependence within the trans-Atlantic region as it elevates the collective power of the US-led West. Yet, why would Russia and China support the EU?

In the 1990s, Russia looked favourably on the EU as the "good West" versus NATO as the "bad West" (Danilov 2005: 87). The underlying assumption being that the EU's strategic autonomy from the US would be beneficial to Russia as the European were more benign due to less militarism and as it did not have the intention or capacity to base security on EU global dominance. However, to preserve its value to the US, the EU aligned its policies with the US by preserving dividing lines in Europe. The EU relied on geoeconomic influence. When military power was used, NATO would do the invasion and the EU the ensuing peacekeeping. The division of labour was said to the US/NATO makes the "dinner" and the EU does the "dishes" (Diez 2005: 623).

In a multipolar world, the EU must engage in inter-regionalism to make Russia and China self-interested stakeholders in preserving a strong and functional EU. In contrast, hostility from the EU and the reluctance to provide any value result in wedge tactics, which ultimately divides and weakens the EU. Failure to reform the sole dedication to the trans-Atlantic partnership as an anti-Eurasian format will be detrimental to the EU's strategic autonomy. As geoeconomic competition intensifies, the US will demand greater loyalty from the Europeans and thus undermine the autonomy of the EU. The EU appears unable to adapt to a multipolar international distribution of power by still pursuing exclusive spheres of influence in contested regions. The EU foreign policy chief, Josep Borrell, continues to insist on an exclusive influence in the Western Balkans as a deeply divided region: "First and foremost, we must anchor solidly the Western Balkans within the EU."

Russia has historically been feared by European states as it did not fit into the Westphalian world for set borders, and for historical reason had an impulse towards expansionism. In the current world, this description best fits Europe. Westphalian concepts are rejected and Europe seemingly has no natural borders and its internal legitimacy rests on relentless expansionism.

The shift from unipolarity to multipolarity demands that the EU shifts from expansionism for exclusive influence to establishing regional borders without the zero-sum aspect.

CONCLUSION

Geoeconomic regions and international institutions are reflections of power, and Europe gravitated towards unity under a bipolar and unipolar international distribution of power. To remain a viable region in Greater Eurasia, Europe must adapt to the multipolar distribution of power by developing strategic autonomy as the foundation for European sovereignty.

Geoeconomic theory stipulates that sovereignty is achieved by strategic autonomy and diversification of partners for economic connectivity to avoid excessive reliance on any one state or region. The Europeans must reinvent the geoeconomic instruments of power by adapting to new technologies and a more complex internal and external balance of dependence. Europe needs a close partnership with the US, although Europe is marginalising itself in the international system when the partnership with the US limits the ability to develop autonomy and diversify economic partners.

Establishing strategic autonomy and European sovereignty is imperative to elevate the relevance of Europe in the world. Furthermore, it would also make the EU a more reliable partner in the world. Russia became disillusioned with Europe as it is not an independent actor to strike a deal with. Moscow must go through Washington for a comprehensive strategic agreement with Europe, which can only result in agreements consistent with US interests that are defined by preserving dividing lines in Europe. China is now in the process of learning the same lesson as the Europeans are falling in line by adapting a military and ideological response to a shifting geoeconomic distribution of power.

Conclusion

Adapting to Greater Eurasia

Even at the cusp of revolutionary change, there is a tendency to expect continuity. Only a year before the collapse of the Soviet Union, neither the Soviets nor its external adversaries predicted the rapid dissolution of the Soviet Union and the international order that defined the second half of the 20th century. In retrospect, the demise of the Soviet Union appears almost to have been inevitable due to its internal socioeconomic and political contradictions.

A one seemingly permanent feature of the international system was suddenly replaced with another—the unipolar era. The permanency of the unipolar was expressed most succinctly by Francis Fukuyama's "end of history" that envisioned the world to gravitate towards liberal democracy under US leadership. The EU imagined a transformative role for itself in the liberal international economy by advancing post-national and post-sovereign ideals. In retrospect, the unipolar era entailed the transfer of wealth to allies in the form of economic agreements and security guarantees, while key adversaries such as Russia and China could not be included as political subjects. Furthermore, as Fukuyama also recognised two decades later, liberalism alone could not organise society. History as the best teacher could have predicted the emergence of new centres of power at the periphery.

Yet, the rapid end of the unipolar era and the five-centuries-long Western-centric order is seemingly occurring as rapid as the end of the bipolar era. China outgrew the US-led order after decades of accumulating productive power and foreign reserves. China is now using these resources to rewire the global economy by establishing a leadership position in the Fourth Industrial Revolution, connecting the Eurasian continent with new transportation corridors, and developing parallel financial institutions. After the Western actions in Ukraine, Russia has abandoned the Greater Europe initiative since the end of the Cold War, walked back the agreements in the Helsinki Accords of 1975, and even abandoned the three-centuries-long Western-centrism that had lasted since Peter the Great. Russia's Greater Eurasia Initiative endeavours to reduce reliance on the West by repositioning itself from the dual periphery of Europe and Asia to the centre of a larger superregion. The end of Russia's aspirations to join Europe has fundamentally changed the balance of power in the world. China has become the principal partner of Russia to create a Greater Eurasian political economy and thus achieve what Russia has never had—an organic path to development. The rise of China and Russia does not merely signify new competing powers. Instead, the rise of these Eurasian giants is a catalyst for the transformation of the entire international economic system—Europe included.

The China-Russia partnership to construct a Greater Eurasian region creates a gravitation pull for the entire supercontinent. Europe is presented with a dilemma as economic competitiveness requires accepting greater reliance on Chinese technologies and Russian energy, new Eurasian transportation corridors, and new financial instruments. The failure to adapt to the changing international distribution of power will thus leave Europe less competitive and compelled to withdraw under US patronage.

These revolutionary changes are occurring at a time of great instability. Western societies are experiencing socioeconomic and political upheavals, the global financial system is seemingly moving towards a major crisis, and the Covid-19 pandemic has greatly exacerbated socioeconomic weaknesses. Rapid and uncontrolled change, rather than gradual and organised, seem increasingly likely as geoeconomic regions risk collapsing. The economic and political crisis is accompanied by an intellectual crisis, in which ideological convictions impede strategic thinking and planning. Most importantly, the belief in liberal hegemony as the foundation of a rules-based order and perpetual peace generates a Manichaean world view.

The unpreparedness for Greater Eurasia is revealed by the West's reactions to Russian and Chinese counter-sanctions. The astonishment and sense of illegitimacy of Russian and Chinese counter-sanctions are worth exploring as these economic sanctions are in response to European and American sanctions. Economic sanctions have been seen as a one-way instrument of power due to the economic primacy of the West, coupled with the assumptions of moral authority. Sanctions have been seen as an instrument to organise the world towards Fukuyama's end of history where the world embraces political and economic liberalism under Western leadership. It has therefore been assumed that the political objects, Russia and China, would recognise the legitimacy of the teacher-student relationship and the tools for punishing the "bad behaviour." In Greater Eurasia, Europe and the US has neither the economic nor moral authority to exercise this socialising role. Calls for sanctions to uphold liberal values becomes merely an exercise of virtue-signalling and self-aggrandising when it does not influence policies of the counterpart but undermines peaceful relations.

The liberal international economic system is also coming to an end, which results in a more state-centric and Eurasian-led format for globalisation. The concentration of economic power is a precondition for a liberal international economy. The hegemonic power has systemic incentives to embrace a liberal economic system as it integrates the world under its geoeconomic levers of power. The benefit for the hegemon is that a liberal economy negates the ability and incentives of other states to challenge the central role of its mature industries, administration over the "freedom of navigation" along transportation corridors, and the national control of the international financial system and reserve currency. Yet, hegemonic stability comes at a price—the requirement to deliver collective goods to the wider world to incentivise compliance with the hegemonic liberal economic system.

The EU is at a crossroads as the status quo of the unipolar order has already come to an end. What does the Greater Eurasian partnership mean for Europe? Should the EU remain committed solely to the trans-Atlantic Region or embrace the dynamics of Greater Eurasia? Strengthening Western solidarity in opposition to Greater Eurasia requires hardening the porous geoeconomic regional border by converting the rivalry into a military and ideological stand-off, or the EU can integrate as a sovereign entity into the multipolar format of Greater Eurasia.

The Greater Eurasian region is gradually adapting to the new international distribution of power according to their national interest. Several states are positioning themselves between US-led regions and Greater Eurasia. Turkey endeavours to remain a part of the trans-Atlantic region, yet also looks towards Greater Eurasia for economic connectivity. India is similarly leaning towards the Indo-Pacific region, although also seeks to participate in Greater Eurasia. Economic coercion and efforts to isolate states in multipolar Greater Eurasia are counter-productive. Case in point, US economic sanctions against Iran have compelled Tehran to align itself squarely within the Greater Eurasian format by developing a strategic partnership with Russia and China.

By aligning itself solely to the trans-Atlantic region, Europe will drift towards a geoeconomic core-periphery relationship with the US and forego regional autonomy. Concurrently, by positioning itself in a zero-sum rivalry against Russia and China, the EU will incentivise Moscow and Beijing to use wedge tactics.

Systemic pressures are incentivising Europe to play a balancing role within Greater Eurasia. By softening the zero-sum format of relations with Russia, the Europeans can prevent Russia from drifting too close to China and thus risk isolating Europe. As the EU fears the consequences of US-China bipolarity, the incentives for reaching out to Russia will become more evident. Preserving the dividing lines in Europe diminishes the relevance of the continent in the new international economy. Yet, a new format of sovereign equality must be reached that is acceptable to Moscow. By comparison, Japan and India are reaching out to Russia to diversify Russia's economic connectivity as a condition for preserving its neutral foreign policy. It appears that the EU is acting according to these systemic pressures. The EU is revising its former economic liberalism and post-sovereign ideals and instead pursuing "strategic autonomy" to enhance "European sovereignty."

Geoeconomic theory stipulates that sovereignty is achieved by a balance of strategic autonomy and diversification to excessive reliance on more powerful actors. European sovereignty in a multipolar world inevitably demands economic connectivity with the various poles of power. This requires a sovereign Europe to position itself between the trans-Atlantic region and Greater Eurasia—thus redefining the EU's relationship with the US, China, and Russia.

Bibliography

Acharya, A., 2007. The emerging regional architecture of world politics. *World Politics, 59*(4): 629–652.

Adams, E.D., 2019. *Great Britain and the American Civil War*. Outlook Verlag GmbH, Frankfurt am Main.

Albright, M., 1997. American Principle and Purpose in East Asia. Forrestal Lecture, *U.S. Naval Academy*, Annapolis, Maryland, 15 April 1997.

Albright, M., 1998. Press Conference by US Secretary of State Albright, *NATO Library*, 8 December 1998.

Alemdaroglu, A. and Tepe, S., 2020. Erdogan is turning Turkey into a Chinese Client State. *Foreign Policy*, 16 September 2020.

Ang, K., 2021. Europe pivots to Indo-Pacific with ""multipolar"" ambitions. *Financial Times*, 8 February 2021.

Arnold, J.R. and Wiener, R., 2016. *Understanding US Military Conflicts through Primary Sources*. ABL-CLIO, Santa Barbara.

Aron, R., 1966. *Peace and War: A Theory of International Relations*. Doubleday, Garden City.

Baer, G.W., 1996. *One Hundred Years of Sea Power: The US Navy, 1890-1990*. Stanford University Press, Stanford.

Baev, P.K. 2018. ""The Russian ''pivot to Asia-Pacific.''" In M. Wigell, S. Scholvin, and M. Aaltola (eds.), *Geo-economics and Power Politics in the 21st Century: The Revival of Economic Statecraft*. Routledge, London, pp. 75–88.

Baker, J.A., 2002. Russia in NATO? *The Washington Quarterly, 25*(1): 95–103.

Baldwin, D.A., 1985. *Economic Statecraft*. Princeton University Press, Princeton.

Baldwin, R.E., 1997. The causes of regionalism. *World Economy, 20*(7): 865–888.

Barbanov, O., and Bordachev, T., 2012. Toward the great ocean, or the new globalization of Russia. *Valdai Discussion Club*, July 2012.

Barigazzi, J., 2019. Borrell urges EU to be foreign policy ""player, not the playground." *Politico*, 9 December 2019.

Baru, S., 2012. Geo-economics and strategy. *Survival, 54*(3): 47–58.

Baruch, L., 2001. *Intangibles: Management, Measuring and Reporting.* Brookings Institution Press, Washington DC.

Bekturganov, N.S. and Bolaev, A.V., 2017. The Eurasia Canal as a factor of economic prosperity for the Caspian Region. *Geography, Environment, Sustainability*, *10*(1): 34–43.

Bell, C., 1997. Thinking the unthinkable: British and American naval strategies for an Anglo-American War, 1918–1931. *The International History Review*, *19*(4): 789–808.

Bell, C., 2000. *The Royal Navy, Seapower and Strategy between the Wars.* Palgrave, London.

Beorn, W.W., 2018. *The Holocaust in Eastern Europe: At the Epicenter of the Final Solution.* Bloomsbury Publishing, London.

Bergsten, C.F., 2012. Why the Euro will survive completing the continent's halfbBuilt house. *Foreign Affairs*, *91*(5): 16–22.

Bertrand, N., 2016. Putin: The deterioration of Russia's relationship with the West is the result of many "mistakes." *Business Insider*, 11 January 2016.

Bhadrakumar, M.K., 2020. Quad won't fly. This is why, *Indian Punchline*, 13 October 2020.

Biegun, S., 2020. Deputy Secretary Biegun Remarks at the U.S.-India Strategic Partnership Forum. *US Department of State*, 31 August 2020.

Bildt, C., 2018. Trump's decision to blow up the Iran deal is a massive attack on Europe. *The Washington Post*, 12 March 2018.

Blackwell, W.L., 2015. *Beginnings of Russian Industrialization, 1800-1860.* Princeton University Press, Princeton.

Blackwill, R.D. and Harris, J.M., 2016. *War by Other Means: Geoeconomics and Statecraft.* Harvard University Press, Cambridge.

Blair, T., 1999. The Blair Doctrine. *Public Broadcasting Service*, 22 April 1999.

Blinken, A.J., 2021. Reaffirming and Reimagining America's Alliances. US Department of State, 24 March 2021.

Bowers, C.G., 1932. *Beveridge and the Progressive Era.* The Literary Guild, Boston.

Bradford, A., 2012. The Brussels Effect. *Northwestern University Law Review, 107(1):* 1–67.

Brattberg, E. and De Lima, B.P., 2015. Germany's unipolar moment. *Berlin Policy Journal*, 21 September 2015.

Brechtefeld, J., 1996. *Mitteleuropa and German Politics, 1848 to the Present.* Macmillan, London.

Breslin, S., 2010. Comparative theory, China, and the future of East Asian regionalism(s). *Review of International Studies*, *36*(3): 709–729.

Bretherton, C. and Vogler, J., 1999. *The European Union as a Global Actor.* Routledge, New York.

Broers, M., Hicks, P. and Guimera, A., eds., 2012. *The Napoleonic Empire and the new European political culture.* Springer, New York.

Brown, J.D., 2016. *Japan, Russia and Their Territorial Dispute: The Northern Delusion.* Routledge, New York.

Browning, C.S., 2003. The Region-Building Approach Revisited: The Continued Othering of Russia in Discourses of Region-Building in the European North. *Geopolitics*, *8*(1): 45–71.

Browning, C.S. and Joenniemi, P., 2008. Geostrategies of the European Neighbourhood Policy. *European Journal of International Relations*, *14*(3): 519–551.

Brzezinski, Z., 1997a. *The Grand Chessboard: American Primacy and its Geopolitical Imperatives*. Basic Books, New York.

Brzezinski, Z., 1997b. Geostrategy for Eurasia. *Foreign Affairs*, *76*(5): 50–64.

Brzezinski, Z., 2009. *The Choice: Global Domination or Global Leadership*. Basic Books, New York.

Brzezinski, Z., 2017. How to Address Strategic Insecurity in a Turbulent Age. *The Huffington Post*, 3 January 2017.

Burrows, M. and Manning, R.A., 2015. Kissinger's nightmare: How an inverted US-China-Russia may be a game-changer. *Valdai Paper*, no.33, 9 November 2015.

Buzan, B., 1984. Economic structure and international security: The limits of the liberal case. *International Organization*, *38*(4): 597–624.

Buzan, B., 2005. ""The security dynamics of a 1+4 world." In E. Aydinli and J.N. Rosenau (eds.), *Globalization, Security, and the Nation State: Paradigms in Transition*. State University of New York Press, Albany, pp. 177–198.

Buzan, B., 2010. China in international society: Is "Peaceful Rise" possible? *The Chinese Journal of International Politics*, *3*(1): 5–36.

Buzan, B. and Wæver, O., 2003. *Regions and Powers: The Structure of International Security*. Cambridge University Press, Cambridge.

Carden, J., 2020. Europe's Gaullist revival. *The American Conservative*, 5 October 2020.

Carpenter, T.G., 1992. *A Search for Enemies: America's Alliances After the Cold War*. Cato Institute, Washington DC.

Carpenter, T.G. and Conry, B., 1998. *NATO Enlargement: Illusions and Reality*. Cato Institute.

CENA, 1998. Founding Declaration of the Coalition Against NATO Expansion. *CANE*, 26 January 1998.

Chang, H.J., 2003. *Rethinking Development Economics*. Anthem Press, New York.

Chaudhury, D.R., 2018. Chennai-Vladivostok sea route: India's effort to counter China's OBOR could soon get a big Russian helping hand. *The* Economic Times, 12 July 2018.

Chen, D., 2014. China's ""Marshall Plan"" is much more. *The* Diplomat, 10 November 2014.

Chen, I.T.Y., 2018. European participation in the Asian Infrastructure Investment Bank: Making a strategic choice and seeking economic opportunities. *Asia Europe Journal*, *16*(4): 297–315.

Cheshire, H.T., 1934. The expansion of Imperial Russia to the Indian border. *The Slavonic and East European Review*, pp. 85–97.

Chizhov, V., 2012. Impact of the Eurasian integration on Russia-EU relations. Speech by Ambassador Chizhov. *Permanent Mission of the Russian Federation to the European Union*, Berlin, 15 June 2012.

Churchill, W.S., 1994. ""The tragedy of Europe." In B.F. Nelsen and A. Stubb (eds.), *The European Union*. Palgrave, London, pp. 5–9.

Clark, G., 2005. Japan-Russia dispute over northern territories highlights flawed diplomacy. *Asia-Pacific Journal*, 3(4): 1–5.

Clinton, H.R., 2011a. Secretary of State Hillary Rodham Clinton Speaks on India and the United States: A Vision for the 21st Century, 20 July 2011.

Clinton, H.R., 2011b. Foreign Policy: America's Pacific Century. *NPR*, 13 October 2011.

Clinton, H.R., 2020. A National Security Reckoning: How Washington Should Think about Power. *Foreign Affairs*, November/December 2020.

Cohen, S.F., 2009. *Soviet fates and lost alternatives: from Stalinism to the new Cold War*. Columbia University Press.

Cohen, S.F., 2018. *War with Russia?: From Putin & Ukraine to Trump & Russiagate*. Simon and Schuster, New York.

Common Spaces Agreement, 2005. Road Map on the Common Space of External Security, Approved on May 10, 2005, in Moscow by President of Russia Vladimir Putin, Prime Minister of Luxembourg Jean-Claude Juncker, President of the European Commission Jose Manuel Durao Barroso, and European Union High Representative for Foreign Policy and Security Javier Solana.

Connolly, R., 2016. The empire strikes back: Economic statecraft and the securitisation of political economy in Russia. *Europe-Asia Studies*, 68(4): 750–773.

Crawford, T.W., 2011. Preventing enemy coalitions: How wedge strategies shape power politics. *International Security*, 35(4): 155–189.

CRS, 2012. Pivot to the Pacific? The Obama Administration's "Rebalancing" Toward Asia. *Congressional Research Service*, 28 March 2012.

Cwik, P.F., 2011. The new neo☐mercantilism: Currency manipulation as a form of protectionism. *Economic Affairs*, 31(3): 7–11.

Daalder, I. and Lindsay, J., 2004. An alliance of democracies. *The Washington Post*, 23 May 2004.

Danilov, D., 2005. Russia and European security. *What Russia Sees. Chaillot Papers,* pp. 79–98.

De Brichambaut and Perrin, Marc, 2009. It's time the EU stopped undermining the OSCE. *Europe's World*, Autumn(13): 48–51.

Deng X., 1990. The international situation and economic problems. *The Selected Works of Deng Xiaoping*, Vol. 3, 3 March 1990.

Diesen, G., 2015. *EU and NATO Relations with Russia: After the Collapse of the Soviet Union*. Routledge, London.

Diesen, G., 2017. *Russia's Geoeconomic Strategy for a Greater Eurasia.* Routledge, London.

Diesen, G., 2018. The geoeconomics of the Russian–Japanese territorial dispute. *Asian Survey*, 58(3): 582–605.

Diesen, G., 2019. The geoeconomics of Russia's Greater Eurasia Initiative. *Asian Politics & Policy*, 11(4): 566–585.

Diesen, G., 2021a. *Great Power Politics in the Fourth Industrial Revolution: The Geoeconomics of Technological Sovereignty.* Bloomsbury, London.

Diesen, G., 2021b. *Russian Conservatism: Managing Change under Permanent Revolution.* Rowman & Littlefield, London.

Diesen, G. and Wood, S., 2012. Russia's proposal for a new security system: Confirming diverse perspectives. *Australian Journal of International Affairs, 66*(4): 450–467.

Diez, T., 2005. Constructing the self and changing others: Reconsidering normative power Europe. *Millennium-Journal of International Studies, 33*(3): 613–636.

Dolgopolov, N. and Fronin, V., 2019. My Vsegda budem vmeste [We will always be together]. *Rossiyskaya Gazeta*, 2 April 2019.

Donnan, S., Ryan, C. and Stearns, J., 2020. U.S. widens tariffs on EU imports in Airbus, Boeing fight. *Bloomberg*, 31 December 2020.

Dostoevsky, F., 1997. *A Writer's Diary — Volume 2: 1877–1881.* Northwestern University Press, Illinois.

DPG 1992. Defense Planning Guidance. Washington, 18 February 1992.

Du Bois, W.E.B., 1941. Neuropa: Hitler's New World Order. *The Journal of Negro Education*, 19(3): 380–386.

Dulles, J.F., 1952. Security in the Pacific. *Foreign Affairs, 30*(2): 175–187.

DW, 2020. NATO's Jens Stoltenberg sounds warning on China's rise. *Deutsche Welle*, 13 June 2020.

DW, 2021. China is a challenge and opportunity, NATO chief tells DW. *Deutsche Welle*, 22 March 2021.

Dzarasov, R.S., Lane, D. and Dadabaev, T., 2017. Russian neo-revisionist strategy and the Eurasian Project. *Cambridge Journal of Eurasian Studies* (1): 1–15.

Earle, E.M., 1943. Friedrich List, forerunner of pan-Germanism. *The American Scholar, 12*(4): 430–443.

Eberlein, B. and Grande, E., 2005. Beyond delegation: Transnational regulatory regimes and the EU regulatory state. *Journal of European Public Policy, 12*(1): 89–112.

Eckes, A.E., 1995. *Opening America's Market: US Foreign Trade Policy Since 1776.* University of North Carolina Press, North Carolina.

Eckes, A.E. 2015. ""U.S. trade history." In W.A. Lovett, A.E. Eckes Jr., and R.L. Brinkman (eds.), *US Trade Policy: History, Theory and the WTO.* Routledge, New York, pp. 36–92.

EEAS, 2018. The European way to connectivity—a new strategy on how to better connect Europe and Asia. *European External Action Service*, 19 September 2018.

EEC, 2018. Connecting Paths: 2018 Annual Report, *Eurasian Economic Commission.*

Eichengreen, B., 2011. *Exorbitant Privilege: The Rise and Fall of the Dollar and the Future of the International Monetary System.* Oxford University Press, Oxford.

Eisemann, J., Heginbotham, E. and Mitchell, D., 2015. *China and the Developing World: Beijing's Strategy for the Twenty-First Century.* Routledge, New York.

Élysée, 2019. Speech by the President of the Republic at the conference of ambassadors [in French: Discours du Président de la République à la conférence des ambassadeurs]. *Élysée*, 27 August 2019.

Élysée, 2020. Dialogue franco-allemand sur la Technologie. *Élysée*, 13 October 2020.

Entin, M. and Zagorsky, A., 2008. Should Russia leave the OSCE? *Russia in Global Affairs*, 6(3): 19–31.

Ercolani, G. and Sciascia, L., 2011. Keeping security and peace: Behind the strategicalization of NATO's "Critical Security Discourse." *The Journal of Security Strategies* (14): 43–85.

Erickson, A.S. and Wuthnow, J., 2016. Barriers, springboards and benchmarks: China conceptualizes the Pacific Island chains. *The China Quarterly*, pp.1–22.

European Commission, 2008a. Eastern Partnership: Commission staff working document accompanying the communication from the Commission to the European Parliament and the Council, 3 December 2008.

European Commission, 2008b. EU-Russia relations: The way forward? *European Commission*, 8 May 2008.

European Commission, 2016. Joint communication to the European Parliament and the Council: Elements for a new EU strategy on China. *European Commission*, 22 June 2016.

European Commission, 2017. State of the Union 2017 –- Trade Package: European Commission proposes framework for screening of foreign direct investments. *European Commission*, 14 September 2017.

European Commission, 2019. EU-China—A strategic outlook. *European Commission*, Strasbourg, 12 March 2019.

European Commission, 2020a. Cybersecurity of 5G networks—EU Toolbox of risk mitigating measures. *European Commission*, 19 January 2020.

European Commission, 2020b. State of the Union 2020: The von der Leyen Commission: One year on. The European Commission

European Council, 2010. Project Europe 2030: A report to the European Council by the Reflection Group on the Future of the EU 2030. May 2010.

European Council, 2019a. A new strategic agenda for the EU. *Council of the European Union*, 21 June 2019.

European Council, 2019b. Council Decision (EU) 2019/ of authorising the opening of negotiations with the United States of America for an agreement on the elimination of tariffs for industrial goods. *Council of the European Union*, 9 April 2019.

European Council, 2020a. Conclusions of the President of the European Council following the video conference of the members of the European Council. *Council of the European Union*, 23 April 2020.

European Council, 2020b. EU-China Summit: Defending EU interests and values in a complex and vital partnership –- Press release by President Michel and President von der Leyen. *Council of the European Union*, 22 June 2020.

European Council, 2020c. Recovery Plan: Powering Europe's strategic autonomy –- Speech by President Charles Michel at the Brussels Economic Forum. *Council of the European Union*, 8 September 2020.

European Council, 2021. Digital sovereignty is central to European strategic autonomy –- Speech by President Charles Michel at ""Masters of digital 2021"" online event. *Council of the European Union*, 3 February 2021.

Evans-Pritchard, A., 2016. Euro "house of cards" to collapse, warns ECB prophet. *The Telegraph*, 16 October 2016.

Fairgrieve, J., 1915. *Geography and World Power*. University of London Press, London.

Farage, N., 2015. Speech at the European Parliament, Strasbourg, 7 October 2015.

Feldstein, M., 2012. The failure of the euro. *Foreign Affairs*, *91*(1): 105–116.

Figaro, 2020. Emmanuel Macron: ""Renforcer notre autonomie stratégique." *Figaro Live*, 23 April 2020.

Fiott, D., 2018. Strategic autonomy: Towards ""European sovereignty"" in defence? *European Union Institute for Security Studies (EUISS)*, November 2018.

Flanagan, S.J., 1992. NATO and central and eastern Europe: From liaison to security partnership. *Washington Quarterly*, *15*(2): 141–151.

Follain, J. and Migliaccio, A., 2020. Something has snapped in Italy's stormy relationship with Europe. *Bloomberg*, 21 April 2020.

Forbes, 2019. For Wall Street, Russia has become ""Bulletproof."" *Forbes Magazine*, 18 November 2019.

FR, 2020. Europe must break ""Chinese-American duopoly," Macron says. *Financial Review*, 17 November 2020.

Freeman, C.P., 2018. China's ""regionalism foreign policy"" and China-India relations in South Asia. *Contemporary Politics*, *24*(1): 81–97.

Friedman, T.L., 1998. Foreign affairs: Now a word from X. *The New York Times*, 2 May 1998.

Friedrich-Ebert-Stiftung, 2020. Russia's ""Generation Z"": Attitudes and values 2019/2020. *Friedrich-Ebert-Stiftung*, 2020.

FT, 2012. Clinton vows to thwart new Soviet Union. *Financial Times*, 12 December 2012.

FT, 2019a. Vladimir Putin says liberalism has ""become obsolete."" *Financial Times*, 28 June 2019.

FT, 2019b. Abide by US sanctions on Iran or drop the dollar, Mnuchin says. *Financial Times*, 18 July 2019.

FT, 2020. Yandex to offer car-sharing in Europe as rivals pull out. *Financial Times*, 12 January 2020.

FT, 2021. Germany's bridges to Russia split open Europe. *Financial Times*, 15 February 2021.

Gabuev, A., 2020. Pax Sinica: Europe's dilemma in facing the Sino-Russian axis. *Carnegie Moscow Centre*, 25 November 2020.

Gaddis, J.L., 1982. *Strategies of containment: A critical appraisal of postwar American national security policy*. Oxford University Press, New York.

Gaddis, J.L., 2005. *Strategies of Containment: A Critical Appraisal of American National Security Policy during the Cold War*. Oxford University Press, Oxford.

Gallagher, J. and Robinson, R., 1953. The imperialism of free trade. *The Economic History Review*, *6*(1): 1–15.

Garcia-Herrero, A., 2020. Macro view of US-China tech competition: WhereaAre we and what to expect? *Valdai Discussion Club*, 16 November 2020.

Garcia-Herrero, A., and Xu, J., 2019. How does China fare on the Russian market? Implications for the European Union. *Bruegel*, working paper issue 08, 18 November 2019.

Gates, D., 1997. *The Napoleonic Wars 1803-1815.* London, Arnold.

Gates, R.M., 2014. *Duty: Memoirs of a Secretary at War.* Knopf Doubleday Publishing Group, New York.

Gatev, I. and Diesen, G., 2016. Eurasian encounters: The Eurasian economic union and the Shanghai cooperation organisation. *European Politics and Society, 17*(1): 133–150.

Geis, A., 2013. The ""concert of democracies"": Why some states are more equal than others. *International Politics, 50*(2): 257–277.

German Federal Ministry of Defence. 2011. Defence Policy Guidelines: Safeguarding National Interests—Assuming International Responsibility—Shaping Security Together. *German Ministry of Defence,* Berlin, 27 May.

Gerschenkron, A., 1963. *Economic Backwardness in Historical Perspective: A Book of Essays.* Harvard University Press, Cambridge.

Gheciu, A., 2005. *NATO in the "New Europe": The* Politics of International Socialization after the Cold War. Stanford University Press.

Gilpin, R., 1975. *U.S. Power and the Multinational Corporation: The Political Economy of Foreign Direct Investment.* Basic Books, New York.

Gilpin, R., 1981. *War and Change in World Politics.* Cambridge University Press, Cambridge.

Gilpin, R., 2011. *Global Political Economy: Understanding the International Economic Order.* Princeton University Press, Princeton.

Goldberg, J., 2016. The Obama Doctrine: The U.S. president talks through his hardest decisions about America's role in the world. *The Atlantic*, April 2016.

Goldstein, L.J., 2021. The Indo-Pacific strategy is a recipe for disaster. *Lawfare*, 18 February 2021.

Gunnarsson, B., 2021. Ten years of international shipping on the Northern Sea route: Trends and challenges. *Arctic Review on Law and Politics* (12): 4–30.

Gvosdev, N., 2008. Parting with illusions: Developing a realistic approach to relations with Russia. *CATO Institute*, 29 February 2008.

Haidt, J. 2012. *The Righteous Mind: Why Good People Are Divided by Politics and Religion.* Penguin Books, London.

Hamilton, A. 1857. *The Federalist: On the New Constitution* (Written in 1788). Hallowell, Masters, Smith & Company.

Hanemann, T., Huotari, M. and Kratz, A., 2019. Chinese FDI in Europe: 2018 trends and impact of new screening policies. *A Report by Rhodium Group (RHG) and the Mercator Institute for China Studies (MERICS)*, pp. 2019–03.

Haukkala, H., 2010. *The EU-Russia Strategic Partnership: The Limits of Post-Sovereignty in International Relations.* Routledge, London.

Haushofer, K., 1924. *Geopolitik des pazifischen Ozeans: Studien über die Wechselbeziehungen zwischen Geographie und Geschichte.* Kurt Vowinckel, Berlin.

He, K. and Li, M., 2020. Understanding the dynamics of the Indo-Pacific: US–China strategic competition, regional actors, and beyond. *International Affairs, 96*(1): 1–7.

Heckscher, E., 1922. *The Continental System.* Clarendon Press, Oxford.

Heilmann, S., Rudolf, M., Huotari, M. and Buckow, J., 2014. China's shadow foreign policy: Parallel structures challenge the established international order. *China Monitor*, *18(*October): 1–9.

Heller, M., 2015. *Histoire de la Russie et de son empire*. Tempus, Paris.

Henderson, W.O., 1975. *The rise of German industrial power, 1834-1914*. University of California Press, Berkeley.

Henderson, W.O., 1983. *Friedrich List, Economist and Visionary, 1789-1846*. Frank Cass, New York.

Herwig, H.H., 2016. *The Demon of Geopolitics: How Karl Haushofer "'Educated'" Hitler and Hess*. Rowman & Littlefield, London.

Hettne, B., 1993. Neo-mercantilism: The pursuit of regionness. *Cooperation and Conflict*, *28*(3): 211–232.

Hettne, B. and Söderbaum, F., 2000. Theorising the rise of regionness. *New Political Economy*, *5*(3): 457–472.

Hilpert, H.G. and Wacker, G., 2015. Geoeconomics meets geopolitics: China's new economic and foreign policy initiatives. *Stiftung Wissenschaft und Politik*, June, pp.1–7.

Hilton, B., 1977. *Corn, Cash, Commerce: The Economic Policies of the Tory Governments, 1815-1830*. Oxford University Press, New York.

Hirschman, A., 1945. *National Power and the Structure of Foreign Trade,*.University of California Press, Berkeley.

Hirschman, A., 1978. Beyond asymmetry: Critical notes on myself as a young man and on some other old friends. *International Organisation*, *32*(1): 45–50.

Hoagland, J., 1989. Europe's destiny. *Foreign Affairs, 69*(1): 33–50.

Hobsbawm, E.J., 1968. *Industry and Empire: An Economic History of Britain since 1750*. Weidenfeld and Nicolson, London.

Holslag, J., 2006. China's new mercantilism in Central Africa. *African and Asian Studies*, *5*(2): 133–169.

Hopkins, M. and Lazonick, W., 2014. Who invests in the high-tech knowledge base. *Institute for New Economic Thinking*, Working Paper no.6.

Hopkirk, P., 2001. *The Great Game: On Secret Service in High Asia*. Oxford University Press, Oxford.

Horn, S., Reinhart, C.M. and Trebesch, C. 2019. China's overseas lending. Working Paper 26050, National Bureau of Economic Research.

Hornby, L., 2018. Mahathir Mohamad warns against "'New Colonialism'" during China visit. *Financial Times*, 20 August 2018.

Hosking, G.A., 2001. *Russia and the Russians: A History*. Harvard University Press, Cambridge.

Huasheng, Z., 2018. Greater Eurasian partnership: China's perspective. *China International Studies* (January/February 2018): 68–84.

Hudson, M., 2010. *America's Protectionist Takeoff, 1815-1914: The Neglected American School of Political Economy*. Islet.

Hughes, C. R., 2005. Nationalism and multilateralism in Chinese foreign policy: Implications for Southeast Asia. *The Pacific Review*, *18*(1): 119–135.

Huntington, S.P., 1993. Why international primacy matters. *International Security*, *17*(4): 68–83.

Huntington, S.P., 1999. The lonely superpower. *Foreign Affairs*, *87*(2): 35–49.

Huntington, S.P., 2004. Dead souls: The denationalization of the American elite. *The National Interest*, 1 March 2004.

Huotari, M. and Heep, S., 2015. Learning geoeconomics: China's experimental financial and monetary initiatives. *Asia Europe Journal*, *14*(2): 153–171.

Hurrell, A., 1995. Explaining the resurgence of regionalism in world politics. *Review of International Studies*, *21*(4): 331–358.

Hyde-Price, A., 2006. "Normative" power Europe: A realist critique. *Journal of European Public Policy*, *13*(2): 217–234.

Ikenberry, G.J., 2008. The rise of China and the future of the West: Can the liberal system survive? *Foreign Affairs*, *87*(1): 23–37.

Ikenberry, G.J. and Slaughter, A.M., 2006. Forging a world of liberty under law. U.S. national security in the 21st century. Princeton, NJ. Final Paper of the Princeton Project on National Security.

Ingram, P., 1998. *Napoleon and Europe*. Stanley Thornes Publishers Ltd., Cheltenham.

Ireland, P.W., 1941. Berlin to Baghdad up-to-date. *Foreign Affairs*, *19*(3): 665–670.

Irwin, D.A., 1989. Political economy and Peel's repeal of the Corn Laws. *Economics & Politics*, *1*(1): 41–59.

Ischinger, W., 2021. A possible solution to the Nord Stream 2 conundrum. *Spiegel International*, 27 February 2021.

Jacobs, E., 2020. Top Chinese professor boasts of operatives in top of US ""core inner circle." *New York Post*, 8 December 2020.

Joffe, J., 2017. Europe's struggle to take its destiny into its own hands. *The Wall Street Journal*, 20 July 2017.

Jones, L. and Hameiri, S., 2020. Debunking the myth of ""Debt-trap Diplomacy"": How recipient countries shape China's Belt and Road Initiative. *Chatham House*, 19 August 2020.

Jones, R.B., 1986. *Conflict and Control in the World Economy: Contemporary Economic Realism and Neo-Mercantilism*. Wheatsheaf Books, Brighton.

Kaczynski, T., 1995. Industrial society and its future. *The Washington Post*, 19 September 1995.

Kaiser, D.E., 2015. *Economic Diplomacy and the Origins of the Second World War: Germany, Britain, France, and Eastern Europe, 1930-1939*. Princeton University Press, Princeton.

Kaplan, R.D., 2012. *The Revenge of Geography: What the Map Tells Us about Coming Conflicts and the Battle against Fate*. Random House, New York.

Kaplan, S.B., 2018. The rise of patient capital: The political economy of Chinese global finance. *Institute for International Economic Policy Working Paper Series, Elliott School of International Affairs and the George Washington University*.

Karaganov, S., 2020. ""The Military Underpinning of the Geopolitical Revolution." In G. Diesen and A. Lukin (eds.), *Russia in a Changing World*. Palgrave Macmillan, Singapore, pp. 1–22.

Kärnfelt, M., 2020. China's currency push: The Chinese Yuan expands its footprint in Europe. *Merics*, 9 January 2020.

Katzenstein, P.J., 2005. *A world of Regions: Asia and Europe in the American Imperium.* Cornell University Press, London.

Kazmin, A., 2016. India watches anxiously as Chinese influence grows. *Financial Times*, 10 May 2016.

Keating, D., 2012. Commissioner urges EU to face down Russia on energy. *Europeanvoice*, 11 October 2012.

Keating, D., 2018. Trump to Europe: Drop Nord Stream or we won't protect you from Russia. *Forbes*, 11 July 2018.

Kennedy, P., 1987. *The Rise and Fall of the Great Powers: Economic Change and Military Conflict from 1500 to 2000.* Vintage.

Keqin, S., 2021. Poll finds Germans diverge from US" anti-China campaign. *Global Times*, 14 January 2021.

Khabar 2015. The next provincial relations, Iran, China and Russia, explained China's readiness to build more power plants in Iran. *Khabar Online*.

Kindleberger, C.P., 1986. *The World in Depression, 1929-1939.* University of California Press, California.

Kipp, J.W. and Lincoln, W.B., 1979. Autocracy and reform bureaucratic absolutism and political modernization in nineteenth-century Russia. *Russian History*, 6(1): 1–21.

Kireeva, A.A., 2020. The Indo-Pacific in the strategies of the US and Japan. *Russia in Global Affairs*, 18(3): 98–127.

Kissinger, H., 1994. *Diplomacy.* Simon and Schuster, New York.

Kissinger, H., 1999. Interview in *The Daily Telegraph*, June 28, 1999.

Kissinger, H., 2015. The interview: Henry Kissinger. *The National Interest*, 19 August 2015.

Kjellén, R., 1900. Inledning till Sveriges geografi. Gothenburg, Wettergren & Kerber.

Klaus, K., 2009. Speech of the President of the Czech Republic Václav Klaus. *European Parliament*, 26 January 2009.

Klinke, I., 2012. Postmodern geopolitics? The European Union eyes Russia. *Europe-Asia Studies*, 64(5): 929–947.

Klug, A., 2001. Why Chamberlain failed and Bismarck succeeded: The political economy of tariffs in British and German elections. *European Review of Economic History*, 5(2): 219–250.

Klyuev, N.N., 2018. Industrial and transport development of the territory of Russia in the post-Soviet period. *Geography and Natural Resources*, 39(1): 1–9.

Knorr, K., 1977. International economic leverage and its uses. *Economic Issues and National Security.* University Press of Kansas, Kansas.

Kolstad, I., 2020. Too big to fault? Effects of the 2010 Nobel Peace Prize on Norwegian exports to China and foreign policy. *International Political Science Review*, 41(2): 207–223.

Koreneva, M., 2013. Russia, China sign ""Unprecedented"" $270 billion oil deal. *Agence France-Presse*, 24 June 2013.

Kortunov, A. 2019. Is Russia over its resentment. *Russian International Affairs Council*, 14 October 2019.

Kowalski, B., 2017. China's foreign policy towards Central and Eastern Europe: The "16+ 1" format in the South–South cooperation perspective. Cases of the Czech Republic and Hungary. *Cambridge Journal of Eurasian Studies, 1*(1): 1–16.

Kramer, A.E., 2012. Sberbank Looks to buy banks in Eastern Europe. *The New York Times*, 14 April 2012.

Krauthammer, C., 1990-1. The unipolar moment. *Foreign Affairs, 70*(1): 23–33.

Kremlin, 2016. Plenary Session of St. Petersburg International Economic Forum, 17 June 2016.

Krickovic, A., 2014. Imperial nostalgia or prudent geopolitics? Russia's efforts to reintegrate the post-Soviet space in geopolitical perspective. *Post-Soviet Affairs, 30*(6): 503–528.

Kristeva, J., 2000. ""Europe Divided: Politics, Ethics, Religion." In *Crisis of the European Subject.* Other Press, New York.

Krugman, P., 2013. Those depressing Germans. *The New York Times*, 3 November 2013.

Kuik, C.C., 2005. Multilateralism in China's ASEAN policy: Its evolution, characteristics, and aspiration. *Contemporary Southeast Asia, 27*(1): 102–122.

Kulintsev, Y.V., Mukambaev, A.A., Rakhimov, K.K. and Zuenko, I.Y., 2020. Sinophobia in the post-Soviet space. *Russia in Global Affairs, 18*(3): 128–151.

Kundnani, H., 2020. Europe's sovereignty conundrum. *Berlin Policy Journal*, 13 May 2020.

Kupchan, C.A., 1994. Expand NATO-And split Europe. *The New York Times*, 27 November 1994.

Kupchan, C.A., 2010. NATO's final frontier: Why Russia should join the Atlantic Alliance. *Foreign Affairs, 89*(3): 100–112.

Kuznetsov, A., 2016. Russian direct investment as a factor of Eurasian integration. *Problems of Economic Transition, 58*(4): 348–361.

Laruelle, M., 2015. The US Silk Road: Geopolitical imaginary or the repackaging of strategic interests? *Eurasian Geography and Economics, 56*(4): 360–375.

Laskar, R., 2020. West has policy to engage India in ""anti-China games," says Russian foreign minister Lavrov. *Hindustan Times*, 9 December 2020.

Lavenex, S., 2011. Concentric circles of flexible ""EUropean"" integration: A typology of EU external governance relations. *Comparative European Politics, 9*(4): 372–393.

Lavrov, S., 2012. Russia in the 21st-century world of power. *Russia in Global Affairs, 4* (October/December).

Lavrov, S., 2013. Speech at 49th Munich Security Conference, February 2013.

Lavrov, S., 2018. Foreign Minister Sergey Lavrov's remarks and answers to media questions at the news conference following the Russia-ASEAN Foreign Ministers' Meeting, Singapore, 2 August 2018.

Lavrov, S., 2020. Foreign Minister Sergey Lavrov's remarks and answers to questions at the presentation of the Valdai International Discussion Club analytical report "History, To Be Continued: The Utopia of a Diverse World," *The Ministry of Foreign Affairs of the Russian Federation*, 14 October 2020.

Layne, C., 1993. The unipolar illusion: Why new great powers will rise. *International security*, *17*(4): 5–51.

Lazonick, W., 2009. *Sustainable Prosperity in the New Economy? Business Organization and High-Tech Employment in the United States.* WE Upjohn Institute for Employment Research Kalamazoo, Michigan.

Le Corre, P., 2018. On Chinese investment and influence in Europe. *Carnegie Endowment for International Peace*, 23 May 2018.

Le Corre, P. and Sepulchre, A., 2016. *China's Offensive in Europe.* Brookings Institution Press, Washington.

Lee, L. and Gill, G., 2015. India, Central Asia and the Eurasian Union: A new ballgame? *India Quarterly: A Journal of International Affairs*, *71*(2): 110–125.

Lehti, 1999. ""Competing or complementary images: The North and the Baltic world from the historical perspective."" In Hiski Haukkala (ed.), *Dynamic Aspects of the Northern Dimension.* Turku: Jean Monnet Unit, University of Turku.

Levada 2021. Rossiya i Evropa [Russia and Europe]. *Levada Centre*, 18 March 2021.

Lissovolik, Y., 2017. A geographical case for the ""One Belt, One Road"" and the Eurasian Economic Union. *Valdai Discussion Club*, 25 May 2017.

List, F. 1827. *Outlines of American Political Economy, in a Series of Letters.* Samuel Parker, Philadelphia.

List, F., 1841. *The National System of Political Economy.* Longmans, Green & Company, London.

List, F., 1846. Über den Wert und die Bedingungen einer Allianz zwischen Großbritannien und Deutschland (On the Value and Conditions of an Alliance between Great Britain and Germany), Presented to the governments of England and Prussia, in Friedrich List's Gesammelte Schriften. Ed Ludwig Haeuffer. Stuttgart and Tübingen, JG Cottascher Verlag, Vol. 2, 435–468.

Löwenhardt, J., 2004. The OSCE, Moldova and Russian diplomacy in 2003. *Journal of Communist Studies and Transition Politics*, *20*(4): 103–112.

Lukin, A., 2000. *Political Culture of the Russian ""Democrats.""* Oxford University Press, Oxford.

Lukin, A., 2016. Russia's pivot to Asia: Myth or reality? *Strategic Analysis*, *40*(6): 573–589.

Lukin, A. and Yakunin, V., 2018. Eurasian integration and the development of Asiatic Russia. *Journal of Eurasian Studies*, *9*(2): 100–113.

Lukyanov, F., 2021. EU-Russia relations: What went wrong? *Carnegie Moscow Center*, 26 February 2021.

Lundestad, G., 1986. Empire by invitation? The United States and Western Europe, 1945-1952. *Journal of Peace Research*, *23*(3): 263–277.

Lustgarten, A., 2020. How Russia wins the climate crisis. *The New York Times*, 16 December 2020.

Luttwak, E.N., 1990. From geopolitics to geo-economics: Logic of conflict, grammar of commerce. *The National Interest* (20): 17–23.

Luttwak, E.N., 1993. Why fascism is the wave of the future. *London Review of Books, 16*(7): 3–6.

Luttwak, E.N., 2010. *Endangered American Dream.* Simon and Schuster, New York.

Lynch, D., 2003. Russia faces Europe. Chaillot Paper No. 60. *Institute for Security Studies,* Paris.

Lyons M., 1994. *Napoleon Bonaparte and Legacy of the French Revolution.* St. Martin's Press, New York.

Ma, T., 2018. Eurasia Canal can link Black, Caspian seas. *China Daily*, 29 July 2018.

Maas, H., 2020. In humility for peace and Europe. *Federal Foreign Office*, 7 December 2020.

Maas, H., 2021. Speech by Foreign Minister Heiko Maas to the German Bundestag at the debate held at the request of the parliamentary group of Alliance 90/The Greens on "What consequences should the Federal Government draw from violence, arbitrary acts and repression in Russia?" *Federal Foreign Office*, 10 February 2021.

Maçães, B., 2019. Why Putin wants to believe in the death of liberalism. *Moscow Times*, 1 July 2019.

Mackinder, H.J., 1904. The Geographical Pivot of History. *The Geographical Journal, 170*(4): 421–444.

Mackinder, H.J., 1919. *Democratic Ideals and Reality: A Study in the Politics of Reconstruction.* Constable, London.

Macron, E., 2019. Ambassador's Conference—Speech by M. Emmanuel Macron, President of the Republic, Paris, 27 August 2019.

Mahan, A.T., 1890. *The Influence of Seapower on History.* Little, Brown and Company, Boston.

Mahan, A.T., 1892. *The Influence of Sea Power upon the French Revolution and Empire.* Little, Brown and Company, Boston.

Makarkin, A., 2010. We have simply redefined the threat. *Eastern Partnership Community*, 10 October 2010.

Mankoff, J., 2013. *The United States and Central Asia after 2014.* Washington, DC: Center for Strategic and International Studies, January.

Manners, Ian, 2002. Normative power Europe: A contradiction in terms? *Journal of Common Market Studies, 40*(2): 235–258.

Manners, Ian, 2006. The European Union as a normative power: A response to Thomas Diez. *Millennium-Journal of International Studies, 35*(1): 167–180.

Mansfield, E.D. and Milner, H.V., 1999. The new wave of regionalism. *International Organization*, pp.589–627.

Marrow, A., 2020. Russia's Sberbank partners with China's Huawei on cloud services. *Reuters*, 3 March 2020.

Mastanduno, M., 1997. Preserving the unipolar moment: Realist theories and US grand strategy after the Cold War. *International Security, 21*(4): 49–88.

Matlock, J.F., 2010. *Superpower Illusions: How Myths and False Ideologies Led America Astray—-and How to Return to Reality.* Yale University Press, New Haven.

Mattich, A., 2011. German mercantilism to rescue the euro. *Wall Street Journal*, 28 June 2011.

Mearsheimer, J.J., 2014. Why the Ukraine crisis is the West's fault: The liberal delusions that provoked Putin. *Foreign Affairs*, *93*(5): 77–89.

Mearsheimer, J.J. and Walt, S.M., 2016. The case for offshore balancing: A superior US grand strategy. *Foreign Affairs, 95*(4): 70–83.

Medcalf, R., 2017. "'Reimagining Asia: From Asia-Pacific to Indo-Pacific.'" In *International Relations and Asia's Southern Tier* (pp. 9–28). Springer, Singapore.

Meissner, K.L., 2019. Leveraging interregionalism: EU strategic interests in Asia, Latin America and the Gulf region. *International Politics*, pp.1–16.

Melenciuc, S., 2020. Romania caught in the middle of the US-China cold war. *Business Review*, 21 August 2020.

Michaels, D. and Pop, V., 2021. China faces European obstacles as somecCohntries Heed U.S. pressure. *The Wall Street Journal*, 23 February 2021.

Miller, C., 2018a. *Putinomics: Power and money in resurgent Russia*. UNC Press Books.

Miller, N., 2018b. China undermining us "'with sticks and carrots'": Outgoing German minister. *The Age*, 19 February 2018.

Mirsky, D.S., 1927. The Eurasian Movement. *The Slavonic Review*, *6*(17): 311–320.

Mitrany, D., 1965. The prospect of integration: Federal or functional. *Journal of Common Market Studies*, *4*(2): 119–149.

MMS, 2020. Rush Limbaugh: "There cannot be a peaceful coexistence" between liberals and conservatives. *Media Matters*, 9 December 2020.

Moe, A., 2020. A new Russian policy for the Northern sea route? State interests, key stakeholders and economic opportunities in changing times. *The Polar Journal*, *10*(2): 209–227.

Momtaz, R., 2019. Merkel sees post-Brexit as "'potential competitor'" to EU. *Politico*, 13 October 2019.

Möller, F., 2003. Capitalizing of difference: A security community or/as a Western project. *Security Dialogue*, *34*(3): 315–328.

Morris, I., 2014. *Why the West Rules—-for Now: The Patterns of History, and What They Reveal About the Future*, Feng Qian, trans. Beijing: China International Trust and Investment Corporation (CITIC) Publishing House.

MTC, 2019. Final report of the Joint Working Group between Finland and Norway on the Arctic Railway. *Ministry of Transport and Communications*, Helsinki, 11 February 2019.

MTI, 2018. Hungary is ready for the opening of a new chapter in Hungarian-Turkic cooperation. *MTI*, 3 September 2018.

Mudde, C., 2016. Europe's populist surge: A long time in the making. *Foreign Affairs*, *95*(6): 25–30.

Münchau, W., 2015. Two mistakes that ruined Europe. *Financial Times*, 1 November 2015.

Mundell, R., 1993. *EMU and the International Monetary System: A Transatlantic Perspective*. Austrian National Bank Working Paper 13, Vienna.

Muraviev, A., 2011. Shadow of the northern giant: Russia's current and future engagement with the Indian Ocean Region. *Journal of the Indian Ocean Region*, *7*(2): 200–219.

NATO, 2020. NATO 2030: United for a new era –- Analysis and recommendations of the Reflection Group appointed by the NATO secretary general. *NATO*, 25 November 2020.

Naumann, F., 1915. *Mitteleuropa.* Reimer, Berlin.

Neumann, I.B., 1994. A region-building approach to Northern Europe. *Review of International Studies*, 20(1): 53–74.

Neumann, I.B., 1999. *Uses of the Other: The '"'East'"' in European identity forma-tion.* Manchester University Press, Manchester.

Neumann, I.B., 2013. ""Russia as a Great Power." In J. Hedenskog, V. Konnander, B. Nygren, I. Oldberg and C. Pursiainen (eds.), *Russia as a Great Power: Dimensions of Security under Putin*. Routledge, New York, pp. 13–28.

Neumann, I.B. and Pouliot, V., 2011. Untimely Russia: Hysteresis in Russian-Western relations over the past millennium. *Security Studies*, 20(1): 105–137.

Nierop, T. and De Vos, S., 1988. Of shrinking empires and changing roles: World trade patterns in the postwar period. *Tijdschrift voor economische en sociale geo-grafie*, 79(5): 343–364.

Novikov, S.V., Lastochkina, V.V. and Solodova, A.D., 2019, May. Import substitution in the industrial sector: Analysis and facts. In *IOP Conference Series: Materials Science and Engineering*, 537(4): 1–5.

NSS, 2002. The National Security Strategy of the United States of America. *The White House*, June 2002.

NSS, 2017. The National Security Strategy of the United States of America. *The White House*, December 2017.

Obama, B., 2016. President Obama: "The TPP would let America, not China, lead the way on global trade." *The Washington Post*, 2 May 2016.

Olson, M., 1965. *The Logic of Collective Action*. Harvard University Press, Cambridge.

Orban, V., 2014. Full text of Viktor Orbán's speech at Băile Tuşnad (Tusnádfürdő) of 26 July 2014. *The Budapest Beacon*, 26 July 2014.

Oreskes, B., 2016. Moscow wary of TTIP talks. *Politico*, 9 May 2016.

Orwell, G., 1940. Review of *Mein Kampf. The New English Weekly*, 21 March 1940.

Padoa-Schioppa, T., 2004. *The Euro and Its Central Bank: Getting United After the Union*. MIT Press, Cambridge.

Paik, K.W., 2018. ""The role of Sino-Russian gas cooperation in China's natural gas expansion." In J.I. Considine and K.W. Paik, (eds.), *Handbook of Energy Politics*. Edward Elgar Publishing, Cheltenham, pp.133–152.

Panda, A., 2016. Trump: ""I Don't Know Why"" US Is bound by ""'One China'"" policy. *The Diplomat*, 12 December 2016.

Paradise, J.F., 2016. The role of "parallel institutions" in China's growing participa-tion in global economic governance. *Journal of Chinese Political Science*, 21(2): 149–175.

Parker, G., 1985. *Western Geopolitical Thought in the Twentieth Century.* Routledge, New York.

Paszak, P., 2020. Not only the Balkans—China enters the CEE infrastructure. *Warsaw Institute*, 14 May 2020.

Perskaya, V.V., 2020. The comparison of the energy markets of the EAEU and the Scandinavian countries: Best practices for the energy integration. *International Journal of Energy Economics and Policy*, *10*(1): 81–88.

Pflanze, O., 2014. *Bismarck and the Development of Germany, Volume II: The Period of Consolidation, 1871-1880*. Princeton University Press, Princeton.

Pisani-Ferry, J., 2019. Europe can take a bigger role in providing public goods. *Financial Times*, 2 December 2019.

Polanyi, K., 1944. *The Great Transformation*. Beacon Press, Boston.

Pompeo, M., 2018. Sec. Pompeo remarks on "America's Indo-Pacific Economic Vision." *U.S. Mission to ASEAN*, 30 July 2018.

Pompeo, M., 2019. Trump administration diplomacy: The untold story. *US Department of State*, 22 October 2019.

Pompeo, M., 2020. Communist China and the Free World's Future. *US Department of State*, 23 July 2020.

Pouliot, V., 2007. Pacification without collective identification: Russia and the Transatlantic Security Community in the post-Cold War era. *Journal of Peace Research*, *44*(5): 605–622.

Pouliot, V., 2010. *International security in practice: The politics of NATO-Russia diplomacy*. Cambridge University Press, Cambridge.

PRC, 2017. Latvia's priorities in 16+1 format are strengthening of cooperation in transport and logistics. *Ministry of Commerce People's Republic of China*, Riga, 26 October 2017.

PRC, 2020. Foreign Ministry Spokesperson Zhao Lijian's regular press conference. *Ministry of Foreign Affairs of the People's Republic of China*, 17 November 2020.

Prechel, H., 1997. Corporate form and the state: Business policy and change from the multidivisional to the multilayered subsidiary form. *Sociological inquiry*, *67*(2): 151–174.

Prestowitz, C., 2012. Mercantilism is a state of mind. *Foreign Policy*, 16 April 2012.

Preziosi, G., 1916. *La Germania alla conquista dell'Italia*. Libreria, Florence.

Prodi, R., 2000. 2000–2005: Shaping the New Europe. *European Parliament*, Strasbourg, 15 February 2000.

Province, C.M., 1983. *The Unknown Patton*. Hippocrene Books, New York.

Putin, V., 2013. Meeting of the Valdai International Discussion Club. *President of Russia*, 19 September 2013.

Putin, V., 2014. Address by President of the Russian Federation. *President of Russia*, 18 March 2014.

Putin, V. 2016. Plenary Session of St. Petersburg International Economic Forum. *President of Russia*, 17 June 2016.

Putin, V., 2018. Meeting of ambassadors and permanent representatives of Russia. *President of Russia*, 19 July 2018.

Putin, V., 2020. Meeting of the Valdai Discussion Club. *President of Russia*, 22 October 2020.

Quigley, C., 1961. *The Evolution of Civilisations: A Historical Analysis*. Liberty Press, Indianapolis.

Rabe, W. and Gippner, O., 2017. Perceptions of China's outward foreign direct investment in European critical infrastructure and strategic industries. *International Politics*, *54*(4): 468–486.

Rand, 2019. Extending Russia competing from advantageous ground. *Rand Corporation*, Santa Monica.

Rastogi, C. and Arvis, J.F., 2014. *The Eurasian Connection: Supply-Chain Efficiency along the Modern Silk Route through Central Asia.* World Bank Publications, Washington.

Ratzel, F., 2019. *Politische geographie.* Walter de Gruyter GmbH & Co KG.

Raza, W., 2007. ""European Union tprade Politics: Pursuit of neo-mercantilism in different flora." In W. Blaas and J. Becker (eds.), Strategic Arena Switching in International Trade Negotiations. Ashgate, Hampshire, pp. 67–96.

Reagan, R., 1984. Remarks at an Ecumenical Prayer Breakfast in Dallas, Texas. *Reagan Library*, 23 August 1984.

Reinert, E.S. and Daastøl, A.M., 2007. ""The Other Canon: The history of Renaissance economics." In E. S. Reinert (ed.), *Globalization, Economic Development and Inequality: An Alternative Perspective*. Edward Elgar Publishing, pp. 21–70.

Ren, X., 2017. The G20: Emerging Chinese leadership in globag Governance? *Global Policy*, *8*(4): 433–442.

Republic of Serbia, 2009. Serbia, China sign framework agreement on economic, technological infrastructure cooperation. *The Government of the Republic of Serbia*, 21 August 2009.

Rettman, A., 2013. D''Estaing: Eurozone should shut its doors after Poland. *EUObserve*r, 26 March 2013.

Ricardo, D., 1821. *On the Principles of Political Economy and Taxation.* John Murray, London.

Rice, C., 2003. Remarks by Dr Condoleeza Rice, Assistant to the President for national security affairs. *International Institute for Strategic Studies*, London, United Kingdom, 16 June 2003.

Riley, J.P., 2013. *Napoleon and the World War of 1813: Lessons in Coalition Warfighting.* Routledge, New York.

Risse-Kappen, T., 1995. *Cooperation among Democracies: The European Influence on U.S. Foreign Policy.* Princeton University Press, New Jersey.

Robinson, P., 2019. *Russian Conservatism.* Northern Illinois University Press.

Rodrik, D., 1997. Has globalization gone too far? *California Management Review*, *39*(3): 29–53.

Rodrik, D., 2011. *The Globalization Paradox: Democracy and the Future of the World Economy.* W.W. Norton, New York.

Röhl, J.C., 2017. *Wilhelm II: Into the Abyss of War and Exile, 1900–1941.* Cambridge University Press, Cambridge.

Rolland, N., 2019. A China–Russia Condominium over Eurasia. *Survival*, *61*(1): 7–22.

Rorty, R., 1998. *Achieving Our Country: Leftist Thought in Twentieth-Century America.* Harvard University Press, Harvard.

Rose, G., 1998. Neoclassical realism and theories of foreign policy. *World Politics*, *51*(1): 144–172.

Rose, M., 2018. China's new ""Silk Road"" cannot be one-way, France's Macron says. Reuters, 8 January 2018.

Roy, S., 2020. India ""object"" of anti-China policy of the West, Russia minister says. *The Indian Express*, 10 December 2020.

RT, 2008. Putin: We must end monopoly in world finance. *RT*, 30 October 2008.

Ruggie, J.G., 1982. International regimes, transactions, and change: Embedded liberalism in the postwar economic order. *International Organization, 36*(2): 379–415.

Rühlig, T., 2021. China, Europe and the new power competition over technical standards. *The Swedish Institute of International Affairs*, No.1, 2021.

Russett, B. and Stam, A.C., 1998. Courting disaster: An expanded NATO vs. Russia and China. *Political Science Quarterly*, *113*(3): 361–382.

Russian Federation. 2015. Plenary session of the 19th St Petersburg International Economic Forum, 19 June 2015.

Sakwa, R., 2017. *Russia Against the Rest: The Post-Cold War Crisis of World Order*. Cambridge University Press, Cambridge.

Sakwa, R., 2020. Greater Russia: Is Moscow out to subvert the West? *International Politics*, pp. 1–29.

Sarotte, M.E., 2011. In victory, magnanimity: US foreign policy, 1989–1991, and the legacy of prefabricated multilateralism. *International Politics, 48*(4/5): 482–495.

Savitsky, P., 1921. Kontinent-Okean (Rossiia i mirovoi rynok) // Iskhod k Vostoku. Sofia.

Savitsky, P., 1996. *Geographical and Geopolitical Foundations of Eurasianism*. Continent EM, Agraf.

Savitsky, P., 1997. *Exodus to the East*. Charles Schlacks, Jr. Publisher, Bakersfield.

Sberbank, 2018. Sberbank strategy, 2020.

Scheuermann, C., 2013. Interview with Tony Blair: Leaving Europe would be very bad for Britain. *Der Spiegel*, 28 January 2013.

Schmidt, H., 1974. The year of economics: The struggle for the world product. *Foreign Affairs*, April 1974.

Schmoller, G., 1897. *The Mercantile System and Its Historical Significance*. Macmillan, London.

Scholvin, S. and Wigell, M., 2018. Power politics by economic means: Geoeconomics as an analytical approach and foreign policy practice. *Comparative Strategy*, *37*(1): 73–84.

Schuman Foundation, 2021. Europe as a power, European sovereignty, strategic autonomy: A debate that is moving towards an assertive Europe. *Foundation Robert Schuman: The Research and Studies Centre on Europe*, 1 February 2021.

Schweller, R.L., 1999. ""Realism and the present great power system: Growth and positional conflict over scarce resources." In E.B. Kapstein and M. Mastanduno (eds.), *Unipolar Politics: Realism and State Strategies after the Cold War*. Columbia University Press, New York, pp. 28–68.

Seaman, J., 2020. China and the new geopolitics of technical standardization. *Ifri*, January 2020.

Sell, S.K., 2003. *Private Power, Public Law: The Globalization of Intellectual Property Rights*. Cambridge University Press, Cambridge.

Semmel, B., 1970. *The Rise of Free Trade Imperialism*. Cambridge University Press, Cambridge.

Senate Reports, 1974. Congressional Serial Set. U.S. *Government Printing Office*, Washington, 1974.

Sender, H. and Stacey, K., 2017. China takes ""Project of the Century"" to Pakistan. *Financial Times*, 18 May 2017.

Shadlen, K., 2005. Policy space for development in the WTO and beyond: The case of intellectual property rights. Global Development and Environment Institute. Working Paper No. 05–06, Tufts University.

Smh, 1999. No turning back now for Alliance. *Sydney Morning Herald*, 31 May 1999.

Smh, 2011. US a ""parasite"" on world economy: Putin. *Sydney Morning Herald*, 2 August 2011.

Smith, A., 2002. Imagining geographies of the ""new Europe"": Geo-economic power and the new European architecture of integration. *Political Geography*, *21*(5): 647–670.

Smith, G., 1984. The Legacy of Monroe's Doctrine. *The New York Times*, 9 September 1984.

Smith, K., 2005a. The EU and Central and Eastern Europe: The absence of interregionalism. *Journal of European Integration*, *27*(3): 347–364.

Smith, K., 2005b. The outsiders: The European neighbourhood policy. *International affairs*, *81*(4): 757–773.

Snidal, D., 1985. The limits of hegemonic stability theory. *International Organization*, pp. 579–614.

SOA, 2016. State Oceanic Administration, 2016 Ocean Development Report. Beijing, Haiyang Press.

Solzhenitsyn, A., 1978. The exhausted West, *Harvard Magazine*, July-August 1978.

Sorhun, E., 2014. *Regional Economic Integration and the Global Financial System.* IGI Global, Hershey.

Spohr, K. and Hamilton, D.S., 2020. *The Arctic and World Order.* Foreign Policy Institute/Henry A. Kissinger Center for Global Affairs, Washington DC.

Spolaore, E., 2013. *What is European integration really about? A political guide for economists,* no. w19122, National Bureau of Economic Research.

Spykman, N.J., 1942. *America's Strategy in World Politics: The United States and the Balance of Power*. Transaction Publishers, New Brunswick.

Squires, N. 2018. Italy risks clash with Britain and EU as it threatens to veto renewal of Russia sanctions. *The Telegraph*, 17 October 2018.

Stiglitz, J., 2016. *The Euro: And Its Threat to the Future of Europe*. Penguin Books, London.

Stockhammer, E., 2014. The Euro crisis and contradictions of neoliberalism in Europe. *Post Keynesian Economics Study Group*, Working Paper 1401, pp.1–18.

Stråth, B., 2008. Mitteleuropa: From List to Naumann. *European Journal of Social Theory*, *11*(2): 171–183.

Straus, I., 2003. NATO: The only west that Russia has? *Demokratizatsiya, 11*(2): 229–269.

Subramanian, A., 2011. The inevitable superpower: Why China's dominance is a sure thing. *Foreign Affairs* (90): 66–78.

Surkov, V., 2018. Odinochastvo polukrovki [The Loneliness of the Half-Blood]. *Russia in Global Affairs*, April 11 2018.

Szabo, S.F., 2015. *Germany, Russia, and the Rise of Geo-Economics*. Bloomsbury Publishing, London.

Talbott, S., 2007. *The Russia Hand: A Memoir of Presidential Diplomacy*. Random House, New York.

Tass, 2019. Mutual interest not money key to Russia-China cooperation in AI, says Putin. *Tass Russian News Agency*, 20 November 2019.

Tass, 2021. EU remains unreliable partner for Russia for now—Lavrov. *Tass Russian News Agency*, 5 February 2021.

Tassinari, F., 2005. Security and integration in the EU neighbourhood: The case for regionalism. *CEPS Working Document*, No. 226.

The Hindu, 2020. China has deployed 60,000 soldiers on India's northern border: Pompeo. *The Hindu*, 10 October 2020.

Thompson, W.R., 1992. Dehio, long cycles, and the geohistorical context of structural transition. *World Politics: A Quarterly Journal of International Relations*, pp.127–152.

Ting, G., 2015. AIIB could be win-win, rather than zero-sum game for China and US. *China Institute of International Studies*, 15 July 2015.

Toby, R.P., 1977. Reopening the question of Sakoku: Diplomacy in the legitimation of the Tokugawa Bakufu. *Journal of Japanese Studies*, 3(2): 323–363.

Towle, P., 1980. British assistance to the Japanese Navy during the Russo-Japanese War of 1904–5. *The Great Circle*, 2(1): 44–54.

Trenin, D., 2009. Russia's spheres of interest, not influence. *The Washington Quarterly*, 32(4): 3–22.

Trenin, D., 2019. 20 Years of Vladimir Putin: How Russian foreign policy has changed. *The Moscow Times*, 27 August 2019.

Trotsky, L., 1934. Nationalism and economic life. *Foreign Affairs* (12): 396–402.

Tsygankov, A., 2003. Mastering space in Eurasia: Russian geopolitical thinking after the Soviet break-up. *Communist and Post-communist Studies (35):* 45–55.

Tsygankov, A.P., 2009. *Russophobia*. Palgrave Macmillan, New York.

Tsygankov, A.P., 2016. *Russia's Foreign Policy: Change and Continuity in National Identity*. Rowman & Littlefield, London.

Tubilewicz, C., 1999. Comrades no more: Sino–Central European relations after the Cold War. *Problems of Post-Communism*, 46(2): 3–14.

Tusk, D., 2016. Speech by President Donald Turk at the event marking the 40th anniversary of European People Party (EEP). *European Council*, 30 May 2016.

Unnikrishnan, N. and Kapoor, N., 2021. India-Russia relations in a Post-Covid world. *Valdai Discussion Club*, 3 March 2021.

US Congress, 2018. 2018 Annual Report to Congress. *U.S.-China Economic and Security Review Commission*, Washington DC, November 2018.

US Department of Defense, 2020. Advantage at sea: Prevailing with integrated all-domain naval power. US Department of Defense, December 2020.

US State Department, 1945. Memorandum by the Under Secretary of State (Acheson) to the Secretary of State. *US State Department*, 9 October.

US Treasury, 2013. Report to Congress on International Economic and Exchange Rate Policies. *US Department of the Treasury Office of International Affairs*, 30 October 2013.

Vahl, M., 2005. ""Lessons from the North for the EU's ''Near Abroad.''"" In Christopher S. Browning (ed.), *Remaking Europe in the Margins: Northern Europe after the Enlargements.* Aldershot, Ashgate, pp. 51–67.

Van der Oye, D.S., 2015. ""Russia, Napoleon and the threat to British India." In J.M. Hartley, P. Keenan, and D. Lieven (eds.), *Russia and the Napoleonic Wars.* Palgrave Macmillan, London.

Veebel, V., 2015. Baltic pathways from liberal trade model to neo-mercantilism in the European Union. *Managing* Global Transitions, *13*(3): 213–229.

Vuksanovic, V., 2020. In Serbia, China's Digital Silk Road might be in trouble very soon. *The Diplomat*, 23 September 2020.

Wæver, O., 1997. ""Imperial metaphors: Emerging European analogies to pre-nation-state imperial systems." In Ola Tunander, Pavel Baev, Victoria Einagel (eds.), *Geopolitics* in Post-Wall Europe: Security, Territory and Identity. Sage, London, pp. 59–93.

Wallander, C. and Keohane, R.O., 1999. ""Risk, threat, and security institutions." In Helga Haftendorn, Robert Owen Keohane, and Celeste A. Wallander (eds.), *Imperfect Unions*. Oxford University Press, pp. 21–47.

Waltz, K.N., 1979. *Theory of International Politics*. McGraw-Hill, New York.

Waltz, K.N., 2000. Structural realism after the Cold War. *International Security*, *25*(1): 5–41.

Waltz, K.N., 2010. *Theory of International Politics*. Addision-Wesley Publishing Company, Massachusetts.

Wang, X. and Chin, G., 2013. Turning point: International money and finance in Chinese IPE. *Review of International Political Economy*, *20*(6): 1244–1275.

Wang, Y., 2013. Exploring the path of major-country diplomacy with Chinese characteristics. *Foreign Affairs Journal* (10): 5–14.

Wang, Z., 2015. China's alternative diplomacy. *The Diplomat*, 30 January 2015.

Weber, M., 1980. The national state and economic policy (Freiburg address) (Inaugural lecture, Freiburg, May 1895). *Economy and Society*, *9*(4): 428–449.

Weigert, H.W., 1942. Haushofer and the Pacific. *Foreign Affairs*, *20*(4): 732–742.

White House, 1988. National Security Strategy of the United States. *White House*, April 1988.

White House, 2021. U.S. Strategic Framework for the Indo-Pacific. *White House Archives*, 5 January 2021.

Wiebe, R.H., 1967. *The Search for Order, 1877-1920*. Hill and Wang, New York.

Wigell, M. and Vihma, A., 2016. Geopolitics versus geoeconomics: The case of Russia's geostrategy and its effects on the EU. *International Affairs*, *92*(3): 605–627.

Williams, M.C. and Neumann, I.B., 2000. From alliance to security community: NATO, Russia, and the power of identity. *Millennium, 29*(2): 357–387.

Wingard, J., 2011. Putin remains untroubled by wave of protests. *Deutsche Welle,* 15 December 2011.

Witte, S., 1954. ""Report of the Minister of Finance to his Majesty on the necessity of formulating and thereafter steadfastly adhering to a definite program of a commercial and industrial policy of the Empire. Extremely secret."" In T.H. Von Laue, A Secret Memorandum of Sergei Witte on the Industrialization of Imperial Russia. *The Journal of Modern History, 26(1):* 60–74.

Wohlforth, W.C., 1999. The stability of a unipolar world. *International Security, 24*(1): 5–41.

Wong, J.Y.W., 2002. *Deadly dreams: Opium and the Arrow war (1856-1860) in China.* Cambridge University Press, Cambridge.

World Bank, 2016. Russia Economic Report 35: The longjJourney to recovery. *The World Bank,* 6 April 2016.

WT, 2015. Read Putin's U.N. General Assembly speech. *The Washington Times,* 28 September 2015.

Xi, J., 2020. Carrying Forward the Shanghai Spirit and Deepening Solidarity and Collaboration for a Stronger Community with a Shared Future. Remarks by H.E. Xi Jinping President of the People's Republic of China At the 20th Meeting of the Council of Heads of State of The Shanghai Cooperation Organization, 10 November 2020.

Xinhua, 2006. China, Russia, India hold 1st trilateral summit. *Xinhua News Agency,* 18 July 2006.

Yan, X., 2014. From Keeping a Low Profile to Striving for Achievement. *The Chinese Journal of International Politics, 7*(2): 153–184.

Yarmolinsky, A., 1921. *The Memoirs of Count Witte.* Doubleday, Toronto.

Yellen, J.A., 2019. *The Greater East Asia Co-Prosperity Sphere: When Total Empire Met Total War.* Cornell University Press.

Yevtushenkov, V., 2015. Import substitution without Self-Isolation. *Russia in Global Affairs,* 19 March 2015.

Youngs, R., 2021. The EU's Strategic Autonomy Trap. *Carnegie Europe,* 8 March 2021.

Yu, X., Tettamanti, M. and Rizzi, C., 2020. *China's Continued Reforms in a New Era: Their Impact on Chinese Foreign Direct Investments and RMB Internationalization.* World Scientific.

Zeng, L., 2021. Conceptual analysis of China's Belt and Road Initiative: A road towards a regional community of common destiny. In *Contemporary International Law and China's Peaceful Development.* Springer, Singapore, pp. 305–331.

Zhao, S., 2013. Delicate balance of power in the Asia-Pacific: The Obama administration's strategic rebalance and the transformation of US-China relationship. *Economic and Political Studies, 1*(2): 109–133.

Ziegler, C.E. and Menon, R., 2014. Neomercantilism and great-power energy competition in Central Asia and the Caspian. *Strategic Studies,* Summer: 17–41.

Zielonka, J., 2013. Europe's new civilizing missions: The EU's normative power discourse. *Journal of Political Ideologies*, *18*(1): 35–55.

Ziguo, L., 2017. Da Ouya huoban guanxi: chongsu Ouya xin zhixu [Greater Eurasian Partnership: Reshaping the Eurasian Order?]. *Guoji Wenti Yanjiu [International Studies]*, vol. 1, 2017.

Zloch-Christy, I., 1987. *Debt Problems of Eastern Europe*. Cambridge University Press, Cambridge.

Zürn, M. and Checkel, J.T., 2005. Getting socialized to build bridges: Constructivism and rationalism, Europe and the nation-state. *International Organization*, 1045–1079.

Index

ABM Treaty, ix
Adams, Brooks, 28
AIIB. *See* Asian Infrastructure
Investment Bank
Airbus Industrie, 157–59
Albright Madeleine, 61, 125
Alexander I, 23
Alexander III, 26
American System, xii, 12, 16, 44;
American System of Manufacturers,
57–58; economic nationalism of, 155
America's Economic Supremacy
(Adams), 28
APEC. *See* Asia-Pacific Economic
Cooperation
Arctic corridor, xvii–xviii, 99–100,
111–12, 123, 138, 144, 180
Aron, R., 74
ASEAN. *See* Association of Southeast
Asian Nations
Asian Development Bank, 59, 82, 101
Asian Infrastructure Investment Bank
(AIIB), xvii, 102, 125, 160–61
Asian Tigers, 79
Asia-Pacific Economic Cooperation
(APEC), 113
Asia-Pacific region, xviii, 65, 68
Association of Southeast Asian Nations
(ASEAN), 113

asymmetrical interdependence, xv, xvii,
1–4, 12, 53–54; Russia and, 73–75;
in Russian-Chinese partnership for
Greater Eurasia, 92
Australia, 86, 181; dispute with
China, 128–29

Baikal-Amur railway, 99
Baker, James, 72
Belgrade-Budapest railway, 124–25
Belt and Road Initiative: call for
cancellation of, 129; cooperation
with, 181; EU and, 123–24, 127;
European countries joining, 160;
in Russian-Chinese partnership for
Greater Eurasia, viii, xv, 97–98,
100, 103–4, 108–10; VCMC
challenging, 112
Berlin-Baghdad Railway, 20, 28–29
Berlin Wall, 73, 132, 184
Beveridge, Albert, 49
Biden, Joseph, 84, 127; on China,
159–60; restoring leadership among
allies, 159
Biegun, Stephen, 86
Bildt, Carl, 160
Bismark, Otto von, 45–46
Blair, Tony, 186, 187
Boeing, 158–59

Bolshevik Revolution, 20, 26
Bonaparte, Napoleon: Civil Code and, 42; defeat of, viii, 4; Russian Tsar and, xvi–xvii. *See also* Continental System
Borrell, Josep, 136, 177, 189
Brandt, Willy, 147
Bretton Woods system, viii, 91–92, 156
Brexit, 121, 157
Briand, Aristide, 48
Brichambaut, Marc Perrin de, 133
Britain: Brexit, 121, 157; China trade and, 57; Continental System and, 40; Eurasian threats to, xix; financial instruments and, 42; free trade and, 43; geoeconomic dominance of, 4; geoeconomic hegemons and, 49; global Britain, 164; oceanic Europe of, 41–44; Russian-British Great Game, xvii, 24; strategic industries and, 42; transportation corridors of, 41–42
Brock, Osmond, 51
Brzezinski, Zbigniew, 34
Burrows, M., 92–93
Bush, George H. W., 70
Bush, George W., 67
Buzan, B., 177

CAATSA. *See* Countering America's Adversaries Through Sanctions Act
CAI. *See* Comprehensive Agreement on Investment
Caillaux, Joseph, 48
capitalism, 171, 185
Carter, Jimmy, 34
Catherine the Great, 22
centralisation of power, 11–14, 118, 165, 187
CFIUS. *See* Committee on Foreign Investments in the United States
China, viii; altering engagement and containment, 82–83; Biden on, 159–60; British trade and, 57; containment of, in Greater Eurasia

political subjectivity, 83–85; debt-trap diplomacy, 102; Digital Silk Road of, 94, 121; EU and, 116–17; Eurasian Russia accommodating, 137–38; as European power, xx; financial instruments in, 101–3; first among equals principle and, ix; genocide accusations, 128; as geoeconomic region, 55–56; Germany and, 130; Going Global Strategy, 80; as great power, xiv; India and, 112; Iran strategic cooperation agreement, 111; multipolarity and, 79; NATO against, 87–88; One-China policy, 84, 128; peaceful rise of, xiv–xv, 66, 78–81; Polar Silk Road of, xvii, xxi; political subjectivity and, 81–82; rejection of unipolar era, xiii–xv; restoring political subjectivity, xix–xx; Silk Road of, 55–56; string of pearls infrastructure, 80; transportation corridors, 97–99; Trump trade war with, 158; Turkey and, 128; US policies and, 65; US rivalry, 151; zero-sum politics and, 87, 110. *See also* Russian-Chinese partnership for Greater Eurasia
China, as European power: Australia dispute and, 128–29; *China 2025* industrial policy, 120; EU responding to, 126–27; financial instruments in, 124–25; 5G networks and, 121; Greater Eurasia and, 115; Greece and, 122; Norway and, 128; political influence in, 127–28; regional formats for economic connectivity, 116–17; Serbia and, 121–22; 17+1 format and, xx, 117–18, 128; strategic industries in, 119–22; transportation corridors in, 122–24; US opposing, 118–19; yuan in, 125–26
China Everbright Limited, 122–23

China National Space Administration (CNSA), 94

China Ocean Shipping Company (COSCO), 122

Churchill, Winston, 51–53

CIS. *See* Commonwealth of Independent States

Clay, Henry, 12

Clinton, Bill, 54, 167

Clinton, Hillary, 35, 84–85, 107, 158

Cloud Act of 2018 (US), 178

CNSA. *See* China National Space Administration

Cold War, xiii–xiv, 2, 20; bipolar power distribution during, 155; capitalism-communism divide in, 171; declared end of, 70–71; Europe as other, 187; Greater Eurasia political subjectivity in post, 70–73; Mackinder policies, 34; opportune conditions of, 4; unipolar region after Cold War, 59–62

collective bargaining, 6

Committee on Foreign Investments in the United States (CFIUS), 182

Common Eurasian Home, 105–6

Common European Home, xv, 70, 105, 132

Common Spaces Agreement (2005), 134

Commonwealth of Independent States (CIS), 35

communism, 52, 117, 149, 166; Communist Revolution (1949), 57, 78

comparative advantage, 43–44, 57

Comprehensive Agreement on Investment (CAI), xvii, 127, 159

Concert of Democracies, 43, 68, 121

Conference on Security and Cooperation in Europe (CSCE), 132–33

Continental System, xix; Britain and, 40; collapse of, 44; Eurasian, 31; geoeconomics of, 42; Germany and, 44, 46; maritime regions and, 41–44; Russia and, 43; weakness of, 162

"Continent-Ocean" (Savitsky), 27

Corn Laws (Britain), 43, 60

COSCO. *See* China Ocean Shipping Company

Countering America's Adversaries Through Sanctions Act (CAATSA), 141

Covid-19 pandemic, 180, 192

Crédit Mobilier, 45

Crimea, 69, 183; reincorporation to Russia, vii, 145

Crimean War, 20, 24, 25, 27, 71, 93

CSCE. *See* Conference on Security and Cooperation in Europe

Daalder, I., 68

DCEP. *See* Digital Currency Electronic Payment

Dead Souls (Huntington), 169

debt-trap diplomacy, 102

de-dollarisation, 92, 102, 104–5, 146

Defense Planning Guidance (DPG), 33–34, 67

De Gaulle, Charles, 16, 54; as Euroseptic, 175; French-German axis and, 177; NATO and, 176

de Hoop Scheffer, Jaap, 133

Deng Xiaoping, 78–79

Digital Currency Electronic Payment (DCEP), 102

Digital Silk Road, 94, 121

Digital Single Market, 174, 178

Dostoyevsky, Fyodor, 23, 24

DPG. *See* Defense Planning Guidance

Dulles, John Foster, 58

Dutch East Company, 56

EAEU. *See* Eurasian Economic Union

Eastern Partnership, 134–35

Eastern Siberian-Pacific Ocean pipeline (ESPO), 96

ECB. *See* European Central Bank

economic liberalism, 5, 17, 166, 168–70, 192, 194

economic nationalism, 12, 79, 126, 155, 173; free trade and, 14
economic regionalism, 6–7
EDB. *See* Eurasian Development Bank
Eisenhower, Dwight, 155
energy corridors, 15–16
ESPO. *See* Eastern Siberian-Pacific Ocean pipeline
EU. *See* European Union
Eurasia, viii; Anglo-American containment of, 31–33; Anglo-German Eurasia, 27–29; as geoeconomic region, xix, 19–37; geoeconomics of, 20; German continental bloc, 29–33; Russia as custodian of backward, 21–23; Russian-French partnership, 23–29; US penetration of, 33–36. *See also* Eurasian Russia; Greater Eurasia; Greater Eurasia, political subjectivity in
Eurasian Development Bank (EDB), 104
Eurasian Economic Union (EAEU), xvi, 7–8, 104, 150–51; bargaining power of, 99; Iran and, 111; one-custom zone in, 108; Putin on, 107–8, 110; Russia and, 10, 116–17, 137; in Russian-Chinese partnership for Greater Eurasia, 108–10
Eurasianism, xx; German Eurasianism, 27–29; maritime dominance and, 37; Russian Eurasianism, 19, 24, 26–27, 36, 149
Eurasian Russia: agriculture in, 140; balance of dependence with, 131–32; China accommodated by, 137–38; EU and US energy war, 141–42; exports of, 141–45; financial instruments of, 145–46; geoeconomic power in, 138–40; from Greater Europe to Greater Eurasia, 132–33; Helsinki Accords cancellation and, 135–37; ideological appeal of, 149–50; as international conservative power, 148–50; political influence of, 146–47; respect and resentment for, 147–48; strategic industries in, 139–40; as swing supplier, 143; transportation corridors of, 144–45; Wider Europe opposing Greater Europe in, 133–35; yuan and, 145
Euro, 161–62, 178
Euro-centrism, xii
Europe: dominance in maritime regions, 39–40; as geoeconomic region, xi–xii, xix; Germany treating as region, 44–48; growing divisions in, 161; marginalising Russia in, 69–70; multipolar system for, xxi; oceanic Britain of, 41–44; Russia restructuring relations with, xx–xxi; sharing of trans-Atlantic region, 155–56; in trans-Atlantic fragmentation, 160–61; in trans-Atlantic region, 65; between trans-Atlantic region and Greater Eurasia, xvii–xviii; United States of Europe, 46–48; as US-led region, 52–55. *See also* China, as European power; European Union
European Central Bank (ECB), 61
European Commission, 174, 179
European Constitution, 170
European Council, xi, 121, 159, 165, 178–80
European Neighborhood Policy, 134
European sovereignty: Covid-19 pandemic and, 180; external balance of dependence for, 186–88; financial instruments for, 182; geoeconomic levers of power for, 177–86; globalisation and, 184–86; as gradual process, 187; militarising EU for, 182–83; multipolarity and, 175–76; strategic autonomy for, 173–75, 194; strategic industries for, 178–80; swing power strategy for, 176–77; transportation corridors for, 180–82; unipolarity or inter-regionalism for, 188–90

European Union (EU): Belt and Road
Initiative and, 123–24, 127; China
and, 116–17; Common Strategy of
the European Union on Russia, 74;
at crossroads, 193; Eurasian Russia
energy war, 141–42; expansion of,
71, 73; federalist approach of, 164;
geoeconomic hegemony and, 60;
as geoeconomic region, xii–xiii,
60–61; INOGATE project, 35,
134; militarising, for European
sovereignty, 182–83; NATO and,
61; as Normative Power of Europe,
186–87; peaceful rise of, xix;
response to China as European
power, 126–27; Russian reliance
and, xv; Single Market in, 61,
178; strategic autonomy and, 116,
126–30, 135; swing power strategy
for, xiii; symmetry sought by, 7;
trans-Atlantic region and, 13; 27+1
format, 134; United States and, xviii;
warning to, xi; Wider Europe and,
133–35; zero-sum policies of, xiii;
zero-sum politics and, 190
European vassalage, 154–55
Export Control Reform Act (US), 179

Fairgrieve, James, 72
fair trade, 13, 44, 45
Fillon, François, 148
financial instruments, 16; Britain
and, 42; in China, 101–3; in China
as European power, 124–25;
of Eurasian Russia, 145–46;
for European sovereignty, 182;
Russia and, 103–5; in Russian-
Chinese partnership for Greater
Eurasia, 101–5
Financial Messaging System of the
Bank of Russia (SPFS), 104–5
5G networks, xvii, 121, 178–79
Fouchet Plan, 175–76
Fourth Industrial Revolution, xv, 84,
94, 175, 191

France: digital service tax of, 179;
NATO reform by, 175–76; Russian-
French Eurasian partnership, 23–29
free-market, 85, 166–68, 175,
180, 184–85
free trade, 12; Britain and, 43; economic
nationalism and, 14; Germany and,
62; US contesting, 48; US using, 63;
after World War II, 48
French Revolution, 23
Fukuyama, Francis, 191

Gabriel, Sigmar, 126–27
Gates, Robert, 75
geoeconomic hegemons, 7, 17, 40;
benefits for, 193; Britain and, 49; EU
and, 60; hegemonic stability theory,
5–6; patronage of, 62–63; prevention
of, 31; reliance on, 40; trans-Atlantic
region as, 154; US and, 52
geoeconomic regions: China as,
55–56; collective bargaining and, 6;
cooperation in, 188–89; EU as, xii–
xiii, 60–61; Eurasia as, xix, 19–37;
Europe as, xi–xii, xix; external
balance of dependence and, 2;
influence and development of, xviii–
xix; internal balance of dependence
in, 8–11; Japan as, xii; loyalties in,
150; United States as, xii; wedge
strategies and, 7–8, 188–89
geoeconomics: balance of dependence
and, 2–4; centralising power in
regions, 11–14; of Continental
System, 42; defined, 1; economic
nationalism and, 12; of Eurasia, 20;
financial instruments as pillar, 16;
geoeconomic regionalism, 1, 154,
161; of liberal economics, 4–11;
modern school of, vii; of nation-
building, xii; roots of, 12; of Russia,
107–8; strategic industries as pillar,
13–15; transportation corridors as
pillar, 15–16; of US, 4, 48–51

Germany: China and, 130; Continental
System and, 44, 46; customs union,
12; Eurasian continental bloc,
29–33; free trade and, 62; German
Eurasianism, 27–29; German
Zollverein, xix, 44–45, 54; Greater
Eurasia and, 20; industrial rise
of, 40; *Industry 4.0* policy, 120,
157; Moldova and, 3; peaceful
rise model of, xiv–xv, 46; Soviet
Union defeating, 43; transportation
corridors, 15; treating Europe as
region, 44–48; Zollverein, xix, 44–45
Giscard d'Estaing, Valéry, 16, 187
Glass-Steagall Act, 167
Global Financial Crisis (2008), 101,
117, 145, 168
Global Financial Crisis (2014), 145
globalisation, 167–69; European
sovereignty and, 184–86; as state-
centric, 176, 193
global warming, 140
Going Global Strategy, 80
gold hoarding, 92
Gorbachev, Mikhail, 86; Common
European Home of, xv, 70, 105, 132
Greater Eurasia, ix; adapting to, 191–94;
borders, x; disunity in, 157–60;
Europe between trans-Atlantic region
and Greater Eurasia, xvii–xviii;
Germany and, 20; Lavrov on, 110;
restructuring China as European
power, 115; Russia connecting space
in, 36–37; Russian Greater Eurasia
Initiative, xvi, 20, 136, 150. *See also*
China, as European power; Eurasian
Russia; Russian-Chinese partnership
for Greater Eurasia
Greater Eurasia, political subjectivity in,
65–67; altering China engagement
and containment, 82–83; Chinese
containment in, 83–85; Chinese
political subjectivity and, 81–82;
containment and engagement
in, 67–69; marginalising Russia

in Europe, 69–70; militarizing
geoeconomic conflict, 85–87; move
from Greater Europe, 76–81; NATO
against China in, 87–88; post-Cold
War Europe and, 70–73; Russian
objectivity and, 73–75
Greater Europe Initiative, xvi, 114,
131; Eurasian Russia move from,
132–33; Greater Eurasia move from,
76–81; Putin on, 77; Wider Europe
opposing, 133–35; Witte on, 46
Greece: Ancient Greece, 39; China as
European power and, 122; Greek
city-states, 11; Mackinder on, 122
GUAM initiative, 35

Hamilton, Alexander, 12, 27, 41, 45;
economic independence and, 48;
ideas of, 57
Hanseatic League, 21–22, 39
Haushofer, Karl, xvii; on Asian
partnerships, 29–30; continental
block of, 20
Havel, Vaclav, 125
heartland theory, 31–33
hegemons. *See* geoeconomic hegemons
Helsinki Accords (1975), 70, 132–33,
191; cancellation of, 135–37;
challenging of, 150
Helsinki-Tallinn tunnel, 123
Herder, Johann Gottfried, 45
Hitler, Adolf, 170; expansion model of,
30–31; power seizure by, 47
Holy Roman Empire, 184
Hong Kong, 84, 102, 127–29
Hoover, Herbert, 52
humanitarian interventionism, 68
Huntington, S.P., 2–3, 169

IMF. *See* International Monetary Fund
India, 114; China and, 112; Hindu
nationalism in, 185; Lavrov on,
112; Russia and, 111–12, 194;
VCMC and, 112
Indo-Pacific region, xviii, 65, 88

Industry 4.0 policy, 157
INOGATE, 35, 134
INSTC. *See* International North-South
  Transportation Corridor
Instrument in Support of Trade
  Exchanges (INSTEX), 182
International Development Finance
  Corporation, 119
International Monetary Fund (IMF), 13,
  54, 82, 83, 156
International North-South
  Transportation Corridor (INSTC),
  100, 111–12
inter-regionalism, xii–xiii, 51, 60–61,
  137, 150, 170, 188–90
Iran: China strategic cooperation
  agreement, 111; EAEU and, 111;
  Joint Comprehensive Plan of
  Action and, 160; Russian-Chinese
  partnership for Greater Eurasia
  and, 110–11
Iraq, viii, 68
Iron Curtain, 53
island states, 41–42, 50, 58, 160, 164
Issing, Otmar, 162
Italy, 10, 16, 60, 125, 162, 164
Ivan the Terrible, 22

Japan, 114; American System of
  Manufacturers and, 57–58;
  failed strategic industries, 59; as
  geoeconomic region, xii; as island
  state, 58; isolation of, 57; Russia
  and, 111, 194; Soviet Union and,
  58; as US rival, 51; Zaibatsu
  system in, 58–59
JCPOA. *See* Joint Comprehensive
  Plan of Action
Johnson, Lyndon, 34
Joint Comprehensive Plan of Action
  (JCPOA), 160
Juncker, Jean-Claude, 126

Kaczynski, Ted, 167
Kaplan, S.B., 124

Karaganov, Sergey, 36
Kazakhstan, 108–9, 114
Kennan, George, 71
Keynes, John Maynard, 82
Khodorkovsky, Mikhail, 141–42
Kievan Rus, 21
Kindleberger, C.P., 6
Kissinger, Henry, 32–33, 72, 92, 127;
  negotiations by, 156; on Russia, 75
Kjellén, Rudolf, 29
Klaus, Václav, 164
Köhler, Horst, 62
Kortunov, A., 148
Kozyrev, Andrey, 74–75
Kristeva, J., 186

Lavrov, Sergey, xv–xvi, 35–36,
  76–77; on Greater Eurasia, 110; on
  India, 112
law of growing spaces, 29–30
League of Nations, 48
Lee Kuan Yew, 117–18
Le Pen, Marine, 148
liberal economics, xxi, 1, 82, 184, 193;
  geoeconomics of, 4–11
liberalism, 69–70, 106, 148; nation-
  states and, 170–71
Libya, viii, 145, 183, 185
Limbaugh, Rush, 170
Lindsay, J., 68
Lissovolik, Yaroslav, 109
List, Friedrich, xvii, 4, 5, 12–13, 31;
  Anglo-German continental bridge
  and, 20; on colonies, 14; on Eurasian
  land quarter, 19; ideas of, 57; on rise
  of America, 48–49; translations of,
  25; vision of Anglo-German Eurasia,
  27–29; on Zollverein, 44
Liu Xiaobo, 128
Long Telegram, 71
Luttwak, Edward, vii, 2

Maas, Heiko, 147
Mackinder, Halford, 19, 20, 26, 99;
  on Greece, 122; heartland theory

of, 31–33; Kissinger influencing, 32–33; language of, 108; post Cold War policies, 34; on transportation corridors, 31–32
Macron, Emmanuel, 124, 146–47, 181; on European vassalage, 154–55; on strategic autonomy, 174
Mahan, Alfred Thayer, 28–29, 31; US as island state and, 50
Manichean world view, 192
Manners, Ian, 186–87
Manning, R.A., 92–93
Mao Zedong, 78
maritime regions: American geoeconomics and, 48–51; Ancient Greece and, 39; Asia as western-led region, 55–59; Continental System of Napoleon and, 41–44; Eurasianism and maritime dominance, 37; Europe as US-led region, 52–55; Europe's dominance in, 39–40; oceanic Europe of Britain, 41–44; regionalisation in, 51–52; unipolar region after Cold War, 59–62. *See also* trans-Atlantic region
market efficiency, 9, 12
Marshal Plan, 53
Matlock, Jack, 71
McCain, John, 68–69
McKinley, William, 50
Mein Kampf (Hitler), 170
mercantilism, 2–3, 56–57
Merkel, Angela, 143–44, 174
Merriam, Gordon, 53–54
Michel, Charles, 174
military blocs, 113–14
Mitrany, D., 165
Mitteleuropa (Naumann), 47
Mnuchin, Steven, 182
Mogherini, Federica, 181
Mongol Empire, 19, 21–22, 55–56
Monroe Doctrine (1823), 49–50
Morgenthau Plan, 52
Mudde, C., 169

multipolarity: China and, 79; European sovereignty and, 175–76; system for Europe, xxi
Mundell, Robert, 16

NAFTA. *See* North American Free-Trade Agreement
nation-states, 45, 107, 118; liberalism and, 170–71; polarisation of, 166–68
NATO, vii, 53; alliances, 113; against China, 87–88; De Gaulle and, 176; Eastern Europe and, 163; energy corridors and, 15–16; EU and, 61; expansionism of, xix, 66, 69, 71–73, 76, 78, 81, 108, 181; France reforming, 175–76; humanitarian interventionism by, 68; increasing presence of, 119; military exercises against, 138; monopoly of, 188; primacy of, 183; Russia joining, 70; Trump addressing, 158–59; Yugoslavia attacked by, 72
Naumann, Friedrich, 47
NDB. *See* New Development Bank
neoclassical realism, 8–9
neoliberalism, 59, 167
Neumann, I.B., 70
New Development Bank (NDB), 101–2
Nicholas II, 46
Nixon, Richard, 65, 127
Nord Stream pipelines, 143–44, 159
Normative Power of Europe, 186–87
North American Free-Trade Agreement (NAFTA), 7, 11, 60, 158
Northern Sea Route, xvii, xxi
Norway, 128

Obama, Barack, 83; pivot to Asia of, 157–58; Trans-Pacific Partnership proposed by, 158
One-China policy, 84, 128
"On the Value and Conditions of an Alliance between Great Britain and Germany" (List), 28
Open Door Policy (US), 50

Opium Wars, 25, 57, 78, 93
Orange Revolution, 142
Orban, Victor, 163
Organisation for Security and
    Cooperation in Europe
    (OSCE), 132–33
Orwell, George, 170–71
OSCE. *See* Organisation for Security
    and Cooperation in Europe
Ostpolitik, 147

Pamir Boundary Commission protocols
    (1895), 25
Pan-German League, 28
Paul I, 23
Pershine Smith, E., 57–58
Petersberg tasks, 183
Peter the Great, 21, 22, 26, 147, 191
Pipes, Richard, 72
pivot to Asia, 157–58
Plato, 169
Polanyi, K., 166
Polar Silk Road, xvii, xxi
political realism theory, 3–4, 8
Politische Geographie (Ratzel), 29
Pompeo, Mike, 85–88
populism, 168–69
positive-sum game, 57
Primakov, Yevgeny, 76
The Problem of Asia (Mahan), 29
Prodi, Romano, 74
Putin, Vladimir, xvi, 66, 69, 70, 148;
    ascension of, 75; on EAEU, 107–8,
    110; on Eurasian integration, 106;
    on failure of liberal ideals, 149;
    on Greater Europe, 77; on world
    finance, 101; Xi Jinping summit and,
    109; on Yugoslavia, 73

Rand Corporation, 75
Ratzel, Friedrich, 29
RCEP. *See* Regional Comprehensive
    Economic Partnership
Reagan, Ronald, 166–67

Regional Comprehensive Economic
    Partnership (RCEP), 84, 159
regionalism: geoeconomic regionalism,
    154, 161; as power instrument, 1
Ricardo, David, 43–44
Rice, Condoleezza, 67
Rimland Theory, 32
Romania, 117, 119
Rorty, R., 169
Roscosmos. *See* Russian State
    Corporation for Space Activities
Rudd, Kevin, 81
rules-based systems, 5, 69, 81, 180,
    185, 186, 192
Russia: asymmetrical interdependence
    and, 73–75; Belt and Road Initiative
    and, viii; Common Strategy of
    the European Union on Russia,
    74; connecting space in Greater
    Eurasia, 36–37; Continental System
    and, 43; Crimea reincorporation,
    vii, 145; as custodian of backward
    Eurasia, 21–23; EAEU and, 10,
    116–17, 137; EU reliance and, xv;
    financial instruments and, 103–5;
    geoeconomics of, 107–8; Greater
    Eurasia Initiative, xvi, 20; as great
    power, xiv; India and, 111–12, 194;
    industrialisation, 12; Japan and, 111,
    194; Kissinger on, 75; marginalising
    in Europe, 69–70; NATO member,
    70; Northern Sea Route, xvii, xxi;
    rejection of unipolar era, xiii–xv;
    restoring political subjectivity,
    xix–xx; restructuring Europe
    relations, xx–xxi; Russian-British
    Great Game, xvii, 24; Russian
    Eurasianism, 19, 24, 26–27, 36, 149;
    safeguarding peace, viii; sovereignty
    and, ix; Spykman on containing,
    23; strategic autonomy and, 114;
    Time of Troubles, 22; transportation
    corridors, 99–100; US policies
    and, 65–66; world GNP and, viii;

zero-sum politics and, 193. *See also*
  Eurasian Russia
Russian-Chinese partnership for Greater
  Eurasia, xi, xv–xvii, xx, 17, 19, 192;
  asymmetrical interdependence in,
  92; balance of Eurasian dependence,
  110–13; Belt and Road Initiative
  in, viii, xv, 97–98, 100, 103–4,
  108–10; Common Eurasian Home
  in, 105–6; EAEU in, 108–10;
  financial instruments in, 101–5;
  geoeconomic levers of power in,
  92–94; harmonising of interests in,
  108–10; International North-South
  Transportation Corridor in, 100;
  Iran and, 110–11; as marriage of
  convenience, 91–92; military blocs
  and, 113–14; Russian geoeconomics
  in, 107–8; strategic industries in,
  93–94; technological leadership
  of China in, 94–95; technological
  preparedness of Russia in, 95–97;
  territorial dispute resolved, 108–9;
  transportation corridors in, 97–100;
  2013 Silk Road Initiative in, 98
Russian-French Eurasian partnership,
  23; German Eurasianism and, 27–29;
  Russia after Crimean War, 24–26;
  Russian Eurasianism in, 26–27
Russian National Technology
  Initiative, 95
Russian State Corporation for Space
  Activities (Roscosmos), 94

Sakoku Edict (Japan), 57
Savitsky, P., 26–27
Sberbank, 146
Schengen agreement, 61
Schmidt, Helmut, 6–7, 54–55
Schmoller, Gustav, 12
SCO. *See* Shanghai Cooperation
  Organisation (SCO)
SDRs. *See* Special Drawing Rights
Serbia, 121–22
17+1 format, xx, 117–18, 128

Shanghai Cooperation Organisation,
  93, 104, 109
Shanghai Spirit, 83
Silk Road, xv, xvii, 19; of China,
  55–56; Digital Silk Road, 94, 121;
  Silk Road Fund, 101–2; spirit, 83;
  2013 Silk Road Initiative, 98; US
  concept, 34–35
Single Market, 61, 174, 178
Smith, Adam, 12
Society for Worldwide Interbank
  Financial Telecommunication
  (SWIFT), xviii, 16, 54, 101–2, 182
South Korea, xvi, 95, 111, 114
Soviet Union, viii–ix, 20; collapse of,
  70–71, 139, 191; Germany defeated
  by, 43; Japan and, 58; new power
  centres and, 36
Special Drawing Rights (SDRs), 156
SPFS. *See* Financial Messaging System
  of the Bank of Russia
Spykman, N.J., 20; on containing
  Russia, 23; Rimland Theory, 32
Stoltenberg, Jens, 87–88
strategic autonomy, xvii, xxi; advance
  of, 14; EDB and, 104; EU and,
  116, 126–30, 135; for European
  sovereignty, 173–75, 190, 194;
  increase of, 4, 6, 12; Macron on,
  174; Russia and, 114
strategic industries: Britain and, 42; in
  China as European power, 119–22;
  defined, 13; in Eurasian Russia,
  139–40; for European sovereignty,
  178–80; failing in Japan, 59; as pillar
  of geoeconomics, 13–15; in Russian-
  Chinese partnership for Greater
  Eurasia, 93–94; of US, 53
Strategic Perspective 2040, xi
string of pearls infrastructure, 80
Suez canal, 15, 31, 54, 100
Surkov, Vladislav, 77
SWIFT. *See* Society for
  Worldwide Interbank Financial
  Telecommunication

swing power strategy, xiii, 176–77

Taiwan Travel Act, 84
Talbott, Strobe, 74
TAPI project, 35
Tatars, 21
Thatcherism, 166–67
Tibet, 128
Tokaev, Kassym-Jomart, 109
TPP. *See* Trans-Pacific Partnership
TRACECA. *See* Transport Corridor
    Europe-Caucasus-Asia
trans-Atlantic fragmentation, 153;
    disunity in Greater Eurasia, 157–60;
    enlargements contributing to, 163;
    Euro in, 161–62; growing divisions
    in Europe, 161; nationalism-
    globalism divide in, 168–71;
    oppositions contributing to, 164–65;
    polarisation of nation-state, 166–68;
    in trans-Atlantic region, 154–57; US
    and Europe in, 160–61
trans-Atlantic region, xvii–xviii; EU
    and, 13; Europe in, 65; formation
    of, 39; fragmentation in, 154–57;
    as geoeconomic hegemon, 154;
    reorganisation of, 63; sustenance of,
    63; United States and, 8, 10, 13; US
    and Europe sharing, 155
Transatlantic Trade and Investment
    Partnership (TTIP), 158–59
Trans-Caspian Railway, 25
Trans-Pacific Partnership (TPP),
    83–84, 158
transportation corridors: of Britain,
    41–42; of China, 97–99; in China
    as European power, 122–24; energy
    corridors, 15–16; of Eurasian Russia,
    144–45; for European sovereignty,
    180–82; of Germany, 15; Mackinder
    on, 31–32; as pillar of geoeconomics,
    15–16; of Russia, 99–100; in
    Russian-Chinese partnership for
    Greater Eurasia, 97–100; US and, 50

Transport Corridor Europe-Caucasus-
    Asia (TRACECA), 35, 135
Trans-Siberian Railway, 26, 28, 99
Treaty of Versailles, 48, 52
triumphalism, 185
Trotsky, L., 47, 50–51
Trubetskoi, Nikolai, 27
Truman, Harry, 31, 155
Trump, Donald, 84–85; addressing
    NATO, 158–59; China trade
    war of, 158
Tsipras, Alexis, 122
TTIP. *See* Transatlantic Trade and
    Investment Partnership
Turkey, ix, xvii, 163, 188, 193; China
    and, 128; Western allies and, 141
Tusk, Donald, 165
27+1 format, 134

Ukraine, 185; coup in, 77; as failed
    state, viii, 131, 139; Orange
    Revolution in, 142
UN. *See* United Nations
unipolarity, 20, 33–34, 41, 73, 79, 82,
    160; Cold War and, 59–62; European
    sovereignty and, 188–90; new
    centres of power, 36–37; perpetuity
    of, 69; Russian rejection of, xiii–xv
unitarianism, viii
United Nations (UN), 68; Chinese
    political subjectivity and, 81–82
United States (US): Asia-Pacific region
    and, 68; China castigating, 65;
    China rivalry, 151; Commonwealth
    of Independent States and, 35;
    containment strategy of, 32–33;
    Cuban Missile Crisis, ix; Defense
    Planning Guidance and, 33–34, 67;
    digital leadership of, 15; economic
    nationalist polices, 41; EU and, xviii;
    Eurasian Russia energy war, 141–42;
    Eurasian threats to, xix; Eurasia
    penetration by, 33–36; Europe as
    US-led region, 52–55; expansion
    model of, 30–31; free trade and, 48,

63; geoeconomic hegemons and, 52; as geoeconomic region, xii; geoeconomics of, 4, 48–51; global supremacy by, xiv; Greek city-states and, 11; Indo-Pacific Strategy Report, 85; as island state, 41–42, 50; Japan as rival, 51; One-China policy, 84; opposition to China as European power, 118–19; Romania and, 119; Russia castigating, 65–66; sharing of trans-Atlantic region, 155–56; Silk Road concept, 34–35; strategic industries, 53; support from, xiii; system-dominance of, 60; in trans-Atlantic fragmentation, 160–61; trans-Atlantic region and, 8, 10, 13; transportation corridors and, 50; War Plan Red of, 52
United States of Europe, 46–48
US. *See* United States

VCMC. *See* Vladivostok-Chennai Maritime Corridor
VKontakte social media, 95
Vladivostok-Chennai Maritime Corridor (VCMC), 112
Von der Leyen, Ursula, 174

Waltz, K.N., 68
Wang Yi, 106
War Plan Red, 52
Weber, Max, 46
wedge strategies, 7–8, 188–89
Wider Europe concept, 133–36

Wilhelm II, 40, 46
Wilson, Woodrow, 51
Witte, Sergei, 12, 25–26; on Greater Europe, 46
Wolfowitz doctrine of global dominance, 33
World Bank, 13, 54, 82, 83
World Trade Organization (WTO), 82
World War I, xii, 26, 29, 47, 50–52, 62; crush zone in, 72
World War II, xii, xvii, 13, 20, 32; devastation of, 41; Europe as US-led region after, 52–55; free trade after, 48; political legitimacy and, 166
WTO. *See* World Trade Organization

Xi Jinping, 66, 98; Putin summit and, 109

Yandex search engine, 95, 141
Yeltsin, Boris, 70, 74, 76–77, 131
yuan, 101–2; Eurasian Russia and, 145; Europeanising of, 125–26
Yugoslavia, viii, 73; NATO attacking, 72; Putin on, 73

Zaibatsu system, 58–59
Zeman, Milos, 125
zero-sum politics, xiii, xviii, 7, 56, 70, 74, 171; China and, 87, 110; EU and, 190; objectives of, 114; rejection of, 77; Russia and, 193
Zollverein, xix, 44–45, 54

www.ingramcontent.com/pod-product-compliance
Lightning Source LLC
Chambersburg PA
CBHW022307280326
41932CB00010B/1016